THE ADULT'S LEARNING PROJECTS

A Fresh Approach to Theory
and Practice in Adult Learning

Allen Tough

Research in Education Series No. 1

The Ontario Institute for Studies in Education

THE ONTARIO INSTITUTE FOR STUDIES IN EDUCATION has three
prime functions: to conduct programs of graduate study in education,
to undertake research in education, and to assist in
the implementation of the findings of educational studies.
The Institute is a college chartered by an Act of the Ontario
Legislature in 1965. It is affiliated with the University of
Toronto for graduate studies purposes.

© The Ontario Institute for Studies in Education 1971
252 Bloor Street West, Toronto 5, Ontario

ISBN 0-7744-0059-5   Printed in Canada

Contents

Experiment with group help for self-planned learning
Reduce the emphasis on credit
Do not rely on a single institution

Preface

During the past seven years, a loosely knit group of researchers in Toronto have conducted several studies of the highly deliberate learning efforts made by men and women. By reporting on and synthesizing these studies, this book provides a broad picture of these learning efforts, which have turned out to be surprisingly common and important.

The findings and implications of the studies, all of which focus on the adult's learning projects, are providing a fresh approach to theory and practice in adult learning. This approach is already proving useful for the researcher and theorist in the fields of adult learning and humanistic psychology. In addition, it provides major implications for the practitioner interested in facilitating the adult's efforts to learn, change, and grow. The book also suggests some implications for youth education in colleges and secondary schools.

My interest in studying the entire range of deliberate adult learning – self-planned learning and private lessons as well as courses and workshops – developed during 1963. During that year, I became strongly interested in several comprehensive questions: what and why adults learn, how they learn, and what help they obtain.

These questions seemed even more important as I reflected on my own previous experiences as a learner and teacher – my years studying psychology and sociology at the University of Toronto; my informal learning as the editor of a college yearbook and while hitchhiking through Europe; my two years as a high school teacher and the surprising contrasts I noticed when teaching my first noncredit adult class; the influence of marriage and a T-group on how I see myself and others; the stimulation of entering a graduate program and of moving to a new city and country. What made some of these learning experiences so fruitful, and others so meaningless? What functions do teachers and other helpers perform in such learning, and what tasks does the learner himself perform?

For my doctoral research at the University of Chicago, I decided to focus my attention on the behavior of adults while planning their own learning projects. With advice and encouragement from Cyril Houle, Philip Jackson, Bruce Joyce, and George Aker, I developed a study focusing on two areas: the teaching tasks that the adult sometimes performs for himself, and the advice and other help he obtains with these tasks from various persons. The study was completed while I was teaching psychology and sociology at the University of Toronto's college of education. As in subsequent studies, I was delighted by the willingness of adults to be interviewed intensively about their learning efforts.

My studies have not relied exclusively on one discipline, or on one school of thought. Although my own background is in psychology and education (especially educational psychology and adult education), I have tried to incorporate insights and approaches from a variety of sources.

Since 1966 I have been in the adult education department of the Ontario Institute for Studies in Education, a department whose members have wide-ranging interests covering many aspects of the learning of men and women. Roby Kidd and other staff members have been helpful in encouraging, broadening, and supporting my studies.

Several studies have been conducted in the department by a loosely knit group interested in the adult's learning projects. This group has concentrated on deliberate efforts to learn in groups and in private lessons, as well as on self-planned learning.

Vida Stanius, a research associate, has been part of the adult learning research team since 1966. Several graduate assistants have spent at least one year on the team, thus contributing much of the thinking and data on which this book is based. They include Heather Knoepfli, Ray Devlin, Stan Searle, Michael Clague, Leonard Shorey, Cressy McCatty, Rosalie Howlett, Jim Fair, Shirley Shipman, and John Morris. In addition, the thesis research projects of Mairi Macdonald, Heather Knoepfli, Cressy McCatty, David Armstrong, Jim Fair, and Larry Denys have made relevant contributions. Students in my courses have supplied additional data and reactions.

Several individuals have also helped me greatly in preparing the manuscript. Portions of the first draft were read critically by David Armstrong, Harold Huston, Roby Kidd, John Morris, Ernest Stabler, Sara Steele, Vida Stanius, Alan Thomas, Anne Tough, and David Tough. In addition, an early plan was discussed with Bill Barnard and Don Blackburn. Editorial assistance was provided by Ellen Choptiany and Myrna Knechtel. Barbara McIntyre and Annemarie Travers transformed thousands of dictated words into a typewritten manuscript, and Barbara McIntyre also performed some of the statistical calculations.

1 Focusing on highly deliberate efforts to learn

Are highly deliberate efforts to learn very common? Why and what do people learn? How much time do they spend at learning? Is their learning self-planned, or do they go to classes and groups? Can we provide better help for individual learners?

During the past few years, these questions have led to several studies with which I have been associated. From the findings of these studies, the following general picture of adult learning emerges.

Almost everyone undertakes at least one or two major learning efforts a year, and some individuals undertake as many as 15 or 20. The median is eight learning projects a year, involving eight distinct areas of knowledge and skill.

A learning project is simply a major, highly deliberate effort to gain certain knowledge and skill (or to change in some other way). Some learning projects are efforts to gain new knowledge, insight, or understanding. Others are attempts to improve one's skill or performance, or to change one's attitudes or emotional reactions. Others involve efforts to change one's overt behavior or to break a habit.

It is common for a man or woman to spend 700 hours a year at learning projects. Some persons spend less than 100 hours, but others spend more than 2000 hours in episodes in which the person's intent to learn or change is clearly his primary motivation.

Many learning projects are initiated for highly practical reasons: to make a good decision, build something, or carry out some task related to one's job, home, family, sport, or hobby. Adult learning is also motivated by curiosity, interest, and enjoyment. A few projects are motivated by credit toward a degree or certificate.

About 70% of all learning projects are planned by the learner himself, who seeks help and subject matter from a variety of acquaintances, experts, and printed resources. Other learning projects rely on a group or instructor, on private lessons, or on some nonhuman resource.

This picture of adult learning has emerged from a series of recent studies, many of which were developed by graduate students and staff members in adult education at the Ontario Institute for Studies in Education. Some members contributed through their own research projects; others played a major role in studies that I initiated.

This book attempts to report and integrate the outcomes of all these efforts. In addition, it incorporates some highly relevant contributions to the field of adult learning made independently by other researchers in the United States, Canada, and the United Kingdom.

THE CENTRAL FOCUS: ALL OF THE ADULT'S LEARNING PROJECTS

In the *Encyclopedia of Educational Research*, Cyril O. Houle (1969) has identified five possible starting points for studying adult learning. One can begin with (1) one or more institutions of adult education; (2) the needs and characteristics of a community or society; (3) the individual learner; (4) a philosophical position; or (5) one or more methods of learning or teaching. An additional starting point could be a body of knowledge and skill to be disseminated to a certain target group.

The starting point of our approach is the adult learner. In particular, we focus on his major efforts to change himself – to learn better ways of doing things, to gain new information and knowledge, to change his perception, behavior, or performance. Our focus includes only highly deliberate learning efforts, not the multitude of phenomena and forces that produce changes in a person without his strong *desire* for learning. Many changes occur in the adult as a result of developmental changes within him, factors beyond his control, his social and physical environment, his casual conversations and television viewing, and his recreational reading. These changes are important to the adult, but they are not the focus of this book. We study only the person's *efforts* to learn: the episodes in which his desire to learn or change is stronger than all his other motivation.

This book encompasses *all* of the adult's learning projects, regardless of what he is trying to learn, why, how, and where. Because we are interested in obtaining a complete picture of the person's total learning effort, we do not restrict our focus to certain methods or places of learning, certain reasons for learning, or certain subject matter.

We do not start, for example, with the notion that learning guided by an instructor or group is somehow better than all other forms of learning. Instead, we have included any learning efforts in which the learner himself does most of the day-to-day planning. We have also included learning that is guided by a set of recordings or printed materials, a correspondence course, or a series of television programs. Learning guided by another person in a one-to-one relationship has also been included, for example, driving lessons, private music lessons, counseling and individul psychotherapy, and some athletic coaching. In addition, of course, we have included classes, conferences, meetings, sensitivity groups, and discussion groups. Some of these may be organized by an adult education agency or extension service, others by a professional association, and others by a service club or church group.

Men and women learn in many ways: by reading books, magazines, and newspapers; by watching television and movies; by seeking subject matter and advice from friends, relatives, neighbors, or fellow workers; by consulting a doctor or lawyer, a salesman or librarian, an extension agent or financial expert. They may also attend discussion groups, lectures, and private lessons.

Sometimes the adult sets out to gain certain knowledge and skill because it will be highly useful in the very near future. At other times he simply wants to possess the knowledge and skill for its own sake, perhaps to have a broad understanding of the world around him. Occasionally the main reason for a learning project is the desire for credit toward some degree or certificate. This book includes all of these reasons for learning and deals with both vocational training and the liberal arts – practical training, and learning for its own sake.

Adults learn a wide range of knowledge and skill. An individual may set out to increase his own self-understanding and self-acceptance, or he may simply want to learn how to refinish a coffee table. He may want to learn about some area of history, philosophy, economics, current affairs, natural science, or social science. He may want to gain more knowledge before making an important decision on the job, or about his own financial affairs. He may learn to play a musical instrument, or to play golf or bridge. He may want to increase his skill in teaching, raising children, supervising, or in some other major task. He may learn in order to plan a trip, buy an appliance, operate a ham radio, deal more effectively with people, or develop a philosophy of life.

Some efforts to learn are relatively brief or superficial. Learning about washing machines in order to buy the best model, for example, hardly seems to involve fundamental changes in personality or behavior. Other learning efforts are aimed at changing one's self-concept, perception and understanding of others, deep feelings, or creativity. Some efforts are aimed at modifying overt behavior, such as a habit, an addiction pattern, or a shoplifting tendency. Some learning projects are primarily cognitive or intellectual, some are aimed primarily at attitudinal and emotional change, some are designed to develop physical skills, and many are a mixture. The term *knowledge and skill* is a convenient way of referring to the entire range of desired changes.

HOW COMMON AND IMPORTANT ARE THESE LEARNING EFFORTS? Highly deliberate efforts to learn take place all around you. The members of your family, your neighbors, colleagues, and acquaintances probably initiate and complete several learning efforts each year, though you may not even be aware of it. When asked about their learning efforts, many of our interviewees recalled none at first, but as the interview proceeded, they recalled several recent efforts to learn. Perhaps this book will open your eyes to some of your own learning efforts, as well as those of your co-workers, your spouse, your students, your colleagues, your political representatives, or your friends.

Highly deliberate learning is a pervasive phenomenon in human life. The 700 hours a year devoted to learning efforts are enormously significant for the adult himself, and for the organization, family, and society in which he works and lives. Although 700 hours constitutes only 10% of an adult's waking time, surely this small percentage affects his life nearly as much as the other 90%. It is during these 700 hours a year, when he sets out to improve his knowledge, skills, perceptions, attitudes, habitual reactions, insight, and perspective, that the adult develops and changes. He resembles an organization that maintains and increases its effectiveness by devoting 10% of its resources to research and development.

Learning projects by members of a society are a means to a better future for that society. When politicians, corporation presidents, and heads of state spend some time learning before making major decisions, their decisions are more likely to be sound. The learning efforts of researchers, journalists, parents, artists, and teachers are clearly important to a society. Several writers have pointed out that adult learning is a crucial factor in achieving peace, reducing poverty and discrimination, increasing the effectiveness of the consumer's decisions, reducing pollution, and reducing population growth.

The individual as well as society benefits from his successful attempts to learn. He gains new abilities and competence, new strength and confidence, an enlarged understanding of the people and environment around him. He can cope better with changes in job, technology, values, and consumer products.

Continuing learning is itself becoming a goal of human life. In advanced nations, more and more men and women are moving beyond material goals, as their lower-order needs such as food are satisfied relatively easily. They are setting a new goal for themselves: self-actualization, the realization of their enormous potential. They are seeking the higher joys of gaining new knowledge and skills, of achieving better self-understanding, of learning to interact more sensitively and honestly with others. The incredible expansion of human growth centers and other means of maximizing human potential is one sign of this shift.

CHILDREN AND ADOLESCENTS Although this book is concerned primarily with adults, we have also interviewed 10-year-olds and 16-year-olds. Their out-of-school learning is extensive, and is similar in some ways to adult learning. Schools and colleges are increasingly recognizing and fostering such learning, thus preparing their students to be competent adult learners.

4

THE SCOPE OF THE BOOK   One emphasis throughout the book is on the *deciding* and *planning* aspects of learning. The learner first has to decide whether and what to learn (and even why). Then he must decide whether to plan most of the learning episodes himself, or whether to select some individual, group, or other resource to perform that responsibility. If he decides that his learning project should be self-planned, as the majority are, he is then responsible for countless detailed decisions and arrangements. In addition, regardless of who is planning the learning, the learner must decide occasionally whether to stop or continue.

Another theme throughout the book is the *help* that the learner seeks and obtains with the various preparations for learning. Often the help available to him is unsuitable or inadequate. Consequently, several chapters suggest innovative programs and procedures that various agencies or institutions may want to experiment with, in order to provide better help for the adult learner, or to develop his competence in making plans and arrangements for learning.

Related topics such as the following have already been discussed by several authors: the various methods of learning; how to teach adult groups; the social psychological processes in those groups; the structure and administration of adult education institutions and growth centers; the detailed cognitive processes during the learning episodes; the effect of certain variables on the behavioral outcomes of the learning episodes; and psychological development during adulthood. Consequently, this book moves on to tackle some other aspects of the adult's learning efforts. In turn, these insights suggest various implications for theory and practice in adult education (including training and development, the human potential movement, extension, and mass media), library science, self-directed change, schools and colleges, and teacher training.

The approach in this book may also contribute to the new conception of man being developed by certain social scientists, who view man as a self-directing organism with initiative, intentions, choices, freedom, energy, and responsibility. This strongly positive view of man's potential sees him as capable of achieving fundamental and far-reaching changes – in his feelings as well as his cognitive knowledge, in his self-insight and relations with others as well as in his physical skills and aesthetic awareness.

According to this view, at times man is a creature pushed and pulled by his environment and by unconscious forces within, but at other times he can effectively develop plans for changing himself and his environment. At times he changes because of coercion, manipulation, or subtle techniques of control and persuasion by others. At other times, though, he detects and resists those forces, and sets his own directions and goals for change.

2 Episodes and learning projects

A learning project – the central focus of this book – is here defined as a series of related episodes, adding up to at least seven hours. In each episode, more than half of the person's total motivation is to gain and retain certain fairly clear knowledge and skill, or to produce some other lasting change in himself.

For convenience, we have adopted the shorthand label *learning project* to refer to this series of related episodes. "A sustained, highly deliberate effort to learn" or some such phrase might communicate the meaning more clearly at first glance, but seems cumbersome after repeated use.

EPISODES The concept of an episode is the foundation on which the definition of a learning project is constructed. Any one day in a person's life may be crowded with a multitude of activities, and one way of grasping or conceptually organizing this variety of activities is to see how they are divided into episodes. An episode is a period of time devoted to a cluster or sequence of similar or related activities, which are not interrupted much by other activities. Each episode has a definite beginning and ending in time. The activities during an episode include all of the person's experiences (everything he does, thinks, feels, hears, and sees) during that period of time.

A concrete example will illustrate the concept of an episode. If we asked an executive to record his activities between 8:10 A.M. and 9:00 A.M. one day, here are the episodes that he might record: 8:10–8:25 read the morning newspaper; 8:25–9:00 drove to the office. To the person himself, and to anyone watching him, it would be clear just when he was moving from the first episode to the second. This transition would be marked by the executive putting down the newspaper and putting on his coat.

In each episode, the intent or activity remains constant throughout the episode. Other aspects, though, may change. The first episode the executive recorded, for example, was reading the morning newspaper. The goal may change from one article to the next, because one article may be relevant to his job and another may be read primarily for pleasure. But the activity of reading and the place remain constant. In

6

the second episode, the intent (reaching the office) remains constant even though the activities may include starting the car, sitting, and walking, and even though the place changes.

An episode, then, is a well-defined period of time that is held together by the similarity in intent, activity, or place of the thoughts and actions that occur during it. The episode has a definite beginning and ending, and is not interrupted for more than two or three minutes by some other activity or purpose. Many episodes are between 30 and 60 minutes in length, but some are shorter or longer.

The concept of an episode emerged in 1966 in some open-ended interviews about adult learning. In these exploratory interviews, I asked people to tell me about their entire range of learning – about all the different things they learned and all the ways they learned. Most people structured their descriptions in the form of episodes. Each person's daily life seemed to consist of activities divided into various "chunks" of time, each period lasting 20 or 30 minutes, two hours, or somewhere in between.

I became aware that many people plan or describe their day in terms of episodes. In this sense, episodes exist in real life: they are not just arbitrarily and artificially imposed on experience by a researcher. I then asked several individuals to record their activities for a day. They found little difficulty in dividing their day into clear-cut episodes; the time of each transition was clear and precise.

It became evident that focusing on episodes was the most appropriate psychological foundation for defining the phenomenon in which I was interested. For most persons, it was fairly easy to recall and describe an episode accurately, and each episode was clear, definite, almost tangible. Our choice of episodes as an especially meaningful piece of reality has not been shaken by our experience in the countless interviews since then.

VERY DELIBERATE LEARNING EPISODES Now let us narrow our focus. Instead of being concerned with the great variety of episodes in a person's life, let us select one sort of episode – episodes in which more than half of the person's intention is to gain and retain certain definite knowledge and skill. Such episodes can include reading, listening, or watching. They can take place in a library, classroom, store, living room, den, kitchen, hotel meeting room, or train. The person can learn with an instructor, in a group, or alone. The desired knowledge and skill can be simple or complex, deeply personal or almost trivial. The person can use the knowledge and skill for solving a problem, obtaining academic credit, or reflecting on the future of mankind.

Despite their variety, these episodes all have one thing in common: an intent that remains dominant throughout the episode. In each episode, the person's desire to gain and retain certain definite knowledge and skill is dominant. It is stronger than the sum of all his other reasons for beginning and continuing that episode.

We have selected this type of episode, which we will term a *very deliberate learning episode*, or sometimes just a *learning episode*, because it seems especially interesting and significant. These short phrases are a label referring to a phenomenon that is described in greater detail in the following sections.

"Knowledge and skill"

When we state that, in a learning episode, the person's intent is to gain certain "knowledge and skill," we intend the phrase to have the following meaning. The term *knowledge and skill* includes any positive or desired changes or improvement in a person's knowledge, understanding, awareness, comprehension, beliefs, ability to apply, ability to analyze and synthesize, ability to evaluate, judgment, perceptual skills, physical skills, competence or performance, response tendencies, habits, attitudes, emotional reactions, recall, awareness, sensitivity, insight, confidence, patience, and self-control, and/or some other personality characteristic, inner behavior, or overt behavior.

These changes result from experience – from what a person sees, hears, feels, thinks, or does. Changes that are produced by a drug, chemical, surgical operation, implanted electrodes, or illness are not included. Also excluded are attempts to improve one's appearance by adding lipstick or dentures, one's health and energy by getting more sleep or refraining from eating or drinking too much, or one's vision by wearing contact lenses.

It is now evident that the meaning conveyed by the phrase "knowledge and skill" is much broader than the bare dictionary definition of these two nouns. Several other terms might have been equally appropriate: learning outcomes, psychological changes, changes in the person, changed behavior. The meaning we have assigned to the term knowledge and skill is similar to the learning theorists' definition of learning. See, for example, Hilgard and Bower (1966, pp. 2-6).

In deciding whether a given episode is a learning episode, we ignore several characteristics of the person's desired changes. They may be large or small, superficial or deep, useful to the individual or harmful, useful to society or useless, intended to last for two days or for a lifetime. Sometimes, at one extreme, a person tries to produce deep and far-reaching changes in himself, as in learning to deal with a major responsibility such as child-raising or a new job. Or learning episodes may involve a broad and fundamental area of competence, such as becoming more effective with other people. At the other extreme, the purpose of certain learning episodes may be to gain relatively simple information or skills that will be useful for only a week or two.

8

"Fairly clear and definite"

One criterion of a learning episode is that the person is trying to gain certain knowledge and skill "that is fairly clear and definite." That is, the person must have certain definite desired knowledge and skill clearly in mind. Alternatively, he could be clear on the desired application of that knowledge and skill, or on the question or puzzle to which he is seeking an answer. The desired knowledge and skill in one particular learning episode, for example, might be to understand the structure of galaxies. Or the person may want to memorize certain French vocabulary, or discover a colleague's opinions about a proposed change.

This criterion excludes episodes in which the person wants to learn *something*, but does not have any definite or clear knowledge and skill in mind. Many people attend a museum or a world's fair primarily in order to learn, but have little or no idea of what the content of that learning will be. The decision to take a certain job or to travel may also be motivated by a desire to learn, but with no definite knowledge and skill in mind. The person expects to benefit somehow from such an experience, but does not have a clear picture of just what changes will occur in him.

"Retain"

The definition of a learning episode specifies that the person wants to gain *and retain* certain knowledge and skill. In many learning episodes, the person wants to retain the knowledge and skill for many weeks or years; in others he hopes to retain it for a lifetime. Sometimes, though, the person wants to remember the knowledge or retain the skill for just a few hours or days. Consequently, we have had to set an arbitrary minimum length of time.

The criterion we chose is simply this: the person must want to retain the knowledge and skill until at least two days later. If he is learning the knowledge and skill on a Tuesday, for example, regardless of whether it is eight o'clock in the morning or just before bedtime, he must want to retain it until at least Thursday morning.

This criterion means that efforts to gain certain knowledge and skill for only a brief time are not regarded as learning episodes. For example, reading a set of instructions one step at a time during one's efforts to assemble something is not a learning episode. In that situation the person wants to remember the instructions only during the next hour or two while he completes the next step.

A similar example involves a person's efforts to learn about new washers or new cars in order to decide about making a purchase. This learning and deciding might be crowded into one or two days. If the person was not strongly motivated to retain the information after making the decision, these efforts would not be considered very deliberate learning episodes.

If the purchaser wanted to retain a *portion* of the knowledge for several days, we would have to discover whether the motivation to gain and retain that portion was at least 51% of the total motivation. Similarly, a newspaper reporter might have some slight desire to remember the gist of an incident for some time, but be primarily motivated by the immediate goal of putting the information into today's story.

A salesman learning about a client and his needs before his first and only contact with that client is another example of an effort to gain, but not retain, certain knowledge. That is, the salesman might have no desire to remember the information after seeing the client that evening or the following morning.

Similarly, a secondary school guidance counselor may spend 25 minutes reading the files of the three students he is about to interview, but has no intention of remembering the information past the end of the interviews. This episode seems to be temporary "information processing": it is not prompted by a desire for relatively permanent knowledge.

The reader may wonder why I chose "two days later" or "until the day after tomorrow" as the minimum length of time for which the person must want to retain the desired knowledge and skill. A shorter time simply seemed too short to me. Gaining certain information in order to use it the next day seems quite different from wanting to remember it for a longer period of time. A longer criterion might make as good sense as the one I have chosen. Wanting to retain the knowledge and skill for at least three or four days, for example, or even for one or two weeks, might be an acceptable criterion. I cannot think of any special reason, though, for choosing one of these times instead of two days. In most learning episodes, in fact, the intent is to retain the knowledge and skill for at least a week or two.

It would be possible to establish 48 hours or some other definite number of hours as the minimum criterion. Although this would be easier to understand and communicate, it seems to me that, if the episode occurs on Tuesday evening, there is not really much difference between wanting to retain the knowledge and skill until Thursday morning compared to Thursday evening. However, I do see a fairly important difference between retaining it until Wednesday ("tomorrow") and retaining it until Thursday.

"More than half of the person's motivation"
With notebook in hand, we could follow a person through a normal day. As he begins each new episode, we could ask "For what reasons are you going to perform this activity?" or "What are your goals for the next 30 or 60 minutes?" Our question would be focusing on his immediate reasons for the episode he is just starting, not on his ultimate or long-term goal or purpose.

One of his immediate goals for the episode might be to gain and retain certain knowledge and skill that is fairly clear and definite. If this reason is stronger than all of his other reasons put together, we consider the episode a very deliberate learning episode.

Let us suppose, for example, that we are interested in four women, each of whom is taking a speed reading course. One evening, each woman picks up a biography or travel book in her home, reads it through quickly at two seconds per page, and then reads it again at five seconds per page. We cannot tell from the overt behavior of the four women whether this is a very deliberate learning episode or not. Consequently, we ask each woman her reasons for the episode, and we ask her to assign a percentage of her total motivation to each reason.

Let us suppose that we obtain the data shown in Table 1. Reading the book was clearly a very deliberate learning episode for the first two women. By adding together the percentages for the first two reasons offered by the third woman, we realize that it was a learning episode for her, too. For the fourth woman, however, even though learning was the strongest *single* reason, this was not a learning episode.

Table 1 / Reasons for Reading a Particular Book

Reason	First woman	Second woman	Third woman	Fourth woman
To gain and retain the main ideas of the book	0	70	30	0
To produce a relatively permanent increase in the ability to grasp the important ideas of a book at high speeds	90	0	30	40
Pleasure, relaxation, escape	0	30	40	30
Immediate interest in the content (apart from a desire to retain it)	10	0	0	30

The underlying concept may stand out more clearly in Figure 1, which uses a continuum to show the data for the same four women. In this figure, all episodes falling to the right of the 50% point are very deliberate learning episodes. All of the numbers refer to the person's conscious motivation just before the beginning of the episode, or very early in the episode. We are not concerned with the motivation several hours or days before the episode begins.

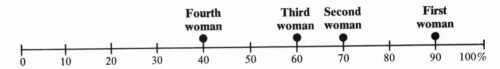

Fig. 1 / A continuum: The portion of a person's total motivation (for beginning and continuing a given episode) that is accounted for by his desire to gain (and to retain until at least two days later) certain fairly clear knowledge and skill.

OUR CENTRAL FOCUS Since our central focus is on the adult's *efforts* to learn, we are interested in episodes in which a certain *intention* (gaining and retaining certain knowledge and skill) accounts for more than half of the person's motivation. These efforts produce a great deal of knowledge, skill, understanding, affective change, and behavioral change in people.

Many other experiences and factors, though, also produce changes in people. Consequently, many researchers define their central focus as any episode or phenomenon that does, in fact, produce some significant change or learning in the person, regardless of the strength of his intent. This is an important and useful focus, but it is not the one chosen for this book.

Instead, for a variety of reasons, we have chosen to focus on the person's highly deliberate *efforts to learn*. In particular, we study his decisions, preparations, reasons for learning, help, problems, and needs.

One reason for our focus is the probability that very deliberate learning efforts account for a large portion of the person's total change over a year. One section in the next chapter speculates on just how large this portion is, compared to the changes produced by episodes in which the person's intent to learn is weaker. A second reason for choosing to study and describe highly deliberate learning efforts is simply that they have been relatively neglected by researchers. The third reason is the most important. The adult's highly deliberate efforts to learn provide an excellent starting point for developing better competence and help in adult learning. A person may be willing to accept help (and accept opportunities for developing his own competence) with something he is *trying* to accomplish. He is not so likely to accept help with something for which his motivation is low.

LEARNING PROJECTS In the earlier part of this chapter, we selected very deliberate learning episodes from the ever changing activity of a person's life, and discussed only single episodes. We now use that concept as a foundation for defining our central phenomenon. That central phenomenon – a learning project – is a *series* of clearly related episodes. Instead of focusing on a single episode, we examine several related episodes, usually spread over a period of time.

These episodes may be related by the desired knowledge and skill. For example, the learner may want to learn about various aspects of India. In one episode he reads about the roles and relationships of men and women in India. In another episode he learns about the current economic and political situation from an Indian graduate student. In a third episode he watches a television program describing the life of an Indian child. These three episodes differ in method of learning, in place of learning, and in the particular aspect of the total subject. Yet in the person's mind, they are clearly related by his overall goal of learning about India.

Very deliberate learning episodes can also be related by the use to which the knowledge and skill will be put. A person might undertake a variety of experiences in order to improve his competence as a parent. Another series of episodes might be aimed at obtaining the knowledge and skill necessary for building a boat, solving a problem, or drawing up a set of recommendations.

Time

A series of related learning episodes might add up to a total of 3, 30, or 300 hours. In order to define a learning project precisely, it is necessary to set a minimum length of time. We have chosen a minimum of seven hours, even though most learning projects are much larger than this. In fact, the mean time for a project is more than 100 hours.

There are several reasons for our choice of seven hours as the minimum size. A seven-hour period is equivalent to one working day, which is a significant amount of time to spend at one particular learning effort. In addition, this minimum seems to work out well in actual interviews. We find that this criterion does not eliminate many learning efforts that are especially important. At the same time, most of the learning efforts that do meet this criterion are quite large or significant.

Of course, one could probably argue quite successfully that six hours or ten hours would be just as appropriate a choice. Either of these criteria would eliminate learning efforts that required only two or three hours.

We also wanted to eliminate learning efforts in which the minimum time was spread over a year or two. Consequently, we set another criterion: the minimum of seven hours must occur within a six-month period. The total learning project might last much longer than six months, of course, but we must be able to identify some six-month period in which the individual spent at least seven hours at this learning effort. Otherwise, the effort does not seem intensive enough to include; it seems too diluted or spread out.

Most learning projects go far beyond the minimum criteria we have set. These criteria seem necessary, however, to separate major learning efforts from those that are not very significant or intensive.

Almost all learning projects consist of more than three or four episodes, and these episodes occur on at least two or three different days. Our definition, though, could include an intensive one-day effort that had very few interruptions.

With most learning efforts mentioned in interviews, there is no doubt about whether they fit our definition of a learning project. Our interviewers found that almost all efforts to learn mentioned by the interviewees either met the criteria for a learning project without any doubt, or clearly did not do so. Only a few examples were borderline or doubtful. Some of these difficulties and borderline cases are discussed in Appendix A.

Laymen grasp the concept

Few people actually call their learning projects by that name; many do not even apply the term *learning* to their efforts. They simply regard the series of learning episodes as an interest or hobby, or as part of some responsibility. During the first few minutes of an interview, helping a person to identify his learning projects is often a challenging task. Few adults see their activities related in this way except when taking a course.

Quite quickly, though, the typical interviewee does grasp the phenomenon we are describing and does identify one or more recent learning projects. Indeed, "clearly related" in our definition of a learning project means that the person himself considers the episodes clearly related (by the desired knowledge and skill or by the responsibility or action for which they will be used). The learning project must be clearly defined in his mind, and he must be able to decide without much difficulty whether any given episode in his life is part of the project or not. The learner, not just the interviewer, must perceive that the various episodes are clearly related to one another, and are fairly distinct from all other episodes.

Even though a person may have some professional interest in learning or education, he may have the same difficulty as others in thinking immediately of his recent learning projects. One way to bring examples to mind is to think of subjects or topics in which one is particularly interested, for example, hobbies and other leisure-time activities. Another way is to recall some major problems or decisions

14

that one may have tackled recently. An effort to learn may have accompanied them. One further way to recall examples of one's own learning projects is to think of certain recent activities; reading, television, travel, meetings, or group discussion may have formed part of a recent learning project.

The concept of a *series* of episodes is not just an arbitrary concept that we impose on experience. People do plan and describe many of their activities in this way. Miller, Galanter, and Pribram (1960), for example, have pointed out that people do have plans, and that these plans provide structure to what a person does during the day. When planning a day, the person may have several possible plans in mind, though the details for each have not yet been established. The person then decides which one to execute or continue that day. Although the authors discuss intention in general rather than intention to learn, their concept of plans seems readily applicable to learning efforts.

3 How common and important are learning projects?

The definition of a learning project presented in the previous chapter enables us to tackle the following question: how common and important are these sustained, highly deliberate efforts to learn, change, and grow? This chapter first describes our 1970 survey of learning projects in seven adult populations, and then presents some highlights from several other studies. After discussing people who learn an exceptional amount, the chapter ends with some speculation about the importance of learning projects compared to all other sorts of learning.

THE 1970 SURVEY   By 1970, several persons in the adult education department at the Ontario Institute for Studies in Education had intensively interviewed more than 200 men and women on a variety of questions, for several different research projects. Throughout all of the interviews, however, we were impressed by how enthusiastically and how often people set out to learn. As a result, in 1970, we decided to focus our attention more precisely on determining how common and important learning projects are.

We did not have enough interviewers or time to cover more than 60 or 70 persons. To spread our resources further, we decided to select small but careful samples from seven populations: blue-collar factory workers, women and men in jobs at the lower end of the white-collar scale, beginning elementary school teachers, municipal politicians, social science professors, and upper-middle-class women with preschool children.

Several individuals helped with the planning of this study and the development of the interview schedule: Jim Fair, Shirley Shipman, Vida Stanius, Cressy McCatty, and David Armstrong. The first three conducted the interviews.

The interviews were intensive and highly structured. Several probing questions and two handout sheets were developed to help people recall their learning efforts, because some self-planned learning efforts are especially hard to recall six or eleven months later. Few previous studies have probed adequately for them. The interviewers used the definition of a learning project outlined in the previous chapter, and were urged to omit any borderline learning efforts. The interview schedule was

16

revised three times. A copy of the final version is available from the OISE Department of Adult Education.

Quantitative findings

First let us get an overview of the findings by combining the data from all seven populations. Then, after looking at some general impressions, we will examine the details of each group.

The typical person conducts about eight learning projects in one year. More precisely, the mean is 8.3 and the median is 8. All but one of the 66 interviewees had conducted at least one learning project in the past year, which produces an astounding "participation rate" of 98%. The detailed data are presented in Table 2.

Table 2 / How Many Learning Projects Does an Adult Conduct in One Year?

Number of projects	Number of persons	Number of projects	Number of persons	Number of projects	Number of persons
0	1	7	6	14	1
1	1	8	6	15	2
2	1	9	9	16	3
3	4	10	4	17	0
4	7	11	3	18	1
5	4	12	3	19	0
6	7	13	1	20	2

These figures are higher than the figures in other surveys of adult learning and adult education. Several factors account for the differences. Our study used extensive probing by interviewers who were thoroughly familiar with the study's purposes and definitions; as a result, they were more successful than other studies at helping people recall self-planned learning efforts. Also, they interviewed the learner himself, not someone else in his household. In addition, our definition of a learning project differs somewhat from the phenomenon on which certain studies have focused. Finally, the seven populations we chose do not provide an unbiased sample of all adults.

To determine how much time people spend at their learning projects, we used a detailed instruction sheet and asked each person to consider carefully just how many hours he had spent at each of his learning projects. By adding together the hours for all of his projects, we obtained the total time the individual devoted to learning

17

during the previous year. The mean of these individual totals was 816 and the median was 687. In short, the average or typical interviewee spent about 700 or 800 hours a year at his learning projects, though the range was very large, from 0 to 2509 hours. Additional details are shown in Table 3.

Table 3 / How Many Hours Do Adults Spend at Learning Projects in One Year?

Number of hours	Number of persons	Number of hours	Number of persons	Number of hours	Number of persons
0–99	7	900–999	5	1800–1899	1
100–199	3	1000–1099	2	1900–1999	0
200–299	6	1100–1199	3	2000–2099	0
300–399	6	1200–1299	0	2100–2199	0
400–499	5	1300–1399	2	2200–2299	1
500–599	3	1400–1499	2	2300–2399	1
600–699	4	1500–1599	1	2400–2499	2
700–799	6	1600–1699	0	2500–2599	1
800–899	2	1700–1799	3		

We were also interested in the length of the typical project. For each person, we calculated the mean number of hours (during the past year) per learning project. If a person had spent 800 hours at 8 projects, for example, his average time per project was 100 hours. The mean of all these individual means was 104, and the median was 81. During a year, then, a representative interviewee spent roughly 90 hours at each of his learning projects.

About two-thirds of all learning projects were still current and active at the time of the interview; only one-third of the projects were completed or dormant. Our data do not include the many hours that would have been spent at some projects during the months after the interview, nor the hours spent more than 12 months before the interview. (Many projects last much longer than 12 months, as found by Tough, 1967.) A study of only *completed* learning projects would probably establish that they are generally much longer than 81 or 104 hours.

Learning for credit
Less than 1% of all the learning projects uncovered by the interviews were undertaken for credit, which included "credit toward some degree or certificate or diploma, . . . toward passing a test or examination, completing an assignment for a course, or producing a thesis, . . . toward some license, or a driving test – or toward

some requirement or examination or upgrading related to a job." If the desire for credit was even 30% of the total motivation for the learning project, it was counted as a credit project.

Despite the detailed questions and the subsequent probing, we found that only 0.7% of all the learning projects were for credit. Apparently learning for credit forms only a small portion of all adult learning. One tends to agree with Johnstone and Rivera (1965) who concluded that "in the main, the earning of formal credit is not an important motive in the educational behavior of American adults [p. 68]." At the same time, one must realize that the actual number of adults taking courses for credit (including full-time students who are at least 21 years old) is rather impressive, even though the percentage is not.

Some "soft" data

Many unsolicited statements and actions during interviews that convey enthusiasm and commitment confirm the quantitative data about the importance of learning projects. A strong determination to succeed, and preserverance despite difficulties, also indicate that many learning projects are very important to the person.

People are eager to talk about their learning projects, partly because they rarely have a chance to describe them to an interested listener. On the one hand, trying to improve oneself – to gain new knowledge or become a better person in some way – is certainly an exciting part of one's life. On the other hand, for some reason, people do not usually discuss this topic at parties or the dinner table. This is unfortunate, because such a discussion can reveal a very positive aspect of a person that is not evident during other conversations. Several times, during an exploratory interview with a family member or friend whom I thought I knew very well, I have discovered an attractive but unsuspected side of the person. Sometimes this impressive new aspect is a goal or an interest, sometimes an earnestness or thoughfulness, and sometimes an intelligent, aggressive striving to become a better person.

Comparing populations

Now let us return to the data collected in our 1970 survey in order to compare the various populations. Table 4 compares the middle or average learner in the various groups by using two measures of central tendency. For each measure and group, Table 5 describes the highest and lowest individual.

Over a one-year period, the faculty members in psychology and sociology spent more time at learning than any other group we interviewed. The typical member of this group spent more than 1700 hours at his 11 or 12 learning projects; one spent 2500 hours. This group was a random sample of associate professors chosen from

19

Table 4 / Comparing Populations: Means and Medians

Population	Total hours at all learning projects	Number of learning projects	Mean number of hours at each learning project
Professors (N = 10)	1491	12.0	117
	1745	11.5	97
Politicians (N = 10)	1189	6.7	190
	908	7.0	135
Lower-white-collar men (N = 10)	907	9.1	111
	827	8.5	114
Factory workers (N = 10)	800	5.5	146
	799	5.5	116
Lower-white-collar women (N = 10)	430	8.2	48
	425	8.5	44
Teachers (N = 6)	395	10.2	42
	371	9.0	43
Mothers (N = 10)	331	7.2	47
	273	6.5	46

Note. – Each cell describes the average or typical learner in the sample. The first figure in each cell is the mean; the figure below it is the median (the "middle" person).

the psychology and sociology departments of three major universities in Ontario.

Politicians were second highest in total hours spent at learning. The typical politician spent about 1000 hours at his 7 learning projects; one spent 2400 hours. This group was composed of full-time elected politicians at the municipal level in two large cities, including the two mayors. All had been in office for more than one year, and their educational level ranged from Grade 8 to a bachelor's degree.

The lower-white-collar men constituted the next highest group in total hours devoted to learning. These men were a random sample from lower-level positions (including a department store salesman, airline passenger agent, and clerk) in large companies. They had been working at least three years, had never attended college, and were earning less than $7000 a year.

The blue-collar factory workers were a random sample from the receiving

Table 5 / Comparing Populations: Ranges

Population	Total hours at all learning projects	Number of learning projects	Mean number of hours at each learning project
Professors	385–2509	6–18	64–209
Politicians	365–2403	4–9	54–464
Lower-white-collar men	452–1494	4–16	49–170
Factory workers	80–2205	1–10	32–433
Lower-white-collar women	30–919	2–15	15–100
Teachers	159–677	5–20	23–62
Mothers	0–1039	0–20	13–115

Note. – Each cell describes the interviewee who was lowest on the given measure, and the interviewee who was highest.

department of a tire and rubber plant. Their jobs did not require a high level of knowledge, training, mental skill, or interpersonal skill. Each man was between 25 and 45 years old, and had not gone beyond Grade 12 in school.

In this survey, the four groups spending the most time at learning were predominantly male. We turn now to the three groups, predominantly or entirely female, that were below average in time spent at learning, though not necessarily in their number of projects.

The group of lower-white-collar women consisted of typists, stenographers, and secretaries in two large companies. They did not have any children, had been working at least two years, and had never attended college. As Table 4 indicates, on the average they conducted eight learning projects, but spent only 430 hours doing so.

Elementary school teachers in one district in their first year of teaching were almost overwhelmed with problems on the job. They conducted a fairly large number of learning projects, but could not find much time for them.

The mothers interviewed were a representative sample of one upper-middle-class neighborhood. During the year before the interview, each woman's primary occupation was that of mother and homemaker. Each mother had at least one young child who was not yet attending school or nursery school.

Some clear differences were evident within each population, as well as between populations. That is, within each population a few individuals were marked by a great deal of learning, and a few by only a relatively small number of projects or hours spent at learning. Our populations were chosen by occupation, social class, age, sex, and educational level. Apparently many other factors also affect how often a person sets out to learn. These influential factors include the individual's past experiences, his current personality or psychological characteristics, the people around him, and certain characteristics of his community and society. Some detailed speculations about these influential factors are presented in Appendix B.

Other populations

Our 1970 interview schedule was used or adapted in four recent unpublished studies. In each one, the findings tend to confirm the general picture presented earlier in this chapter.

Cressy McCatty, in a Ph.D. study that is still in progress, has interviewed 54 men in engineering, medicine, and other professions. Chosen at random from the assessment rolls of a large suburb, these men spent an average of 1240 hours per year at 11.1 learning projects.

Alex Drdul interviewed 12 successful IBM salesmen. They spent a mean of 1113 hours a year (lowest man: 630) at 13 learning projects; the medians were 1013 hours and 12.5 projects. Approximately two-thirds of the learning was job-related.

David Armstrong, in a current Ph.D. project, interviewed 40 men enrolled as full-time students in an academic upgrading program designed to provide sufficient skills for employment. The 40 men were selected by their instructors: 20 of them because they spent a great deal of time at learning, and the other 20 because they spent an average amount. The higher group, during the year before the interview, spent a mean of 1340 hours at class-related learning and another 1121 hours (13.9 projects) at nonschool learning. The lower group spent 1177 hours at school learning, and conducted 3.4 projects (100 hours altogether) at noncredit learning.

Elementary school teachers approaching the end of their first year of teaching are being interviewed by Jim Fair for his Ph.D. study. His data include only learning that is intended primarily to improve the person's professional performance and that occurred during the first seven months of the school year. The 35 teachers he has interviewed spent a mean of 500 hours at 9 projects.

CHILDREN AND ADOLESCENTS In our 1970 survey, to provide an interesting comparison with adults, we interviewed 16-year-old boys and 10-year-old children. The same interviewers and basic interview procedures were used, but a few minor changes were made in the details of the

22

interview schedule. Only out-of-school learning was included; we did not include any learning projects designed to please the teacher or to get credit toward passing the year at school.

The 16-year-old boys who were interviewed were suggested by the interviewer's friends. She asked her friends to suggest acquaintances who were a little more energetic, busy, and active than average 16-year-olds, and who were reasonably well liked by others. In short, she tried to obtain boys who were above average in activity, but normal in other ways.

About half of the 10-year-olds were chosen randomly from the same neighborhood as the group of upper-middle-class mothers. The others were obtained through a lower-middle-class school. There were equal numbers of boys and girls.

The data indicate that the out-of-school learning projects of young learners are fairly similar to adult projects. Indeed, the 16-year-olds conducted more learning projects than most of the adult groups, but spent only 70 hours at the average project. Further details are provided by Tables 6 and 7.

Table 6 / Youth Out-of-School Learning: Means and Medians

Population	Total hours at all learning projects	Number of learning projects	Mean number of hours at each learning project
16-year-olds ($N = 10$)	609	9.4	66
	680	9.5	72
10-year-olds ($N = 10$)	139	6.2	23
	113	5.5	18

Note. – Each cell describes the average or typical learner in the sample. The first figure in each cell is the mean; the figure below it is the median (the "middle" person).

Table 7 / Youth Out-of-School Learning: Ranges

Population	Total hours at all learning projects	Number of learning projects	Mean number of hours at each learning project
16-year-olds	140–922	4–14	32–102
10-year-olds	14–432	2–13	7–61

Note. – Each cell describes the interviewee who was lowest on the given measure, and the interviewee who was highest.

Several differences between the learning efforts of 10-year-olds and of adults emerged from the interviews. First, a child learns a far greater variety of knowledge and skill than the adult. This occurs partly because the adult no longer needs to learn anything further on certain topics, and partly because he has become more selective in his areas of interest. The child, in contrast, has a great deal to learn, and has interests that are scattered rather than focused.

Second, most of the child's learning episodes are relatively short. The child asks a few questions or reflects briefly when his interest is aroused by some remark or phenomenon. Or he reads about some topic for 15 minutes, or watches a 30-minute television program. His learning episodes are rarely longer than one hour, except when taking part in some sort of visit or expedition, or perhaps when practicing a sport.

Third, the total number of hours spent at these learning episodes often does not total seven hours over a half-year period. As one interviewer reported, "Many learning efforts are too short in time to fit our definition. Children tend to flit from one interest to another without devoting a great deal of time to any one area."

Fourth, many other episodes result in a great deal of actual knowledge and skill, but the intent to learn is not especially strong. The 10-year-old tends to choose an activity, hobby, or sport because it will be interesting or fun, not consciously because it will produce certain knowledge and skill or help him become a better person. Perhaps he simply does not think often about the future, and has no thought of how he will change during the next few months or years.

Several of these characteristics of the 10-year-olds are also typical of the out-of-school learning of younger children. By the time a person reaches the age of 16, though, some clear changes have occurred. During his hours away from school and homework, the 16-year-old spends far more time at sustained learning efforts than he did at an earlier age. These efforts are marked more clearly and strongly by the intent to learn. Also, he learns more often in order to handle effectively his new responsibilities and the major problems and decisions that are not faced by a 10-year-old. In many ways the 16-year-old is closer to the adult than he is to the 10-year-old. At the same time, though, much of his learning continues to be devoted to athletic skills, musical instruments, and topics of general interest about which he is curious.

Some clues about new roles for school teachers emerged from interviewing the 10-year-olds. Their out-of-school ("noncredit") learning was often influenced by their teachers. Many learning projects, especially for the girls, grew out of an activity or topic at school, or a question or book suggested by the teacher. The interviewer, Jim Fair, has also suggested that schools can help the child develop the wide range of learning skills and the familiarity with various resources that are necessary for effective self-planned learning. It also became evident in the interviews that the human and physical environment, at home and school, has an enormous impact on the 10-year-old's learning.

NEEDED RESEARCH Our 1970 study has provided an estimate of the frequency and importance of learning projects in various populations. Its strengths included a carefully developed interview schedule with sufficient probing, and interviewers who became thoroughly familiar with the background and definitions of the study. The samples were very small, however, and not all of them were chosen on a completely random basis from a large population. Despite the inadequacies of the samples, the data are encouraging enough to indicate that further research could be very valuable.

There is an obvious need for a study of a very large adult population. The ideal would be a large-scale survey using sophisticated sampling techniques to draw a representative sample of the total adult population in several countries. As part of that study, or before it, several smaller populations might be interviewed. In our 1970 study, we did not reach the highest-level corporation president, the top politicians in a country, the unemployed, the functionally illiterate, the criminal, the very old and the very young, and recent immigrants. In addition, we overlooked student radicals, graduates from schools that emphasize various innovations, and 10-year-olds who have never attended school. And our knowledge about the differences between the self-planned, out-of-school learning efforts of children and adults is very primitive.

A researcher with a fresh approach could probably improve the interview schedule used in our study. The interviewers felt several learners were not recalling or revealing all their learning projects, especially their self-planned efforts. We could not think of any other means, however, of stimulating recall or of reducing the person's hesitation to mention a personal, mundane, or offbeat project. Recall might be improved by interviewing the person every three or four months, instead of hoping he can remember an entire 12-month period.

EARLIER STUDIES Several studies during the 1960s, and even earlier, have noted that many adults make highly deliberate efforts to learn. Some of the studies are primarily concerned with adult education programs, others with adult reading.

Adult education programs
Some of the studies of adult education programs have measured the number of adults in various classes and in other programs sponsored by certain institutions, but have

omitted the 70% or so of all highly deliberate adult learning that is self-planned. Although most of these surveys find thousands of adults in educational programs, these numbers constitute a disappointingly small proportion of the total adult population.

Dramatic increases have already occurred, and will continue to occur, in enrollments in organized courses for adults. Moses (1969), who calls this sort of education "the educational periphery," estimates its total enrollment in the United States as 22 million in 1950, 28 million in 1960, and 82 million in 1975. Cohen (1967) provides some interesting estimates of the total "learning force," which is defined as the total number of learners in schools and colleges as well as in the educational periphery. He compared the size of the learning force and of the labor force in the United States, and estimated this ratio at about 83 to 100 in 1940 and 1950. By 1965, the ratio had shifted dramatically to 127 to 100; the learning force was, by 1965, greater than the total labor force. Cohen's projected ratio for 1974 is 159 to 100.

At least three studies have included learning projects that were self-planned as well as those sponsored by adult education institutions. Depending on the procedures and definitions used during the interviews conducted in the different studies, the percentage of the total adult population that had recently conducted a learning project was 25 (Johnstone & Rivera, 1965), 71 (Blackburn, 1968), and 82 (Blackburn, 1967).

Reading
Several American surveys of adult reading point up the widespread use of this method for learning. Parker and Paisley (1966), for example, found that most adults read at least one newspaper each day. They found that 40% spend at least one hour a day doing so, which works out to more than 300 hours a year. Three-quarters of the interviewees mentioned information for practical use as their first reason for reading the newspaper, with only 12% mentioning relaxation or habit.

Magazines turned out to be an important source of knowledge for adults (Smith, 1963). All but 18% of the adults in the Parker and Paisley study read a news or general magazine, a woman's or home magazine, or some other magazine, such as a hobby or travel magazine.

The average executive spends four hours a day reading business reports and correspondence, business magazines, and other business material. He devotes another 10 hours a week to newspapers, newsmagazines, general magazines, and non-business books such as histories and biographies. "All in all," reported Strong (1957), "he spends at least a quarter of his waking hours with eyes glued to the printed – or

26

typewritten – page [p. 60]."

Books, too, are an important source of learning for at least some adults (Campbell & Metzner, 1950; Parker & Paisley, 1966; Porcella, 1964). Some nonfiction books become best sellers even though written in a technical style, and even though originally written for an audience of specialists. Such books include the following: *Secular City*, *Games People Play*, *Human Sexual Inadequacy*, and *Honest to God*. Their popularity suggests that many people are interested in advanced thinking about such fields as social problems, psychology, sex, and theology.

Let us look for a moment at the person who writes the book, not the one who reads it. Some nonfiction writers conduct enormous learning projects in order to write one book. Vance Packard, for example, took four years to write *The Sexual Wilderness*; he talked or corresponded with 400 authorities, traveled to 10 countries and 130 campuses, read thousands of reports, and read many questionnaire responses. Another example is provided by John Pearson. In order to write a book about Ian Fleming, he traveled more than 100,000 miles, interviewed about 150 people, and made an extensive study of Fleming's private papers.

An economist's view

A noted economist, Fritz Machlup, had already written a dozen books when he decided to turn his attention to estimating the production and distribution of knowledge in the United States. The resulting book (Machlup, 1962) is so sweeping and comprehensive in scope that it is almost breathtaking, especially if read through rapidly at one sitting.

After outlining his meaning of "the production of knowledge," Machlup carefully estimated the number of dollars and workers in more than 30 knowledge industries in the United States. He estimated the amounts of money spent on (1) the education of youth and adults in schools and colleges, on the job and in the armed services, in the home, and in the church; (2) basic and applied research and development; (3) newspapers, periodicals, and books; (4) conventions; (5) other media of communication (radio, television, telephone, and so on); (6) a variety of information machines and instruments; and (7) information services provided by lawyers, doctors, engineers, insurance agents, and governments.

The grand total expenditure for the production and distribution of knowledge was a surprisingly high proportion of the Gross National Product, as adjusted by Machlup: about 29%. Moreover, Machlup estimated that expenditures on knowledge production have been increasing rapidly for some time: by 8.8% a year over a short period and by 10.6% a year over an 11-year period. If knowledge production really constitutes 28.7% of the GNP, Machlup argues, then the production of *other* goods and services included in the GNP increased by only 3.7% (or 4.1% over the longer period).

The number of individuals in occupations that produce and transmit knowledge has also been increasing dramatically. In 1959, Machlup calculates, 21,754,000 persons (32% of the civilian labor force) worked in such occupations. That is, an astounding one-third of all persons who worked spent their time producing, transforming, or transmitting knowledge and information rather than producing something else or performing some other service. No doubt the figures today are even larger: Machlup's figures show a consistent increase throughout the past seven decades.

HIGH LEARNERS   Some men and women learn to an extraordinary degree. They are the individuals who spend 2,000 hours a year at learning and who complete 15 or 20 different projects in one year. In their lives, learning is a central activity; such individuals are marked by extraordinary growth.

Several social scientists have detected and studied adult populations marked by especially high achievement, learning, or affective growth. Examples include gifted adults who are also high achievers (Terman & Oden, 1947), the self-actualizing adults studied by Maslow (1954), the outstanding creative scientists interviewed by Roe (1953), men and women conspicuously engaged in continuing learning (Houle, 1961), and the fully functioning person (Rogers, 1961). Describing "the beautiful and noble person," Landsman (1969) said that the same kind of person is also sometimes called productive, efficient, self-fulfilled, self-realized, or a super-person. Maslow (1969 b) has added these phrases: the Good Person, the self-evolving person, the responsible-for-himself-and-his-own-evolution person, the fully awakened man, and the fully human person.

These populations are marked by learning, by efforts to achieve their inherent potential, and by curiosity and joie de vivre. Yet, at the same time, these people like their present job, understand and accept their own characteristics, and are not strongly dissatisfied with their present self. They have the confidence and courage to reveal their real self. They have clearly directed interests: they choose their own career and activities and are not pushed by external forces. They have a strong but realistic commitment to some mission in life. They strive to achieve certain major goals, are spurred on rather than blocked by obstacles, and are productive and successful. Their relationship with at least a few people tends to be compassionate, loving, frank, and effective.

What proportion of the total adult population are we talking about? Perhaps it is the top 10% or even 20%. Or perhaps it is only 1% or 5%. Even these estimates may be too high. Let us suppose, as a very low estimate, that only one adult in a thousand is included. That would still be a fairly large number of persons in any one country: about 110,000 in the United States, 35,000 in the United Kingdom, or 11,000 in Canada, for example.

Behavioral scientists will make many important contributions to knowledge as they continue to study these populations of high learners. The members of this group are especially competent, efficient, and successful at learning. They probably set clear action goals, choose appropriate knowledge and skill, plan their learning episodes fairly easily, and learn without undue effort or frustration. These characteristics make them excellent subjects for studies of effective learning. They are the "growing tip" described by Maslow (1969 a). How can more of these persons be produced? How can other adults gain some of their effectiveness and happiness?

COMPARING OTHER SORTS OF LEARNING   In trying to determine how common and important adult learning projects are, we have discussed such factors as number of hours, number of projects per person, amount of money, and proportion of the labor force. One may also approach the question by asking how much of the change in a person occurs through his highly deliberate, sustained efforts to learn, and how much through all the other ways we have just listed.

A small but intensive study in 1966 provided a tentative answer. After listing the most important things they had learned since finishing secondary school, 20 educators listed the most important activities that had produced those changes. More than *half* of all their choices were learning projects (mostly self-planned learning and courses). Clearly, though, much more research is needed before we feel very confident about this answer.

Learning projects may be especially important for certain persons. If a man or woman spends 1,000 hours a year trying to grow in certain ways, these learning projects will probably change him greatly. The person who conducts only one brief learning project a year, however, is probably affected much more by other activities and factors.

Certain sorts of changes may typically occur through learning projects, and other sorts of changes through other activities. In what ways does a person learn about sex and marriage, raising children, human nature, political issues, his job? What develops his appreciation, sensitivity, mental health, concern for others, self-understanding, self-acceptance? A research or theory-building project might aim to produce a two-dimensional chart: various clusters of knowledge, skill, attitudes, and so on would be on one dimension; various sorts of episodes and factors that produce changes would form the other dimension. It would probably become evident that

29

certain sorts of major changes tend to result from certain sorts of episodes.

The following are some of the forces and activities, aside from learning projects, that produce changes in people.

1. Conversations, newspapers, books, periodicals, television, radio, movies, drama, and travel greatly influence the person's information and attitudes. Although these resources and activities are sometimes part of a learning project, they are often motivated by immediate pleasure, habit, sociability, or a desire for relaxation and entertainment.

2. Sometimes a person learns by observing the world around him, even when the *intent* to learn is not as strong as his other motivation – his curiosity or his desire for immediate enjoyment, for example. The world he observes might include a construction project, art display, sports event, zoo, factory, or trade show. More often, though, he learns through alert observation of human behavior and other common events in his everyday environment, and through thoughtful reflection on what he sees and hears.

3. Often the acquired knowledge and skill is a by-product of some task or responsibility. A person's primary or sole motivation might be to successfully finish a home repair project, chair a meeting, or supervise children. In addition, though, these activities may add to his information or skill, or change his attitudes or awareness.

4. Sometimes a person chooses a job, task, or responsibility because he thinks it will produce some desirable changes in him, or will be "a valuable experience." Other choices, too, are sometimes made primarily because of the beneficial changes they will produce: choosing a marriage partner, a group to join, or a neighborhood.

5. Sometimes episodes that no one intended to occur can greatly influence future behavior. After a traffic accident, for example, the driver may alter some aspect of his future driving in order to avoid having another similar accident. After a child has a fall or burn, his parents may change their behavior in order to prevent a recurrence. Embarrassing moments and frightening experiences also affect the person a great deal.

6. A pervasive, sometimes subtle, influence on the person is summed up in the word *environment*. This includes the people with whom he interacts (usually people of the same social class, neighborhood, age, sex, or occupation), the appearance and resources of his city or town, the political climate of his country, the expectations and norms of his society and employer.

7. The person's brain may be influenced directly by a chemical or by electricity. Psychedelic drugs can produce expanded consciousness, and certain sensations

and images. Some experimental chemical compounds may strengthen memory. Electricity transmitted through electrodes implanted in the brain has made shy women flirtatious, and other people happy or talkative. Brain surgery, or the removal of a gland, can also change a person's typical responses or mood.

8. At least some persons receive information through certain means beyond the normal, well-understood channels. Evidence suggests that some especially sensitive persons can see an object in another room, foresee a distant or future event, or communicate with a dead person. A few individuals can perceive the electrochemical force field around another person's body; in this way they can diagnose his medical problem, know his current mood, or evaluate him for a responsible position.

9. Sometimes a major insight comes from the unconscious mind. After intensive disciplined work at some problem, for example, the solution may suddenly jump into the person's mind while he is sleeping or golfing. Dreams also help us work out emotional conflicts and develop new insights.

ALL WAYS OF LEARNING AND CHANGING ARE IMPORTANT

All of these ways of learning, changing, and growing add up to a rapidly changing individual. The changes that occur over a 10-year span in most men and women are enormous. It is clear that the adult can change very quickly in basic characteristics and insights, knowledge, skills, beliefs, and attitudes.

Changes in adults are a necessary part of social change: the major problems of society cannot be solved without certain changes in people. Without an emphasis on helping people to learn or change, how can we move toward peace, economic development, productivity, zero population growth, more effective government, better cities, widespread physical and mental health, satisfactory race relations – and away from poverty, crime, urban problems, and pollution?

The importance to society of adult learning efforts can perhaps best be grasped by imagining what would happen to our society if all learning projects ceased. What would happen to industrial firms, business corporations, and government departments if the executives made all decisions as soon as they were told of a problem or issue, without bothering to learn anything more about it? Suppose new employees, or those recently promoted, did not bother trying to learn how to handle their new responsibilities. What would happen eventually to our health if all medical personnel refused to make any effort to keep up with new drugs, procedures, and knowledge in medicine? Actually, there would not be many new drugs and procedures in medicine; after all, no researchers would be trying to learn. What would eventually happen in our society if no parents read about child care, if no one attended sensitivity training groups, if no one went to counselors and lawyers for

31

help? What if no leader or citizen tried hard to learn about history, philosophy, religion, evolution, alternative futures, social problems, recreational activities, or the arts?

It is also hard to imagine that one could serve usefully in certain occupations without frequent efforts to learn. The medical doctor and college teacher, for example, must continue learning in order to keep abreast of changes in their fields of expertise. Without spending at least a day or two at learning, a journalist could not write a comprehensive article, an actor could not undertake a new part, a lawyer could not handle a complex case, a political leader could not make a difficult decision, a researcher could not plan a new research project.

It is clear, then, that adult learning and change are important to society and to the individual himself. As a result, many fields of practice and research are concerned with understanding or producing changes in men and women. These fields include personality theory, behavior modification, developmental psychology, adult education, humanistic psychology, organization development, communications and mass media, social psychology and attitude change, learning theory, psychotherapy and psychoanalysis, rehabilitation, manager development, counseling, manpower training, and agricultural extension. Realizing the importance of practice and theory in these areas, foundations and governments as well as universities have supported research and development efforts aimed at understanding how to encourage and facilitate certain changes in adults. Such research and development efforts should continue to encompass the entire range of activities that produce changes in the person's knowledge, skills, attitudes, behavior, and awareness.

At the same time, though, it is becoming evident that learning projects have been a relatively neglected area for comprehensive research and development efforts. Learning projects are far more common and important than anyone realized a few years ago. Studies in this area could make a very high contribution if additional researchers and support were found. Focusing on the person's *efforts* to learn may be a highly fruitful line of research or innovation: only when he has the *intent* to learn will the adult seek new sorts of help and resources that might be developed for him.

4 What people learn

Men and women set out to learn a wide range of knowledge and skill. Some of the subject matter sought in learning projects is complex, difficult, advanced, and abstract; some is esoteric, highbrow, or exotic; and other subject matter is simple, routine, even trivial.

The individual may set out to create major changes in his feelings and attitudes, in his cognitive knowledge, or in his physical skills and overt behavior. He may want these changes to last for a lifetime, or only for a few days. When the adult wants to produce major, far-reaching changes in himself, these desired changes will affect his self-concept, confidence, or mental health. Other learning projects may require only short-term and shallow changes, related only to routine or external goals.

In certain learning projects, the adult merely seeks some specific information that can be used as is. At other times, he must integrate or transform the information before applying it. Most learning projects seek established knowledge, which is gained directly or indirectly from other people who already possess it; a research scientist, though, may set out to gain some original knowledge or insight.

Preparing for an occupation, and then keeping up
A great many learning projects are related to the person's job or occupation. Because performance and attitudes on the job are of great importance to the economy of any nation, this type of learning is very significant to society.

Before entering a new occupation or job, an individual may have to take many courses or learn in other ways. In order to obtain a promotion or major new responsibility, the person may need to undertake an intensive learning effort. Job-related learning projects will probably continue to be important after the person enters the occupation or obtains a new job. At times, he may maintain or upgrade his competence by gaining general background knowledge or learning new skills. Also, as new knowledge is discovered in his field, and as procedures change, he will have to learn in order to keep up.

The range of trade, business, vocational, and professional subject matter is very wide. The fields of learning include electronics, tool design, blueprint reading,

33

business administration, real estate, finance, salesmanship, accounting, law, agriculture, teaching methods, office management, typing, shorthand, bookkeeping, automobile and television repair, foreman training, practical nursing, welding, data processing, and countless others.

Specific tasks and problems on the job

Attempts to update and upgrade one's knowledge and skill are only a part of job-related learning efforts. Many other learning projects consist of just one step in dealing with an immediate problem, case, or task. The person's goal is to prepare a report, make a decision, solve a problem, handle a case, or complete a short-term project. In order to do so successfully, he may decide to spend a great deal of time learning about certain aspects first.

In this situation, the knowledge and skill are acquired for some immediate and definite use or application. The person is preparing for an immediate task or decision, not for some rather vague situation in the distant future. This sort of learning project is often self-planned, because the desired knowledge and skill is rather unique or because the person wants it immediately.

A politician, senior government employee, or top executive, for example, may be faced with a decision that will have a great impact on many individuals, or on the future of his organization or country. Before making that decision, he may devote many hours to learning about it. Many teachers of youth and adults want to improve their performance as an instructor. In order to do so, the person might set out to learn the content to be taught, learn how to use certain teaching methods, or study the background characteristics of the people he teaches. In addition, the instructor can seek feedback concerning his weaknesses by asking his students and others to react to his teaching, or by watching himself in a videotape recording.

Several other examples of specific job-related learning projects are provided by men and women we have interviewed.

1. A lawyer set out to learn a great deal about air crash law after a client walked into his office and announced that her husband had been killed in a plane accident.
2. A community development worker had to read a great deal about the organization and family patterns of the Indian tribe with which she was working.
3. A senior school administrator traveled a thousand miles and expended much effort to learn about possible solutions for dealing with disadvantaged adolescents in his schools.
4. One learning project for an engineer began when he was asked to design a new type of sturdy tape recorder to measure certain factors in an antisubmarine projectile.

5. Aware that his company might begin its first advertising campaign, an investment dealer offered to learn the knowledge necessary for preparing recommendations concerning media, content, and budget.
6. An especially important learning project for a woman working for a children's aid society began when she was assigned several battered child cases. She had to learn the correct legal procedures and how to understand and help the child and the parents.
7. A nursing educator was a leader in planning a new nursing curriculum. In order to plan an effective program, she learned about the characteristics of nursing duties, and about the curriculum and organization of instruction in other schools of nursing.

Learning for home and personal responsibilities
In many learning projects, the person expects to use the knowledge and skill in managing the home and family rather than on a job. In one year, for example, 1,890,000 Americans made a sustained attempt (with or without an instructor) to learn about sewing or cooking (Johnstone & Rivera, 1965). Adults also learn about furniture, rugs, drapes, and other aspects of decorating and furnishing their home. Before buying a house, car, washing machine, tape recorder, or hobby equipment they may learn about the cost and characteristics of various available items. Men and women also learn about budgets, insurance, the stock market, and investing. Other learning projects may begin just before a wedding, childbirth, or moving to a new neighborhood. Through reading, counseling, discussion, or encounter groups, an adult may try to become more effective in communicating and sharing with his or her mate, in achieving a closer and more joyful relationship, and in handling conflicts.

The characteristics of children and youth are greatly influenced by the competence, attitudes, and goals of today's parents. Fortunately, many parents make an effort to learn about caring for a child's health, about the emotional and social development of children, and about helping them develop into effective adults. Parents also learn about changes in schools and society that will affect their children, and later they learn how to set their adolescent children free.

Before making certain decisions of intense personal importance, some adults set out to learn and think a great deal about such decisions. This may occur when choosing a career, deciding which university and course to enter, considering whether or whom to marry, deciding whether to have an additional child, selecting a place to live, or planning for retirement.

The astounding number of practical, how-to-do-it books purchased in Western countries points up just how common it is for adults to learn for home and personal responsibilities. An American study indicates that Dr. Spock's book on baby and child care has been bought by more than 19,000,000 adults (Hackett, 1967). The third most popular book in the period 1895-1965 was a cookbook, and the fourth an atlas. Another cookbook, and Dale Carnegie's *How to Win Friends and Influence People*, were also among the top ten. The lists provided by Hackett also indicate that adults have used more than one million copies of each of the following: several cookbooks, a bartender's guide, several atlases, several foreign and English dictionaries, books for developing vocabulary, home reference books on certain topics (medicine, home repairs and maintenance, housekeeping, marriage and sex, etiquette, gardening), and several encyclopedias.

Improving some broad area of competence

Sometimes an individual sets out to improve his competence in some broad area. The desired knowledge and skill are fairly definite, but may be applied in several areas of the person's life: in his home and family, while interacting with friends and acquaintances, on his job, and in his voluntary responsibilities in his community or some organization.

The individual, for example, may set out to improve his understanding of groups and individuals. This will enable him to be more effective as a group member or leader and in other interpersonal relationships. As a related or separate project, he may try to increase his understanding and acceptance of his own feelings, reactions, blocks, strengths, and weaknesses. He may try to decrease his defensiveness, increase his self-confidence or creativity, or overcome certain fears. He may attend a T-group or a Dale Carnegie course. The person may also try to work out his own meaning or values or goals in life. These may then be useful in guiding many practical decisions.

There are other areas in which learning projects are undertaken to improve one's competence in a broad area. Many adults work at improving their writing style, speaking ability, and vocabulary. Many learn about health, physical fitness, decreasing tension, dieting, or adjusting to bodily changes. The adult may also set out to become more creative and flexible when diagnosing and solving problems, more efficient in all his responsibilities, more imaginative, or less selfish throughout his life.

Learning for interest or leisure

Many learning projects are related to some hobby or other leisure-time activity. In one year, more than a million American adults took lessons in golf, swimming, bowling, tennis, skiing, sailing, scuba diving, surfing, curling, squash, or some other athletic activity (Johnstone & Rivera, 1965). A very large number learned some decorative art or craft such as ceramics and flower arranging. Others tried to improve their painting, drawing, sketching, or photography. Each year, a large number of adults learn to play a musical instrument, take singing lessons, or take dancing lessons. One of every 4.8 Americans play a musical instrument, "making self-made music second only to reading as the nation's most popular leisure-time activity (*Time*, January 14, 1966, p. 49)." Other adults learn about stereo equipment, stamps, hiking, bridge, or pets. Some adults who plan a trip spend many hours gaining information about where to go and what to see.

Some of these recreational interests will lead the person into whole new worlds that were almost invisible before. His new sport, hobby, or interest may lead him to join certain organizations such as a naturalists' club, an orchid growers' association, or a sailing club. A whole world of expertise, technical terms, magazines and newsletters, meetings, like-minded people, standards of excellence, and competitions may suddenly open up before him.

Curiosity or a question about certain subject matter
Many learning projects begin with a question, a feeling of puzzlement or curiosity, or just a general interest in a certain body of subject matter. Some people, for example, want to understand the physical or geographical world, and do so by learning about various regions and perhaps by traveling. Others study the behavioral or social sciences in order to understand society or human nature. Other common areas of learning are English literature, the physical and biological sciences, political science and politics, current events, and economics.

Persons who want to gain some notion of the likely future of mankind may read about probable trends during the next few decades or centuries. In order to gain some perspective about the future, they may also read about past history, about the evolution of man, and about the origin and structure of the universe. Some people want to work out their own set of religious beliefs or philosophy of life. They may learn about their own religion, other religions, or humanism.

Sometimes a dramatic event will puzzle or upset an adult, and he will then begin a major effort to understand what happened and why. A person who is suddenly asked for a divorce or separation, for example, may set out to understand the behavior and events that led to the other person's feelings.

In France, a survey found that geography and history were relatively frequent topics for study (Dumazedier, 1967). In the United States, approximately 3,500,000 people study the basic teachings of a particular religion, or some other religious or moral topic (Johnstone & Rivera, 1965).

37

A number of studies in several Western countries have shown that some anticipated use or application of the knowledge and skill is the strongest motivation for the majority of learning projects. Most adults, in most learning projects, are motivated by some fairly immediate problem, task, or decision that demands certain knowledge and skill. In relatively few learning projects is the person interested in mastering an entire body of subject matter.

In the United Kingdom, Robinson (1965) found that most adult learning arises from the personal, practical needs of everyday life, not from some intellectual curiosity about an academic body of knowledge. Most people "do not at some stage decide that they would like to know more about economics or psychology: they are concerned about how much it will cost them to redecorate their homes or why their children behave in the way they do. These interests might well lead them quite far into economics and psychology, but they will start with concerns of a personal kind [p. 181]."

In France, a survey conducted by Dumazedier (1967) also found an emphasis on practical and technical knowledge: "The preferred topics are connected to *utilitarian* preoccupations, answering a need for information about matters affecting daily life [p. 205]."

In Canada, a study of 35 learning projects found that the desire to use or apply the knowledge and skill was the strongest motivation in 71% of the projects and was present in every other project (Tough, 1968). In many learning projects, this reason was even stronger for continuing than for beginning. Apparently some learners, as they proceed with a project, discover some unexpected uses for the knowledge and skill.

Also in Canada, Knoepfli (1971) interviewed 21 women who were responsible for forming 21 autonomous learning groups, and found that each of the women, to at least some extent, was motivated by this reason. The 21 women mentioned a total of 66 specific applications of the acquired knowledge and skill.

An early lecturer in the United States (Channing, 1838) declared that self-education or self-culture is practical. "It proposes, as one of its chief ends, to fit us for action, to make us efficient in whatever we undertake [p. 18]."

Knowles (1967) has pointed out that adults "engage in learning largely in response to pressures they feel from current life problems; their time perspective is one of immediate application. . . . They tend to enter any educational activity in a *problem-centered* [not subject-centered] frame of mind [p. 278]." The practical nature of adult learning has also been pointed out by Love (1953), Johnstone and Rivera (1965), and Parker and Paisley (1966, p. III/22).

Houle (1961) found several goal-oriented learners – people who gain knowledge in order to put it to use in achieving some goal. Sheffield (1964) and Flaherty (1968), using factor analysis, subsequently found two sorts of goal orientations: in one the knowledge and skill are to be used in achieving a personal goal; in the other they are to be used for a societal or community goal.

With children, too, the desire to achieve some action goal may be an especially strong motivation for learning. Holt (1967) has suggested that "if we begin by helping children feel that reading and writing are ways of talking to and reaching other people, we will not have to bribe and bully them into acquiring the skills; they will want them for what they can do with them [p. 112]."

DERIDING ONE TYPE OF SUBJECT MATTER OR MOTIVATION

Some people denounce or ridicule one sort of learning or another: they scoff at liberal education because it seems useless to the individual and to society, or they express contempt for vocational education because it is just narrow, practical training.

Many of the scoffers divide all learning into two categories: vocational and liberal, training and education, learning for use and learning for its own sake. They assume that any given learning project or course falls into either one category or the other. They fail to realize that both sorts of reasons are present in the typical learning project (Tough, 1968, section 16). It is rare for an adult to learn exclusively in order to use the knowledge and skill, or exclusively in order to acquire the affective benefits inherent in the knowledge itself.

When discussing preparatory education for an occupation or profession, some persons insist that many liberal courses should be included, and other individuals insist that these are a waste of time. Again, the approach taken by both sides presupposes that a simple dichotomy exists. When one looks more carefully at the various sorts of knowledge and skill that are learned for an occupation, the picture becomes more complex.

In a current master's study, for example, Tom Norton distinguishes several types of objectives in the post-secondary training of technicians. These include: (1) manual skills and the use of tools and machines; (2) the scientific theory and principles on which the specific technology is based; (3) general mathematics and science; (4) clear communication orally and on paper; (5) the contributions and context of the particular technology, and its relationships with management and with other technologies; (6) human relations; (7) political science and economics; and (8) the ability and willingness to continue learning about the occupation.

All of these clusters of knowledge and skill are relevant to a technician's performance. Surely it is absurd to declare that any one of them is unimportant to the individual and society, or lacks dignity and prestige. It also seems absurd to deride all these areas as simply "vocational," thus ignoring the range of knowledge and skill that is included.

It seems clear that people do – and should – learn all sorts of things. Some learning will be broad or shallow or superficial; some will be deep or narrow. Some will be practical, related to the job, or useful in some other area of life; some will result from curiosity, puzzlement, a thirst for knowledge, a seeking after truth. Much learning will combine several of these elements.

THE USEFULNESS OF LEARNING PROJECTS IN A CHANGING SOCIETY

Deliberate learning would be important even if there were no changes in the world surrounding the individual. Rapid changes do occur in that world, of course, but first let us look at certain sorts of learning that would occur even without those societal changes.

Some learning projects are initiated because of certain changes that occur in the individual as he moves through the life cycle. He marries and has children. His interests change with age, and he engages in new sports or leisure activities. As he achieves one goal, he moves on to another. As his savings increase, he buys a house or a new car. He receives a promotion because other people in the company retire or die. He receives new responsibilities on the job as his experience and competence increase. These changes and stages in the person's life, and the learning projects they spark, would occur even in a completely unchanging society.

In addition, though, rapid changes do occur in the world around the individual. These social, economic, political, and technological changes not only make an increase in learning necessary or desirable, but also influence the content of that learning.

Some learning projects are necessary to help the individual to *adjust* to changes in knowledge, processes, technology, values, and social organization. These changes affect him on the job, in the home, and elsewhere. He may have to prepare several times for a new occupation, or at least for new procedures and responsibilities in a single job. In his daily life, he must become familiar with new products, laws, recreational and cultural opportunities, and transportation procedures.

The pace and direction of future change in society will be influenced by the adult's resistance or willingness to change in certain ways as a parent, teacher, worker, or consumer. Changes in society will, in turn, result in people learning certain knowledge and skills that are not common at present.

Some learning projects are designed to *produce* or *direct* certain changes in society, not merely to adjust to them. They are oriented toward the future, toward planning or producing social or other change in an organization, curriculum, city, or region. For example, many learning projects occur throughout the sequence of

40

research, development, invention, innovation, adoption. Planning for community or organizational change is often preceded by careful study.

In fact, any major decision of great public importance may be preceded by an intensive learning project. In this way, the most beneficial courses of action can be determined for achieving peace, controlling population growth, reducing pollution and other problems of urban industrial living, and promoting international development. By studying the possible wide-ranging consequences of various routes to achieve a specified goal, public officials can make the decision within a wider and longer-term context.

FURTHER EXPLORATIONS THAT ARE NEEDED

As one reflects on what people learn, the need for several further contributions to theory and practice becomes evident. There are many approaches that can be taken to arrive at an adequate picture of what adults learn.

Developing lists

Because most surveys of adult learning have missed so many learning projects, there is a need for a large-scale survey of what people learn. One task of this survey would be to work out an appropriate way of describing, clustering, or categorizing the diversity of knowledge, skills, attitudes, and affective changes in learning projects.

This survey, or a subsequent one, might include adult populations in many countries. Do people learn different sorts of things in France, Germany, Scandinavia, England, Canada, and the United States? Do people learn quite different knowledge and skills, and for quite different reasons, in developing countries? To what extent do people learn different things in Africa, South America, India, and Southeast Asia?

The survey might also include all ages, even children. It would be interesting to know at what age or stage most people learn each cluster of knowledge and skill. In what ways does a person's language change as he moves through the life cycle?

Instead of studying the actual present learning of adults, an investigator might ask what adults *should* learn. Several lists of what children and adolescents should learn have already been developed; for example, *Cardinal Principles* (1918), Bobbitt (1924), National Education Association of the United States, Educational Policies Commission (1938), Kearney (1953), and French (1957). Perhaps, if it is possible to develop one, a comprehensive list of what adults should learn would also be useful. This list might include things that adults should learn for their own benefit, things they should learn for society's benefit, and things they should learn in 1990 or some other future time. By comparing such a list with the results of the proposed survey of actual learning, the gaps between what adults do and should learn would become evident.

41

New ways of learning new subject matter

The next 20 years might see the development of new ways of learning new things. Developing new ways of learning subject matter that few people now try to learn is a very exciting prospect – it may turn out to be one of the most significant areas of new practice in adult learning.

The last 20 years have produced some important new additions to the content of adult learning projects. Through group and individual methods, many adults now set out to increase their self-insight, their awareness and sensitivity with other persons, and their interpersonal competence. They learn to "listen to themselves," to free their body and their conversations from certain restrictions and tensions, to take a risk, to be open and congruent. Attempting to learn this sort of knowledge and skill seemed incredible to most people 20 years ago. Great changes in our conception of what people can and should set out to learn have been created by T-groups, the human potential movement, humanistic psychology, and transpersonal psychology.

Perhaps the next 20 years will produce several important additions to what we try to learn. In 1990, when people look back to our conception of what adults can learn, will they be amused by how narrow it is?

It is natural for many things to seem incredible to us. Perhaps it is not really impossible, though, to develop ways and resources for an adult to learn how to relax or go to sleep in 10 minutes anytime, anywhere; how to set and modify his life goals; how to perform his daily tasks with half the effort and tension; how to control his heartbeat and brain waves; how to eliminate any bad habit he chooses; how to deal effectively with his own emotional problems and interpersonal difficulties; how to assume effective control over his own physical health; how to assess political candidates and their speeches and decisions; how to choose the best environment and style for any particular task or activity. Already efforts are being made in some of these directions.

In the future, perhaps it will also be far more common for an adult to set out to become a highly sensitive and joyful spouse or parent; to become a much more competent learner or helper; to gain an accurate feeling for his own place in history and in the universe; to express himself in music, poetry, film, and sculpture; to become competent at planning travel and recreation; to expand his consciousness or develop competence at meditation; to become less selfish or more committed to some mission in life; and to learn how it feels to be a corporation president or an Asian peasant.

One of the greatest challenges for the innovative practitioner is to develop new materials and methods that will increase the amount and ease of learning in these areas.

A personal inventory

In addition to global surveys, it might be useful to explore better ways of helping each individual see clearly what he already learns and what else he should learn. Constantin A. Doxiadis, the noted planner, raised this possibility in 1968. While writing his chapter for the book *What I Have Learned*, he realized that "we cannot make an inventory of our intellectual gains as easily as we can of our material ones – perhaps because there is no internal revenue department to keep track of them.

Is it not time to think of an annual declaration of our gains in learning, not in order to pay tax on them, but so that we may know how far behind we are and what we need to catch up [p. 36]?"

5 Why people learn

Several times during the year, an adult initiates a major effort to learn or change. What sorts of reasons provide the impetus to learn? What do people expect to gain from their learning efforts? There are many other ways in which a man or woman could spend the hundreds of hours devoted to learning, some of which would provide more pleasure or income than the learning projects. Instead, the adult spends several hundred hours a year at learning.

The question of why men and women learn is extremely important, for it is hard to develop better help for adult learners without understanding their reasons for learning. The question has been discussed by many writers (Hall, 1965, Appendix A), going back as far as Socrates.

A complete picture of why adults learn will require many approaches, focusing on various aspects. Even understanding why one particular adult begins one particular learning project is an enormous task. He may anticipate a variety of benefits from the learning project. One might also have to study his childhood, his basic personality characteristics, and his long-term goals and responsibilities. Strong irrational forces within him may be influential, though he may not even be conscious of them. His age, previous education, socioeconomic status, occupation, intelligence, optimism, or mobility might be part of the explanation. Various events and individuals in his environment may also increase his motivation.

OUR APPROACH The goal of this chapter is to fill in a small but significant portion of the total picture: the benefits that the person intends to obtain through the learning project. These desired outcomes are present in his conscious mind when he decides to begin the project.

Some of the intended benefits are immediate; others are expected to result from a chain of consequences. The benefits anticipated by the learner are not only intellectual, cognitive, and material; many are emotional or psychological, including pleasure, satisfaction, self-esteem, impressing others, and receiving praise.

44

Rationale

There are several reasons for choosing this portion of the total picture, that is, for trying to determine which benefits a person anticipates in undertaking a learning project.

First, exploratory interviews indicated that the anticipated benefits constitute a significant portion of the person's total motivation for learning. Though subconscious forces deep inside the person and the stimuli in his environment affect his decision to learn, in most learning projects the person's clear anticipation of certain likely benefits is even more important.

Second, the appropriateness of our approach is supported by a certain view of man that is becoming more widespread in psychological literature. Man, according to this view, can be active, energetic, free, and aware. He often chooses his goals, direction, and behavior; he is not always pushed and pulled by his environment and by unconscious inner forces.

Third, in many of our efforts to teach certain knowledge and skill and to change attitudes and behavior, we do something *to* the person regardless of his needs and even his wishes. When beginning a learning project, however, the person often has fairly accurate and complete information, and makes a fairly free and conscious decision to undertake the project. Many episodes in which someone else is trying to influence the adult do not fit our criteria of a learning project; in such cases, the person's intent may be vague, or the person may even be trying to *resist* the persuasion.

Fourth, our approach to understanding why adults learn fits in with our definition of a learning project. That definition emphasizes one sort of anticipated outcome: certain fairly clear knowledge and skill that the person wants to have a few days or weeks later. Also, the definition requires that the person be fairly clear about his motivation for beginning the episodes: if he feels uncertain or doubtful, he cannot meet our criteria.

There is an interesting parallel between the individual level and the societal level. A growing corps of futurists point out the importance of a society examining alternative futures. A society, or all mankind, should study the consequences that are likely to result from each decision that is possible at the present time. By making appropriate selections today, society can influence its future, rather than merely wait for the inevitable to occur. The individual, too, can consider what sort of person he wants to become, and what goals he wants to achieve, before making a choice between various alternatives. He can set out to produce a certain future for himself, instead of feeling that his life is completely determined by forces over which he has little control.

OVERVIEW A person begins a learning project because he anticipates several desired outcomes or benefits that are interrelated. Figure 2 shows the various possible chains of positive consequences that a learner might anticipate and summarizes the various benefits that might motivate a person to begin a learning project. The various routes (chains of events) show the possible relationships among these benefits. An arrow means that the event or feeling at the left produces the event or feeling at the head of the arrow.

An illustration

Let us suppose a man has decided to landscape the front yard of his new suburban home. He realizes his actions will include deciding whether to grade his yard, deciding the location of the flower beds and shrubs, choosing certain plants, and actually doing the grading and planting. He also realizes that he could learn about grading and landscaping from books, magazines, friends, neighbors, and salesmen.

The sequence of future events being considered in the amateur landscaper's mind is represented by A-B-C in Figure 2. That is, box A leads to box B, which in turn leads to better decisions and performance (box C). In addition, the man might expect to have a better image of himself just as a result of possessing his new knowledge of landscaping. This anticipated benefit is represented by the arrow from box B to *self-esteem*. Finally, the man may anticipate certain sorts of enjoyment or satisfaction while actually reading the landscaping magazines and talking with his neighbors. These expected benefits are summarized by the *pleasure* growing out of box A.

For this particular learning project, all the other reasons presented in Figure 2 might be irrelevant. The amateur landscaper is not interested in credit (box F) or some material reward (box D) for undertaking his learning project.

If we were interviewing the amateur landscaper, we might ask him to imagine that his motivation for the learning project could be measured in some sort of unit. We could then arbitrarily define 100 units as the strength of his total motivation for all the episodes in the project. After helping him to understand our diagram, we could ask him to distribute the 100 units throughout the diagram to show the relative strength of the various expected outcomes. His distribution would show which expected outcomes were especially important in his mind when he decided to begin, which were moderately important, and which were of no importance.

There are at least 18 or 20 possible locations in Figure 2 to which he might assign several units. He would assign them to the end-points of his various chains of benefits. In most learning projects the person is influenced by several possible benefits, but certainly not by all. Alternate routes to some of the benefits are available, and the learner might choose one or both of them.

46

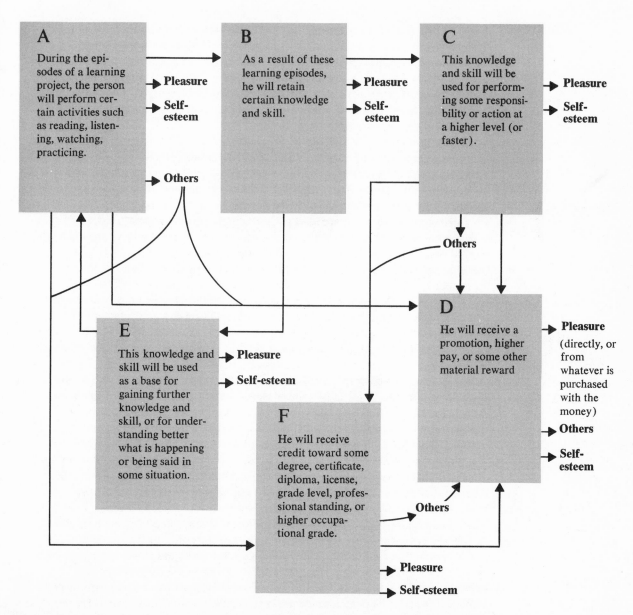

Fig. 2 / The relationships among the benefits that a learner may expect from a learning project.

As he proceeds in his learning, the landscaper will actually experience some of the benefits that he predicted. When deciding whether to continue his learning efforts, he will probably be able to predict benefits more accurately than at the beginning of the project. In addition, however, he may experience some unexpected benefits during the learning project, which will increase his motivation for continuing. The typical adult learner, in fact, has more reasons for continuing his learning than for beginning a learning project.

Figure 2 presents only the positive outcomes of learning projects: its purpose is to describe why people begin and continue learning, not to point out their obstacles and frustrations. The process of estimating the cost of the learning project in terms of money, time, and frustration is discussed in the next chapter. Here we are concerned only with the individual's reasons for beginning.

Three words in Figure 2 are used as convenient shorthand terms for describing a large cluster of ultimate benefits. One of these terms, representing the ultimate benefit occurring at the end of several chains of consequences, is *pleasure*. This benefit can include an increase in pleasure, joy, "feeling good," happiness, delight, satisfaction, enjoyment, or other positive emotions. It could also include avoiding or reducing some unpleasant or negative feeling. In Figure 2 and throughout this chapter, we will simply use the term *pleasure* to indicate this large cluster of benefits.

Several chains of events end in another sort of benefit: the person regards himself more highly, feels more confident, feels he is a better person than before, and/or avoids a damaging blow to his self-esteem or self-image. This benefit also might include maintaining one's self-image as a good parent, a knowledgeable man, an informed citizen, a person who always does a good job, or a curious person. We will use the term *self-esteem* to refer to this cluster of benefits.

One other cluster of benefits appears fairly often in Figure 2. Like the two just mentioned, it often comes at the end of a chain of events. Sometimes it is an ultimate benefit in that no further benefit flows from it. That is, it is sometimes an end in itself, rather than a means to some other end. This third benefit is simply the following: other persons, when they become aware of the adult's learning or accomplishments, regard him more highly, like him more, feel pleased, or feel grateful. These other persons may then praise the learner or express their positive feelings or high regard in some other manner. Our shorthand term *others* can also mean avoiding displeasing others, or avoiding reducing their regard.

Any one of the three clusters of benefits just mentioned can, in turn, produce the other two benefits. A person's new self-esteem, for example, may lead to greater happiness, and may please or impress others.

Procedure

This way of understanding why adults learn was developed in 1967 at the Ontario Institute for Studies in Education, by a research team consisting of Heather Knoepfli, Vida Stanius, Ray Devlin, and Allen Tough.

In developing our thinking about why adults learn, we tried to remain open to all possible sources of insight and data, including our own experiences and those of people we knew well, published biographical material, and research and theoretical literature. In addition, we interviewed a fairly broad range of adults, and asked several other adults to write an account of their learning projects for us.

Our starting point was any adult who made a highly deliberate, sustained attempt to learn something, regardless of how or what he learned. His methods of learning could include reading, listening, attending a conference, taking lessons, practicing, and watching a television documentary.

Our interviewing moved from an early exploratory stage to a testing stage. After revising the interview schedule, we conducted intensive, semi-structured interviews with 35 adults. During the two hours he was interviewed, the adult was guided by detailed lay descriptions of the various benefits that might have influenced his decision to begin. Then, on a four-point scale, he rated the strength of each reason for beginning and for continuing the learning project. Our procedures and findings are presented in an early detailed report of this study (Tough, 1968). Much of the report, however, is superseded by the present chapter.

In our study, we were able to identify several reasons for undertaking learning projects. To discuss them, we will turn first to box C in Figure 2: *using* the desired knowledge and skill, a very common reason for learning. Then we will turn to box E, which includes future learning or understanding. Two other benefits flow from retaining certain knowledge or skill (box B): the pleasure and self-esteem that result from merely possessing the knowledge and skill. Credit toward some degree or certificate is a fourth outcome that a learner may expect; the various routes leading toward box F will be discussed. Finally, several benefits may flow immediately and directly from certain characteristics of the learning activities themselves.

THE INTENTION OF USING THE KNOWLEDGE AND SKILL

It is common for an adult to face some task or responsibility. He may have to make a decision, develop a set of recommendations, build something, or produce something. In order to perform the action at a higher level of performance, he may spend some time beforehand gaining certain knowledge and skill. He will then use or apply the knowledge when he is performing the action (box C in Figure 2).

This is the strongest reason in the majority of adult learning projects, as has been demonstrated by several studies that were mentioned in the previous chapter.

49

Even when it is not the strongest reason, the intention of using or applying the knowledge and skill is often present to some extent in a learning project. The relevant portion of the total diagram is reproduced as Figure 3.

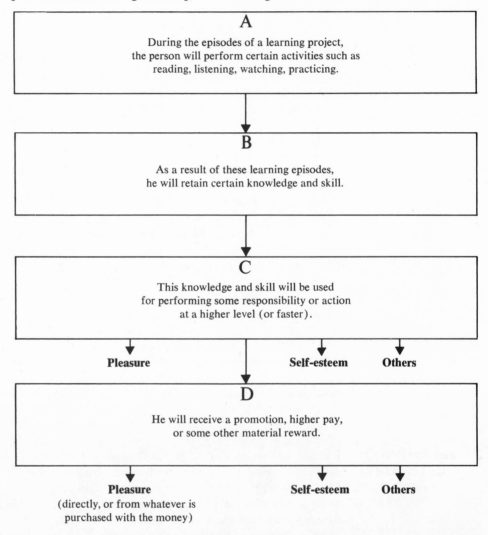

Fig. 3 / The intention of using or applying the knowledge and skill.

When the person's central concern is a task or decision, he will not be very interested in learning a complete body of subject matter. Instead, he will want just the knowledge and skill that will be useful to him in dealing with the particular responsibility of the moment.

The variety of applications

Knowledge and skill are gained for a wide variety of uses and applications. One man we interviewed was asked to draw up recommendations on the most suitable computer installation for his company's personnel department. In order to prepare an excellent report, he set out to learn about computers, systems, and his company's needs. A young woman wanted to make certain clothes that could not be bought. Consequently, she had to learn how to operate a sewing machine and how to choose appropriate materials and patterns. A young singer who had agreed to sing in six operas wanted to perform very well. He therefore worked hard at learning the words, music, and stage movements for his six parts.

All three of these adults wanted to take some action: to plan, to sew, or to sing. Their action goals or desired end-products were, respectively, a good set of recommendations, some pieces of clothing, and a good operatic performance. In order to achieve these action goals more efficiently or successfully, they set out to gain certain knowledge and skill.

The action goal was chosen or assigned first; it then became clear that certain new knowledge and skill would be useful in achieving it. The knowledge and skill provide a means or tool for dealing successfully with some task, situation, decision, or activity: the adult learns because he expects to use or apply the knowledge and skill directly in order to achieve something.

The person may go back and forth, from learning to application, throughout the learning project. These alternating episodes can be illustrated by the previous example of the man who decided to landscape his property himself in order to save money. First he spent two episodes learning about grading. Then he spent one or two afternoons actually doing the grading near his house, using the knowledge that he had gained earlier. In the next learning episodes he read about topsoil. In subsequent episodes he bought and spread some topsoil. Before choosing shrubs for his property, or making other decisions, he also spent some time learning.

Why was the learning desirable for taking the action?

Once a person has decided to carry out a responsibility or perform an action, why does he not just go ahead and do it? Why does he decide to spend many hours of effort, and perhaps some money, trying to gain certain knowledge and skill first? In short, why is the learning desirable for taking the action?

The question becomes even more puzzling when we discover that in most cases the person could go right ahead without bothering at all to gain any knowledge and skill. When interviewed about their learning projects, almost all adults reported that the learning efforts definitely were not necessary for performing the action at a low level (Tough, 1968).

Instead, their reason for learning was to raise the level at which they performed the task or action. They *could* have completed it at a bare minimum level without learning, but they learned in order to perform it more successfully.

Why does a person want to perform the responsibility or action at a higher level? The various benefits that result from the higher level of performance flow from box C in Figure 3.

The individual may expect some pleasure or satisfaction *during* the application episodes. His pleasure or satisfaction may come from feeling he is "doing a good job" in performing the responsibility. He may feel pleased with his successful performance. He may feel more relaxed or confident, or feel more optimistic about completing the task successfully.

The expectation that he will experience some pleasure *afterwards*, too, may motivate him. After making a decision, for instance, he may feel pleased that it was a good one. His better decision might avoid certain undesirable consequences, for himself or his employer, that would have resulted from a hastier decision. His pleasure may also come partly from realizing that his better performance or decision is useful: it makes a contribution to his organization, or helps to improve the world.

In addition to providing pleasure, the improved performance may increase the person's self-esteem. It may also impress or please other people.

There is one other arrow leading from box C. It is possible, though not especially common, for an adult to initiate a learning project because he expects to reach box D. The fact that his performance has been recognized and rewarded in some way can lead in turn to pleasure, self-esteem, and pleasing or impressing additional persons. A person with very long-range plans might even be motivated at the beginning of the learning project by the pleasure he will receive from the trip, activities, or purchases that the additional money or promotion will make possible.

Efficiency is a supplementary motive for some learners. They expect to achieve the action goal faster, in the long run, by spending some early time at learning. The learning will save more time than it will cost. By making a better decision based on learning, for example, the person may save time or money in the future for himself or his company. Also, by learning more effective techniques, he may perform his responsibilities in much less time.

52

IMPARTING THE KNOWLEDGE AND SKILL

When a person expects to use certain knowledge or skill, he usually plans to produce, decide, or complete something. Sometimes, though, he has a somewhat different use in mind for the knowledge and skill – he wants to impart it to others by means of a speech, conversation, written article or report, lecture, broadcast, lesson, or demonstration. This may be his primary reason for learning the knowledge and skill, or just a small part of his total motivation.

Here are three actual learning projects in which the desire to impart the knowledge or skill was the *primary* reason for beginning and continuing. A secondary school teacher learned about the stages and problems in a family in order to teach this content to the students in her family living course. Another teacher had a different target audience – some of his fellow teachers. Having noticed some incompetence in their teaching, he learned about better teaching methods so he could discuss them with certain colleagues. A third person wanted to teach her two supervisors about a revised accounting procedure for the hospital in which they worked. To their request for help, she responded with a written report as well as several conversations after she herself had gained the necessary knowledge.

In the typical pattern, the first decision is to impart certain knowledge and skill to certain people. For example, the person may commit himself to write an article, deliver a speech, or teach a lesson on a certain topic. The subsequent decision is to make certain efforts to learn the knowledge and skill before imparting it.

A second possibility is that the motivation to impart the knowledge and skill will arise (or become stronger) after the learner has already gained the knowledge for other reasons. As he proceeds, he realizes how useful or important or interesting the knowledge and skill could be for other people.

We have also found a few examples of a third possibility. In this situation, the person accepts a commitment *because* it will provide motivation (or an excuse) for learning about some topic of great relevance to him. He may deliberately accept a commitment to teach a class, for example, or to write an article or report, in order to make himself learn something that he already wants to learn. One man offered to teach a Sunday school class because it would give him a chance to explore the question of the existence and nature of God. A woman volunteered to write an article about certain political leaders of the past in order to make herself learn about her country's history.

FUTURE UNDERSTANDING OR LEARNING

We turn now to a different use for knowledge and skill: to help the person to understand what will happen, or what will be said, in some future situation. This reason for wanting to gain and retain certain knowledge and skill is shown in box E (Figure 2). It can be a small part of the total motivation, or a fairly strong part.

In the previous sections, the person was using the knowledge and skill to produce something or impart something in the outside world. In this section, he is using the knowledge and skill in order to take in something.

Future learning

Sometimes a person tries to gain certain knowledge and skill that will be used, in some future learning episode, as a base on which to build further knowledge or develop further skill. For example, a person may first learn certain technical terms in a field so that he will be able to read advanced books in that field. Or he may improve his algebraic skills before beginning a statistics course. In Figure 2, the arrow that goes from box E to box A represents this type of learning.

The future learning episode may be the next episode in the same learning project or a much later episode in that learning project. Alternatively, it could be part of some other learning project.

A person may also work hard at developing some general learning skills. One teacher, for example, who wanted to increase his effectiveness at reading a large amount of material each week, took a course to improve his reading speed and comprehension. A person might set out to gain some other skill, information, mental capacity, awareness, or sensitivity that will be useful in a variety of future learning situations.

Future understanding

The person may want to use the knowledge and skill in some future situation in which he is listening, reading, or observing, even though learning is not his primary intention in that situation. Sometimes the person faces some specific situation in which he wants to be able to understand better what is happening, or what he is seeing, hearing, or reading. In this future situation he will be primarily receiving certain stimuli rather than trying to accomplish something. His new knowledge and skill will help him do so with greater understanding, insight, or appreciation. He wants the greater understanding for its own sake – because he is interested or curious, because he will feel happier or more relaxed – not to impress someone or take some action.

A man who had to attend several concerts, for example, decided to study music appreciation in order to receive more benefit from them. An adult educator who had to go as an observer to several meetings about educational television wanted to understand better the discussion about issues and policies. She set out to learn more about the topic beforehand. A housewife wanted to understand what goes on behind the scenes during a national election campaign. A woman learned about electronic music so that she would be able to understand it and know how it is composed and produced, whenever listening to electronic music in the future. A librarian attended a human relations training lab partly in order to understand her own behavior and feelings, and those of others, in all future group situations.

PLEASURE AND SELF-ESTEEM FROM POSSESSION

The second box in Figure 2 represents the learner's expectation of retaining certain knowledge and skill. In previous sections, we have traced the anticipated consequences of this box through one or more subsequent boxes. That is, we have looked at one way or another of using or building on the knowledge and skill.

We have not yet discussed the pleasure and self-esteem that flow directly from box B. We turn now to those two important clusters of benefits that a person can feel by merely possessing or retaining certain knowledge and skill.

These benefits – pleasure and self-esteem – flow directly from the possession itself. No intermediate step or box intervenes. The pleasure or self-esteem comes from simply possessing the knowledge and skill – from having it, not from using it and not from other people being aware of it. The pleasure or self-esteem from possession may be the primary reason for beginning and continuing a project, or may just supplement some other stronger reason.

We are referring here to benefits that are expected to occur at least two days after the learning episode. Benefits that are expected to occur while actually gaining the knowledge and skill, or within a few hours of gaining it, are discussed later in this chapter.

Pleasure

In this chapter, the term *pleasure* refers to the large cluster of positive feelings that a person may expect from certain aspects of a learning project. These positive feelings – pleasure, joy, happiness, or whatever – can arise directly from possessing the knowledge itself. Several interviewees describe their positive feelings as enjoyment, satisfaction, or interest. Other learners have a strong desire for possessing the knowledge, but cannot find precise words to describe or explain it.

In some learning projects, the person is puzzled or curious about something, and wants to remember the resulting knowledge for at least two days. Sometimes the pleasure seems to come, as one man put it, simply from "knowing something I didn't know before – something new."

Some men and women have a strong drive to achieve certain basic understanding or perspective. They want to develop their own set of beliefs about religion, the nature and future of man, some controversial contemporary issue, or some proposed innovation. One woman, for example, wanted not only to understand the background of the war in Vietnam, but also to have an answer to a crucial question: "Must man continually kill his own kind?" A man expected great personal satisfaction from having an answer about the existence and nature of God, which he regarded as "the most fundamental question in one's religion."

Sometimes a person wants to remember certain subject matter because it seems so important or significant. He may feel that knowing certain things about mankind, history, the universe, philosophy, or other nations is part of being human – or that this knowledge makes him "more" human. He may feel he is learning the most important things in the world: truth, reality, what the world is really like, a true and complete picture of mankind or of God. Indeed, he may become so enthusiastic about the subject matter that he comes to believe that all human beings should learn it.

Another important topic is oneself. It is fairly common for a person to have an interest in learning about himself – to gain insight into how he reacts to others, and how others react to him. Human relations training groups, sensitivity training groups, and encounter groups are designed to help individuals gain this sort of knowledge.

Self-esteem and confidence
The other direct benefit from possessing certain knowledge is an increase in one's self-esteem or confidence. The person expects to regard himself more highly after he gains and retains the knowledge.

Sometimes the increased self-esteem is general. That is, the adult feels he is "a better person" because he possesses the knowledge (or because he possessed it sometime in the past). Learning about one's community or about certain geographical regions, and perhaps learning to read faster or to drive a car, are examples of learning efforts that increase one's overall self-esteem.

More often, the self-esteem seems to be related to some particular role. The person sets out to gain certain knowledge and skill because he perceives it as part of being a good parent, citizen, teacher, nurse, Christian, musician, or spouse. A man may feel that "all Christians should have an opinion about the existence and nature of God," or a woman may believe that skill at sewing is "part of the wife identity – it is a good thing for young women to know," quite apart from its usefulness.

A person's picture of the ideal parent or citizen, or at least of the sort of parent or citizen he wants to become, may include certain knowledge that he does not now possess. Consequently he sets out to reduce this gap between his actual self (as he perceives it) and his ideal self.

The person may also expect that, as a result of gaining self-esteem, he will feel more confident or self-assured. A woman who took a modeling course, for example,

56

expected to "feel even more self-confident as an individual." A man who greatly improved his reading speed also expected his "self-assurance and confidence" to increase.

LEARNING FOR CREDIT

In some learning projects, a large part of the motivation comes from the expectation of receiving credit for the learning. This is shown in box F in Figure 2. The credit may be toward some degree, certificate, diploma, license, academic grade level, professional standing, or higher occupational grade. The credit may be granted and recorded by any one of a variety of agencies: an academic educational institution, a government, a civil service commission (or the military), or a professional association.

There are four routes to credit. Two of these routes flow from box C. In both routes, the learner uses his new knowledge and skill in performing some action, such as passing an examination, and obtains credit for his satisfactory performance. The only difference between the two routes is the extent to which someone has to be aware of the learner's performance. In some situations, no human being plays a major evaluative role: an objective test may be marked by a machine, and the marks recorded and reported by a computer. In other situations, the learner is definitely conscious of the individual who is assessing his performance.

The product or performance that is used to assess the person's knowledge and skill may be a test, examination, assignment, case or project (field work or practical work), or thesis. Performing successfully on an examination, assignment, case, or thesis may produce various benefits in addition to academic credit, as shown in Figure 2.

One common examination situation is an automobile driving test. When learning to drive, a person may be strongly motivated by wanting to demonstrate a sufficient level of skill during the driving test, as well as wanting to use that skill throughout the rest of his life.

Many examinations are related to one's job or occupation. Employees in the civil service and the armed forces can achieve higher levels of work and pay by passing certain examinations. Several occupations, such as accounting, have a series of examinations for entry to certain levels in the field. A correspondence course, textbook, workbook, or other materials may be available for anyone preparing for a certain examination.

The other two routes toward credit flow directly from performing the learning activities (box A). In order to pass a course or a grade, the student may have to attend class regularly, refrain from talking or laughing during class, and do certain exercises for homework. Regardless of whether he wants to retain the resulting knowledge and skill, he may be hoping that the instructor will be more likely to pass him if he performs the learning activities as expected.

A machine rather than an instructor could monitor the learning activities. A computer, for example, can record how quickly and successfully a person is going through certain programmed instruction material. This is shown in Figure 2 by the arrow going directly from box A rather than going through *others*.

<table>
<tr><td>IMMEDIATE
BENEFITS</td><td>

Before undertaking a learning project, the person may expect to enjoy the reading, watching, practicing, and other learning activities involved. He may also expect that these activities will increase his self-esteem, or will impress and please other people. These benefits flow directly from the learning episode itself. They do not depend on retaining or using the knowledge and skill.

</td></tr>
</table>

As the learning proceeds, the person may actually experience some of the immediate benefits that he anticipated earlier. Unexpected benefits may also occur. As the person becomes more realistic about the likely benefits flowing directly from future learning episodes, his motivation for those episodes may increase.

Various aspects of the learning episodes may produce the pleasure, the self-esteem, or the impact on others. We have identified seven aspects, each of which adds to the motivation of at least some learners for beginning and continuing a learning project.

These anticipated benefits, however, do not depend on retaining the knowledge and skill for at least two days. Consequently, they are not included when deciding whether a particular episode meets our criteria for a learning project. Only the motivation that flows through box B is included when estimating whether at least half of the person's intention was to gain and retain certain definite knowledge and skill. The subsidiary benefits discussed in this section are excluded because they flow directly from box A.

We will now examine, in turn, each of the seven aspects of learning activities, such as reading, listening, and practicing, that sometimes contribute to the person's motivation for the learning episodes. Each of these aspects can lead to certain feelings of pleasure or satisfaction, an increase in self-esteem, or a sense of pleasing and impressing others. These three sorts of benefits are shown in Figure 2 by the short arrows from box A.

1. Satisfying curiosity, puzzlement, or a question

A person may look forward to a learning episode because it will help to satisfy his curiosity or puzzlement about something. In this case, he anticipates some psychological benefit from discovering part or all of the answer to a particular question. The psychological benefit may be the positive pleasure or satisfaction of finding the answer. Feelings of mystery, ignorance of the unknown, indecision, ambiguity, and the resulting doubt or unhappiness may be reduced.

The pleasure will come immediately from discovering the knowledge or information. The person may also want to retain the answer, but the benefits we are concerned with here are independent of retaining certain knowledge. In a few projects, increasing self-esteem or even impressing others may also result from working toward an answer to one's curiosity, puzzlement, or question.

The source of the puzzlement or curiosity is often a controversial issue, decision, or procedure. The person may frequently encounter two contradictory sets of beliefs on some question: God is dead, or God is important; UFOs are nonsense, or they are real. The person wants to work out his own set of beliefs about the existence and nature of the phenomenon. There is a second possibility: the person may wonder how effective some current or proposed procedure will be in his job or organization. We interviewed four persons, for example, who felt some skepticism or doubt about a new procedure (a teaching method, accounting system, or set of tests for personnel selection). In a fair and open-minded way they wanted to learn how effective the procedure would be. Third, a person may frequently encounter both positive and negative evaluations of a particular government policy, such as the government's stand on some current international crisis.

In other learning projects, the curiosity seems to arise from a fascinating, exciting, glamorous, or puzzling phenomenon. Some of these topics seem to be new fads that may lose some of their appeal during the next few years or decades. The following are examples of phenomena about which our interviewees were curious: electronic music, sensitivity training groups, and the mass media.

Learning efforts are one possible reaction to a personal crisis in one's life. For instance, a person may want to discover and understand the causes of an accident or a medical condition. A request from one's spouse for a divorce may set off an attempt to find out the underlying reasons. After the birth of a defective child, the parents may set out to learn everything possible about this defect.

2. Enjoyment from the content itself

We have just seen that the content of a learning effort may provide pleasure by moving the learner toward an answer to his curiosity, puzzlement, or question. In addition, he may enjoy the content itself, finding it interesting, fascinating, or stimulating.

When we list the content of the various projects in which this occurred, most of the items are not surprising. They are interesting to many people. Our interviewees found the following topics enjoyable to read or hear about: the tourist attractions of a certain city, anecdotes about individuals in history, human nature (oneself and others), new sorts of music, golf, educational television, unidentified flying objects.

Some authors on child-raising provide as much entertainment and humor as fiction writers do. Biographies and nonfiction accounts of mountain climbing can be more exciting than adventure stories. The excitement and interest of many news reports are enjoyable for many people.

3. Enjoyment from practicing the skill

Pleasure during the learning episode may come from practicing the skill rather than from learning the content. That is, the learner may enjoy performing the activity in which he is trying to improve his skill. Our interviewees, for example, enjoyed practicing the following skills: golf, interviewing potential employees, singing and acting in an opera, producing electronic music by operating various machines, posing for fashion photographs, proofreading, sewing, and operating effectively in a group. When telling us why they enjoyed practicing the skill, they used a variety of phrases: it was just fun; it feels great; thoroughly enjoyed it; new and different; a challenge.

4. The activity of learning

Pleasure, self-esteem, and impressing others may arise directly from the activity of learning – from the mere fact that the person is, at that particular time, engaged in learning rather than in some other activity.

First, many people derive pleasure from learning. They feel the activity of learning is fun, enjoyable, satisfying, mentally stimulating, challenging, pleasant. They enjoy the adventures and problems that a learner experiences. These feelings are closely connected to the activity of learning, although some of them would occur while the person engaged in certain other activities as well.

Second, several persons found that the activity of learning increased their self-esteem. One said, for example, "I think more highly of myself when I'm learning." Another felt he was putting his time to good use, and doing the right thing, whenever he learned. Perhaps being a learner was central to his self-concept.

Third, some other person may notice one's efforts to learn. That other person may be pleased or impressed by the learning activities, and may regard the learner more highly. The other persons may include the learner's wife, husband, employer, colleagues, or acquaintances. They may be pleased or impressed by the mere fact that he is trying to learn, by the particular method or resources he is using, or by the subject matter. Figure 2 indicates that when others develop a higher regard or greater respect for the learner because of his learning activities, other benefits may

60

follow. For instance, he may receive a promotion or some other reward.

5. Learning successfully

Sometimes, during a learning episode, a person is pleased or "feels good" because he is learning quickly, easily, or successfully. He has proved to himself that he can master the knowledge and skill, or he has faced the challenge of planning and conducting his own learning, and feels proud because he progresses well.

In short, the learner is pleased by the effectiveness or speed of his attempt to learn. He enjoys meeting a challenge and feeling successful as a learner. The pleasure arises directly and immediately from his own success at learning. It is distinct from the realization that he will retain the knowledge and skill, and be able to use it.

6. Completing unfinished learning

In a few learning projects, part of the motivation for continuing is the desire to finish certain learning activities once they have been started. After enrolling in a course and perhaps paying a fee, for example, the adult may feel a strong commitment to finish it. Some people feel such a commitment after starting to read a book: because they have started it, they strongly want to finish reading it. Indeed, some people feel the need to complete any sort of task or project they have started.

7. Aspects unrelated to learning

Some learning activities provide benefits that could easily be obtained through other activities. These benefits are not closely related to the activity of learning or to the particular knowledge and skill. The importance of such benefits was pointed out by Houle (1961), who found that some adults engaged in many educational activities primarily because "they find in the circumstances of the learning a meaning which has no necessary connection, and often no connection at all, with the content or the announced purposes of the activity [pp. 15-16]." Using factor analysis, Sheffield (1964) and Flaherty (1968) found similar orientations to learning.

Such benefits usually arise from one's association with other people. Adults find that learning in a group provides opportunities for companionship, meeting new people, or making good friends. Sometimes one develops a special closeness with one or more persons when learning with them.

Adult learners sometimes benefit from the change in routine, respite, or escape that learning activities can provide. They may enjoy the quiet, peaceful atmosphere while reading in a den or library. At other times they may enjoy "getting away from the house" to a class or library, or traveling to visit some other institution or city. They may simply enjoy any new activity, thus avoiding boredom.

61

FURTHER WORK   What further inquiries should have the highest priority? Three possible directions seem especially promising.

One clear need, in moving toward a more complete picture of why people learn, is a rigorous testing of the framework presented in this chapter. Most portions of Figure 2 should be tested with a refined procedure and with a more representative sample than the earlier study. The three clusters of benefits (pleasure, self-esteem, and others) that emerged as the end-point of several routes need to be confirmed, and described more precisely.

A subsidiary study might examine the different kinds of perceived discrepancies that are related to self-concept. In explaining why adults learn, some writers emphasize the gap between a person's present self (as he perceives it) and the sort of person he would like to be. If these two perceptions of self are not congruent, the person may try to achieve certain knowledge and skill in order to change his present self or performance. It is also possible for him to foresee a gap occurring in some future situation, and then avoid this anticipated discrepancy by learning beforehand (Tough, 1969). Figure 2 suggests that there may be at least six different kinds of gaps or discrepancies (at each of the *self-esteem* points). These might fruitfully be explored.

A second priority is an accurate picture of the relative weight of the various anticipated benefits presented in Figure 2. In what percentage of learning projects does each anticipated benefit contribute to the motivation? How strong is that anticipated benefit in most projects? Perhaps the interviewee should be asked to indicate relative strength by assigning a total of 100 points or units (or 10 or 20) to the various boxes and end-points. Large samples could be chosen to represent various groups and nations. The typical pattern of motivation (distribution of units in Figure 2) may differ enormously among various groups and cultures.

A third possibility is to speculate about other areas of human choice to which this framework might apply. People choose many goals and activities in addition to learning projects. Perhaps some elements of the framework could help us understand those choices.

6 Deciding to begin

"Which of all these things is really my *strongest* interest?" "What's the most useful knowledge for finishing this job successfully?" "What books should I take home this time?" "Which course should I take this year?" Before he even begins a learning project, a person faces questions like these. He must decide whether to proceed and what to learn.

As part of this decision-making process, he may take several steps. For example, he may set an action goal, assess his interests, seek information on certain opportunities, choose the most appropriate knowledge and skill, establish the desired level or amount, and estimate the costs and benefits of obtaining it.

Throughout the book, to refer to these steps or tasks or decisions, we will use the term *preparatory steps*, or simply *steps*. These terms have the important advantage of being brief and convenient. Other terms, though, could have communicated the meaning just as well. Such phrases include (1) the learner's planning, deciding, and arranging steps; (2) the learner's decisions, tasks, and arrangements; (3) the steps in the learner's decision-making process; and (4) the learner's program-planning steps.

This chapter discusses the preparatory steps involved in deciding whether to proceed with a given learning project, and in deciding just what knowledge and skill to learn in that project. The learner's competence at performing these steps, and the help he needs, are emphasized.

Deciding whether and what to learn is crucially important in most learning projects. Thoughtful, appropriate decisions lead to successful projects; a poor decision may lead to failure or quitting.

The steps involved in deciding to begin a learning project are often difficult. At the same time, surprisingly little help is available for the adult when he is deciding what to learn or whether to proceed. Efforts are needed to develop better ways of helping adults with these crucial steps. This is a relatively unexplored frontier. Creative and innovative developments could dramatically increase the appropriateness and effectiveness of adult learning.

63

How thoughtful, competent, and successful are adults in setting their learning goals? Do they usually spend sufficient time and effort at this stage, or do they just "jump into" a learning project without much thought? Even if the adult does perform this task, does he have much skill at it? Or does he lack the ability to define his real problems, interests, needs, and long-term goals?

As with other decisions in his life, the adult may make the decision to begin a learning project without much thought or effort. All of us probably begin a few of our learning projects "on the spur of the moment." Some major decisions in life are made without careful thought and clear goals in mind.

Some persons seem to drift into many decisions and activities without being aware of their own major characteristics and problems, and without realizing the long-term consequences of their decisions. Their learning projects may lack clear goals, or may be based on a superficial or inaccurate understanding of their real problems, interests, and needs. Their learning goals may be almost clichés or slogans: they want to "learn about other countries" or about "human nature"; they feel they should "keep up with the news" or "become a better parent." They probably do not have any long-term action goals or learning goals. Some persons seem to fill or kill time rather than striving to move ahead in some way. They may choose a course or book, for example, as soon as they hear about it, without much thought about its appropriateness.

Not all quick decisions are poor decisions, of course. When moving to a new country, an individual may just assume that he will try to learn the language and customs of that country. Sometimes we just "know" that a certain book or course is right for us.

On the other hand, some adults think very hard about their decision before beginning a learning project. They may jot down the various possibilities, and may carefully consider the positive and negative aspects of each possibility. In order to make a better decision, the person may even gather certain information or advice. For example, he might attend a demonstration lesson or a special gathering for meeting the instructors.

Many of the preparatory steps will occur before the first learning episode, or shortly afterwards. Throughout the learning project, though, the learner may occasionally spend some time at these steps. For example, he may reexamine some of his original decisions and estimates, consider switching to related subject matter, or decide whether to continue and when to stop. Even when he has turned the detailed day-to-day planning over to someone else, he will occasionally think about whether he should continue the project.

There may be certain "types" of persons who generally are more thoughtful or competent than others at setting their action or learning goals. Such a person may be marked by the ability to think conditionally about himself, and by a lack of confusion or tentativeness about his present self (Winter, Griffith, & Kolb, 1968). He may tend to be quite open-minded (Rokeach, 1960). Such a person may also fit into the fourth stage (positive interdependence) of conceptual development in the framework developed by Harvey, Hunt, and Schroder (1961). He may also have some of the characteristics listed in Appendix B.

It is sometimes said that a person's present beliefs and attitudes will make him shy away from any effort to learn subject matter that might challenge them. A militaristic person, for example, may be reluctant to read about peaceful ways of handling conflict. In addition, when he does happen to meet beliefs and attitudes that are not compatible with his own, he may ignore or reject them.

Although these problems do occur, at least two factors present a more encouraging side of the picture. First, the phenomenon is not as widespread as some pessimists suggest. Rokeach (1960), for example, argues: "We do not agree with those who hold that people selectively distort their cognitive functioning so that they will see, remember, and think only what they want to. Instead we hold to the view that people will do so only to the extent that they have to, and no more. For we are all motivated by the desire . . . to see reality as it actually is, even if it hurts [pp. 400-401]." Second, we have found several examples of a person setting out to develop or change his beliefs and attitudes. As other people become more competent at goal-setting and planning, they may increasingly initiate efforts to change their own beliefs and attitudes.

THE PREPARATORY STEPS

At first thought, deciding to begin a learning project seems a fairly simple matter, consisting of only two or three steps. Interviews suggest that just the opposite is true in many cases: the decision-making is complex and may entail a large variety of steps.

A tentative list of possible steps that may occur as part of deciding whether to begin a learning project has grown out of interviews and observations. No one learner will perform all these steps, of course. In fact, it is quite common for a person to perform only a few of these steps, and to do so fairly easily and quickly. Each step in the list, however, is performed by at least *some* learners. The following list can give the reader a sense of the complexity of some decisions to begin learning.

1. The person decides to turn his attention to the question of what or whether to learn.
2. He tries to increase his general competence at performing these preparatory steps.

3. The person decides which steps to perform, and in what sequence. He may also decide how carefully to perform each step, or how much time to spend at each.
4. He tentatively or definitely adopts, modifies, or drops some action goal (or some desired *level* for an action goal). Or he assesses the strength of his desire for achieving that action goal or level. The action goal could be to perform some responsibility or task at a certain level, to accomplish something, to pass an examination for credit, or to impart something to others.

   As part of this step, the person may perform several other detailed steps. Perhaps, for example, he (a) sets long-term life goals or career goals, or examines his philosophy of life or his basic values; (b) estimates the probable benefits from some action goal or level (that is, estimates the benefits flowing from box C in Figure 2); (c) estimates the present or future needs or problems of some organization or of society; (d) tries to assess his own major strengths and weaknesses, and to develop a more accurate and precise perception of himself, perhaps by comparing himself to certain other persons; (e) estimates the effectiveness or suitability of his current actions or policies in one particular area of his life, or becomes aware of (or dissatisfied with) errors or weaknesses in his performance (or its consequences) in that area; (f) becomes more clearly aware of some problem or decision that he should tackle, or of its importance or urgency; (g) arranges his action goals according to their relative priority, or establishes a schedule or sequence for accomplishing certain action goals; (h) makes an action goal precise and specific rather than general and vague; (i) gains information about the level of performance that he is potentially capable of attaining, or about his probable ability to attain the action goal; (j) sets a very specific level of performance that he wants to achieve; (k) narrows or limits or decreases his action goal to a more realistic level; (l) adopts a supplementary action goal that will require relatively little efforts if he is working at the major action goal anyhow; (m) modifies an original action goal into something more elaborate or complex; (n) tries to become clear about the goals and perceptions of the individual for whom he is performing the task; or (o) develops greater confidence or hope in his ability to achieve the action goal at the desired level.
5. Because he believes that *some* sort of knowledge and skill will help him proceed toward his action goal, the person tentatively or definitely decides to spend some time learning *something* useful, but is not yet certain just what. His next step might then be 11 or 12.
6. Without having any particular knowledge and skill in mind yet, the person recognizes his need for some additional knowledge and skill as a base for

(a) certain further knowledge and skill that he definitely wants, or for (b) a better understanding of the events or contents in some definite future situation. His next step might then be 11 or 12.

7. The person decides to gain some pleasure or self-esteem by just possessing some additional knowledge or skill, apart from any desire to use it. As part of this step, the person might reflect on his personal characteristics, his basic values, his philosophy of life, his ideal self, or his long-term goals. The next step might then be 11 or 12.

8. Without having any particular knowledge and skill in mind, and without having any idea whether the major benefits will come from using or possessing it, the individual tentatively decides to learn *something*, or to improve himself *somehow*, or to take *some* course, or to read *some* book.

9. Because he is considering certain learning activities or opportunities, the person tries to estimate more accurately or precisely just what knowledge and skill he will probably gain from them. (This step can be important when the triggering event for a learning project is a specific opportunity, method, resource, or group for learning.)

10. Because he is already considering setting out to gain certain knowledge and skill, the person tries to estimate more accurately and precisely the probable benefits. For example, he tries to estimate just how relevant the knowledge or skill could be as a means of achieving a particular action goal, as a base for further learning, or as a means of obtaining the benefits that flow directly from box B in Figure 2. The knowledge and skill are considered only at a very comprehensive level. The learner might actually list his educational objectives (learning objectives, or desired changes in overt and inner behavior), or he might simply want to learn "the contents of those two books" or "the subject matter covered by that course."

11. The person tries to increase his awareness of the range and variety of relevant knowledge and skill available to him (and even of certain knowledge and skill that might become available to him if he took certain additional steps).

    As part of this step, he might try to remove some self-imposed restriction. That is, he might test his assumptions about certain knowledge and skill being inappropriate. Eliminating these inaccurate assumptions is often a significant step for learners within an educational institution (when choosing a topic for an individual learning project, for example, or when choosing a thesis topic).

12. The person tries to become more accurate or precise about just what knowledge and skill would be especially relevant for his purposes or desired benefits. Although the knowledge and skill are still considered at a global level, they

become clearer and more refined.

13. The person tentatively selects certain definite (but comprehensive) knowledge and skill to learn during at least the first few learning episodes. This enables him to proceed further with his thinking; in particular, he can now estimate the additional benefits and the costs of this knowledge and skill.

14. The person develops a more precise or accurate estimate of the direct benefits he is likely to receive (pleasure, self-esteem, pleasing or impressing others) from certain aspects of the learning episodes themselves – from box A in Figure 2. Or he tries to become more certain that the learning project will actually produce these benefits, or that he wants them. Often the person will have certain knowledge and skill in mind before considering these benefits; at other times, though, the person will experience one of these needs or desires first, and will then tentatively select the most appropriate knowledge and skill for providing the desired benefit.

15. The person estimates more precisely or accurately (a) his previous level of relevant knowledge and skill, (b) how far he has progressed from that previous level, (c) his current level, (d) the desired or required level, (e) whether there is still a gap between the current and desired level, and/or (f) the amount of knowledge and skill needed to close the gap.

16. He estimates the probability of being able to learn the desired knowledge and skill successfully, or he tries to increase his confidence in his ability to do so.

17. The person tries to find out whether this particular learning project (or learning projects in general) seems appropriate, normal, and acceptable to others. His certainty may increase dramatically if one other person supports or encourages his intention to learn.

18. The person becomes more precise or accurate in his estimates of the various costs of the learning project. These costs can include (a) time for planning, arranging, and learning; (b) money; (c) the sacrifice of other things that would be possible if that time or money had not been spent at the learning project; (d) space for equipment or books; (e) frustration, difficulty, effort, the need to perform boring or unpleasant learning activities, or other negative feelings; (f) unpleasant physical consequences (such as aching muscles after practicing tennis, or an odor in the apartment after cooking); (g) negative reactions in other persons, including their feeling that the learning project is strange or peculiar; and (h) the need to accept help from others, or to put himself in the hands of some person or group.

19. The person decides how to find the time (how to fit the learning project into his daily life) or how to obtain the money.

20. He tries to think of some way of increasing certain benefits or reducing certain costs, either by making some changes in his environment or by dealing with his emotional reactions.
21. The person estimates the probable cost-benefit ratio, or payoff, for the learning project. He may also compare the probable payoffs from various possible activities, and then select one of them or set priorities among them.
22. He decides whether to actually begin or continue the learning project, or at least whether to proceed with the next few learning episodes.
23. He decides the amount to be learned (or the level of knowledge and skill to be achieved, or the readings or other activities to be completed) within a certain period of time. Or he sets or accepts a final deadline and/or a series of intermediate deadlines. Examples of target dates are (a) the starting date for a new job, (b) the departure date for a trip, (c) the expected date of birth of a child, and (d) the date on which the person is scheduled to deliver a speech.
24. The person frees himself for learning (or decides how to free himself) by reducing (a) his fears, (b) his problems or mental blocks, (c) any strong needs that interfere with his commitment to learning, (d) any demands on his time and energy that reduce the amount available for learning.
25. He tries to understand his occasional lack of motivation for learning something that he "should" learn (learning to care for a first child, for example), or figures out how to deal with his worry or concern about this lack of motivation.
26. The person assesses how satisfied or dissatisfied he is with his general progress in a learning project.

Any given learner will omit several of these steps, and may perform several others very quickly. Some of the steps, though, may be performed several times during a learning project. As he proceeds with the learning, for example, the person's estimates will be revised as a result of actual experience. At various times, too, he may reconsider whether to proceed with learning the same knowledge and skill, whether to stop, or whether to shift to a related but different body of knowledge.

It is clear that deciding whether and what to learn can be a very complex process. In fact, our list contains more than 60 conceptually distinct steps if we add the various steps included in 4, 14, and 18 to the total.

ACTUAL HELP   A person may experience some difficulty or doubt when deciding what to learn, or when deciding whether to begin or continue learning. Consequently, he might benefit greatly from some advice, information, encouragement, or other help.

As the learner becomes aware of just which of the preparatory steps are most

69

troublesome, he may plan how to get help with them. Then he may actually seek and obtain that help. A helper (or printed materials) may simply encourage the learner to spend a little more time thinking about whether and what to learn. Or the helper may make him aware of the benefits to be gained from performing one of the 26 steps. At other times a helper will correct certain erroneous perceptions or assumptions, will stimulate or encourage the person to consider learning certain subject matter, or will respond to a request for specific information or advice.

A helper can also point out learning objectives that are too ambitious, that will not really be relevant to the action goal, that are not important enough to sustain the motivation for very long, or that will be almost impossible to attain because of a lack of resources. In several interviews concerning such problems, Heather Knoepfli found in an unpublished study that the learner will actively deal with such a problem as soon as he becomes aware of it. This means the helper can be open and direct, and can operate at a rational, cognitive level. There is little need for him to operate at an emotional, subtle, or subconscious level.

ADDITIONAL NEEDED HELP   Although adult learners do obtain some help while deciding whether and what to learn, they need even more help than they now receive. This was demonstrated in one study (Tough, 1967) that asked college graduates the following question about choosing the goal in one of their learning projects: "With this task, would you have liked *more* assistance than you actually did receive from other people?" More than one quarter replied affirmatively.

Perhaps difficulty in obtaining appropriate help at the goal-setting stage is common in various aspects of life, not just in learning. In particular, it may be that people in our society are generally incompetent at diagnosing what is wrong or what should be improved. As I reflect on my experiences with certain auto mechanics, furnace repairmen, and medical doctors, I wonder whether they diagnose a problem too quickly. They do not seem to ask many questions, nor gather many data by observation. They do not seem to list a variety of hypotheses, and then eliminate some by gathering additional data through questions, observations, or tests. Perhaps many adults also lack competence or thoughtfulness in diagnosing their own action problems and learning needs, and in helping others do the same; they could benefit from appropriate help in this area.

The need for help in setting learning goals is common in some independent study programs in schools and colleges. Educators sometimes assume that the essence of these programs is simply to give the students more freedom. They sometimes overlook the need for helping the students, with skill but without subtle influence, in deciding just what to learn.

MOVING TOWARD BETTER HELP   Certain learners already have expert help available while setting their learning goals. Certain athletes, for example, receive a great deal of help from their coaches (and from films of their performance) in diagnosing their weaknesses. Their coaches help them determine which aspects of their performance to improve. The professional football quarterback is helped to decide what proportion of his time to spend at improving such skills as passing, running, and ball-handling. The boxer, the baseball pitcher, and the hockey player also receive a great deal of help with diagnosing weaknesses and setting specific goals for improvement. The political candidate facing a major election campaign, and a person setting out on a career as a writer, may seek and obtain expert help in selecting specific characteristics to be improved. Throughout the world there are no doubt many other examples as well.

In many other situations, though, expert help is rarely sought or even available, despite the enormous dividends (to the individual himself, his employing organization, or his society) that could result from such help. Suppose we could provide expert, intensive, inexpensive help to the promising young researcher or theorist, to young teachers and professors, or to students beginning a doctoral program. Suppose a company, government department, university, or other organization provided such help to any executive who was facing major new responsibilities. Suppose that all couples could obtain free but competent help in setting their learning goals during the year before their wedding and during the first two years of their marriage, or when expecting and raising their first child. Surely the small investment made by society or an employer in these cases would produce considerable benefits.

Perhaps a competent "learning consultant" should be available to any person in a community who wants help in setting either life goals or learning objectives. A small amount from local taxes could be provided for this service, and a small fee could be charged.

Learning consultants should also be provided by companies for their key personnel, and by associations for their members. Very few of the 70 managers interviewed in one study had any clear aims or learning goals, let alone priorities among them (Dill, Crowston, & Elton, 1965). They lacked practice and skill in formulating learning goals, and certainly did not have access to a specially trained learning consultant.

School teachers would also benefit greatly from competent help (when they want it – not just when an "inspector" arrives) in diagnosing their highest priority areas for improvement. Not every teacher's needs can be met by a large-group, in-service training program.

Goal-setting consultants could also be provided for certain specific subject matter areas. One agency might provide a consultant for anyone who wanted to become a

71

better parent. Another agency might specialize in helping people choose their particular goals in understanding themselves and others. Another might help with plans for learning that are connected with various home improvement projects. All of these consultants would help the person to establish his *specific* learning goals, and might also help him with certain subsequent steps in the learning project.

A shift

Manufacturers, governments, special interest groups, and even adult educators have typically had certain messages or other subject matter as their starting point. They have then done their best to spread that subject matter to as many persons as possible, regardless of whether the content is useful to them. The typical methods have included advertising campaigns, mass media, lectures and speeches, and content-centered courses. Impressed by the size of this barrage of messages, Whyte (1952) asked *Is Anybody Listening*?

Perhaps there is now some shift toward accepting the individual's needs and interests as a more appropriate starting point. Communication theory now recognizes that communication can be a dialogue and can include listening (Matson & Montagu, 1967). "Student-centered" (usually, though, in the sense of group-centered) teaching has become more popular. Adult educators have increasingly realized that most adult learning begins because of a problem or responsibility, or at least a question or puzzle, not because of a grand desire for a liberal education. They have at least paid lip service to beginning with the needs of the learners, though this often means assessing the needs of a group of learners (or an even larger clientele) rather than individual learners.

We must become much more competent at helping individuals to clarify their life goals and their related learning goals. Some persons are very vague or even inaccurate in defining their goals. Many persons could become clearer and more accurate about their unique goals. What gives them pleasure, happiness, and self-esteem? In what ways can they best contribute to the world? What assumptions, perceptions, and unrecognized long-term goals are, in fact, affecting their decisions about career, family, housing, possessions, entertainment, and learning? A book edited by Buhler and Massarik (1968) has shown the complexity of the process of goal-setting, and of achieving some suitable integration of major goals. A person's entire life seems to be guided by certain subconscious or conscious directions and goals, which might be called "the human being's intentionality toward fulfillment [p. 403]." As his real goals become clearer and more detailed, the person can discover conflicting goals, detect clusters of related goals, set priorities, and begin to feel that his goals are integrated and his life is whole.

Once the person has selected his action goals, the learning counselor could then help him select the knowledge and skill needed to achieve them. Some defenses, fears, and other obstacles to learning may have to be reduced. The counselor could help him estimate the costs, and the benefits for *his* goals, of various possible learning projects. Indeed, the person could be helped with any of the 26 detailed steps listed earlier. In addition, the person could be encouraged and helped to gain more knowledge and insight from many aspects of his daily life. He can learn from people, television, casual reading, entertainment, and work, even when the desire to learn is only 10% or 30% of his total motivation.

Let us hope, then, that there is some shift from coercing or persuading people to learn, and from shouting our messages at them through advertising and lectures, toward helping the person decide what learning is best for *him*, and then helping him pursue it.

Who can provide the help?

In many learning projects the person does not need any help in deciding what knowledge and skill to gain. In some learning projects, a spouse, friend, neighbor, or colleague can provide sufficient help. In other learning projects that are immediate and short-term, the person would probably not spend much time seeking help in deciding whether and what to learn. (Developing his general competence beforehand at goal-setting is probably a more useful approach for this sort of learning project than immediate counseling.)

Help in selecting certain learning projects can be provided only by an expert in the problem area or subject matter. For many other learning projects, though, more competent general help is clearly needed. Such counseling is especially beneficial when the individual is selecting his major areas of interest or when he is deciding about *major* learning projects and priorities.

Various sorts of printed materials, as well as a human counselor or consultant, can help a person set his goals. A workbook could be developed to outline the entire range of knowledge and skill open to mankind – the complete potential curriculum for adult learning. It could help the reader to determine his own high priority interest and needs. A simpler version of the book might be entitled "What are *you* going to learn this year?"

A few recent developments in the field of adult learning are intended to help an adult determine his own goals and priorities. In the graduate program in adult education at Boston University, for example, a student uses a "self-diagnosis" sheet to rate himself on more than 30 characteristics, and develops a corresponding list of relevant learning experiences. Malcolm Knowles (1968) has pointed out that some imaginative procedures are being invented for helping the adult diagnose his own strengths, weaknesses, and learning needs. These procedures include role-playing, critical incident process, simulation exercises, skill practice exercises, group observations, and self-rating scales.

Ideal characteristics

To ensure that the adult receives the best possible help in deciding whether and what to learn, the following factors are important:

1. None of the helper's influence results from providing inaccurate or unrealistic information.
2. None of his influence is harmful.
3. Most of the influence is sought by the learner, or at least eventually welcomed by him.
4. The helper does not try to produce much more influence than he actually succeeds in producing, and his concern for what or how much is learned is not greater than the learner's concern.
5. The help is designed for the particular learner.
6. Any influence exerted by the helper results from the learner's trust in his judgment, or from the helper's contagious enthusiasm, not from his control over certain future rewards or other consequences for the learner.
7. As a result of his interaction with the helper, the person develops a stronger tendency to learn in the future whenever he becomes aware of some problem, responsibility, or significant subject matter.

Pilot programs

At present, most attempts to help adult learners merely provide instruction and resources for them. There are few organized attempts to help adults make decisions about what to learn, or about which learning possibilities are highest priority. One of the most significant challenges that we now face is to develop pilot programs to provide better help with goal-setting.

Several psychologists have pointed out the importance of helping a person develop a clear picture of his real self. That picture could include the goals that are already, in fact, influencing his decisions and other behavior. In addition, we could help him develop additional action and learning goals that are especially appropriate for him.

An effective counseling service would also be an excellent way of discovering certain needs of an entire community. New programs of adult education could be developed to meet these needs. Also, several adults with a common interest could be encouraged to form an autonomous learning group.

Let us turn now to the possibility of encouraging and facilitating the development of competence at goal-setting. In an earlier section, we raised the question of how successful men and women are in setting their goals. We turn now to the notion of increasing their success.

This can be a very efficient route to increasing the appropriateness and amount of adult learning. The cost-benefit ratio or payoff from resources directed at developing competence is probably even greater than it would be if the same resources were directed at providing better help.

At an early stage of helping an individual become more thoughtful and successful at setting his goals, we might simply try to increase his awareness. We find in our interviews that most adults have never recognized or examined the entire range of their learning projects. They have never seen the relationship between going to a conference, reading a serious book, taking a music lesson, and collecting information on the job. In fact, when we asked them to list their highly deliberate efforts to learn, these examples only emerged after a great deal of probing and stimulating.

As the person becomes more aware of all the things he has learned intentionally recently, and of all his current learning projects, he may become more thoughtful and careful in selecting the knowledge and skill for his future learning projects. The person's increased awareness of his recent and current learning may also lead to an enhanced self-image. He may become more aware of his potential. He may begin to develop an exciting image of what he can become. He will realize, for example, that it is quite possible for him to become a dramatically better parent or shopper. He will see important possibilities for improving on the job. He will see a vision of the well-informed person that he could become in his knowledge of the world, its people, its past, and its future. He may see further possibilities for learning how to achieve greater joy and happiness, greater love and satisfaction in personal relationships, better understanding and expression of his emotions and body.

As part of his competence at goal-setting, the highly effective learner pays attention to his deepest inner feelings, drives, hopes, images of the future, needs, and dreams. He looks for these, sees them accurately, and accepts them. Throughout his lifetime, he will also be highly responsive to the requirements of the world around him. In the various organizations to which he contributes, he will be aware of his responsibilities and decisions that could be improved by learning beforehand. He will then set correct priorities among the various possibilities.

Four areas in which further work is needed emerge as highest priority.
1. Use exploratory interviews and relevant literature to modify the list of detailed preparatory steps. Using a lay version of the revised list, investigate the relative

frequency with which each step is performed. When is each step performed, and how much time does the learner spend at it? How thoughtfully and successfully does he perform each step?

2. Study the help that competent learners want and need with the steps. Examine the actual help they receive, and their process of considering and seeking help. Which steps are especially troublesome? What goes wrong? With which steps do competent learners need additional help?

3. Design and test better help for the steps involved in deciding whether to begin a particular learning project. Provide the best possible help in a pilot program, and simultaneously collect data on its effectiveness and weaknesses. Design an even better program.

4. Develop effective ways of helping individuals become more competent at setting action goals and learning goals. One possibility is to provide excellent help while the learner is actually setting goals. In addition, various sorts of learning episodes *about* goal-setting might greatly increase the learner's competence. The learner might benefit from feedback on his strengths and weaknesses as a goal-setter. Perhaps we need a booklet on how to set goals.

7 Choosing the planner

In the previous chapter, the learner faced one or two basic questions: Should I proceed with the learning project? What (generally) should I learn?

We turn now to another basic question he must face at the beginning of a learning project: Who will be responsible for the detailed planning? That is, who will decide just what and how I should learn during each session?

In many adult learning projects, the learner himself handles most of his detailed planning. In some projects, he turns over this responsibility to a group, or to the leader or instructor of that group. In others he relies on an individual with whom he interacts in a one-to-one situation. In a few projects the learner follows the sequence determined by a set of materials or recordings.

THE CONCEPT OF THE PLANNER Let us adopt the label *planner* to refer to the person (or group or object) that does most of the detailed day-to-day planning in the learning project. To be more precise, the *planner* is the person or thing responsible for more than half of the detailed day-to-day planning and deciding in a learning project. That is, the planner makes the majority of the decisions about what to learn (the detailed knowledge and skill) in each learning episode, and/or about how to learn (the detailed strategy, activities, and resources). In addition, the planner may also decide when to begin each learning episode, and the pace at which to proceed.

To find out who the planner was when a person learned to speak French, for example, we would seek the answer to the following question: Who decided exactly what vocabulary and grammar he should learn, what sequence he should follow, and what activities (conversation, written exercises, listening to a record, repeating words onto a tape) should be performed in each session? If a person learned about the history of England, we would ask this question: Who or what was responsible for the day-to-day planning, for deciding the precise information to be learned during each episode, and for choosing the reading materials or other resources and methods to use each time?

We do *not* ask who made the initial decision to begin the learning project. The planner is not necessarily the person who decides that French conversation or the history of England should be the content of the learning project. We are not concerned here with what motivates the learner, or with who influences his motivation. We do not ask who made the original decision about how to learn or what resource to use. And we do not assume that the person or resource that provides the subject matter is necessarily the planner.

Instead, we define the planner as the person or thing that is primarily responsible for the detailed (rather than comprehensive) planning (decisions, not motivation or subject matter) for the majority of the learning episodes (from day to day, not just at the early stages). In a sense, the planner is the teacher (in the sense of preparing a lesson plan), curriculum planner, or program planner for this particular learning project.

In some projects, no single person, group, or object dominates the planning. Such learning projects do not have a planner, as we define the term, because no one is *primarily* responsible for the detailed planning of the learning episodes. Instead, a mixture or combination of two or more individuals and things is responsible for the planning.

Over a year, an individual may use several different planners. Several of his learning projects may be self-planned; others may rely on a course or on private lessons.

DISTINGUISHING DIFFERENT TYPES OF PLANNERS

For discussion and understanding, as well as for research and theory, it is useful to classify particular planners. The learner's behavior and needs may be very different with different types of planners.

I distinguish four types of planners. From the learner's point of view, this is a logically complete list . That is, no other category could be added, though some of the present categories could be subdivided. The learner can choose either a human or nonhuman resource as his planner. If human, the resource can logically be only the learner himself, some other person in a one-to-one situation, or one or more persons in a group situation. These four types of planners will now be discussed in turn.

1. One possible planner is the learner himself. He may make most of the decisions, from one learning episode to the next, about what and how to learn. He may seek information and advice about these decisions from various individuals and materials, but still retain control of and responsibility for the decisions. He may obtain the knowledge and skill from a variety of individuals, books, and programs without giving up the responsibility for *deciding* which resources and activities to use each time. To refer to a project where the learner himself is clearly the planner, we will use the term *self-planned* learning project.

2. Instead of making most of the day-to-day decisions himself, the learner may decide to follow the sequence of detailed subject matter and activities provided by some object. This nonhuman resource might be a programmed instruction book, a workbook, a set of tape recordings in a language lab, or a series of television programs. The learner turns over the planning responsibility to the object (or, in a sense, to the person who earlier created the object). The plans reside in the object: it provides the decisions and sequence. The set of materials or series of programs will direct the learner's activities and the content during most of his learning episodes. Generally, the object will provide much of the subject matter in addition to directing the learning project.

3. A third type of planner is a person who interacts with the learner in a one-to-one situation, rather than in a group situation. The interaction may be face-to-face, by mail, or by telephone. The person might be a professional instructor, consultant, counselor, athlete, doctor, or lawyer. He might be a friend, neighbor, relative, or colleague. He might provide much of the subject matter, or none at all. Individual lessons from a golf pro, private music lessons, and driving lessons from a friend are examples of learning projects planned by another person in a one-to-one relationship.

4. One other possibility is open to the learner. He may decide to attend a face-to-face group, and to let the group (especially its leader or instructor) determine what and how he learns during each session. The group could be a group of his peers who decide and conduct their activities without a professional instructor or authority. Or the group could be a class, discussion group, workshop, or other group led by a trained leader or instructor. A large portion of the knowledge and skill will typically be provided by the group or its instructor during the group sessions. The group may be of any size from five persons to several thousand.

Sometimes an instructor or other person may help two or three individuals learn. Do we classify this as a group situation or a one-to-one relationship? I classify this as closer to a one-to-one situation, because each of the learners will be receiving a great deal of individualized help and instruction from the person.

Mixed planning

In most learning projects there is clearly a single planner. That is, when one looks at the entire series of learning episodes, it is clear that the learner himself, some nonhuman resource, a certain person, or a certain group was primarily responsible for deciding what and how he learned. The overall planner may be clearly identified, even though the learning project included at least one episode planned by a group, another episode directed by a book or other object, and a few planned by the learner himself.

A few learning projects, however, are not clearly marked by a single planner. The dominant planner may have shifted once or twice during the project. Or perhaps, looking over all the learning episodes, 30% of the day-to-day planning was provided by the learner, 30% by a series of television programs, and 40% by a group and its leader. That is, no one person or object accounted for the majority of the planning. Let us establish a residual category for any project that does not fit clearly into one of the four categories outlined above. We will call this *mixed* planning.

An example

Let us return to the example of the person who decided to learn some conversational French. What might his planning and learning be like with each of the four types of planners?

1. If he decided to plan his own learning project, he would probably use a variety of resources and learning activities. He might listen to French songs and television programs, repeat French words after they are pronounced on a vocabulary record, read French aloud, try to speak French in a few social situations, and attend a few classes or private lessons. He might ask several friends and colleagues to suggest appropriate books and records.

2. Instead, the person might decide fairly early that a nonhuman resource would be far more effective for learning French. He would then locate a suitable series of tape recordings in a language lab, or a set of phonograph records, and would work his way through them. Alternatively, he might depend almost entirely on a series of instructional films or television programs.

3. If he decided that the increased effectiveness was worth the money, he might pay for a series of private lessons with a French instructor, or he might persuade a French-speaking friend to become his tutor. This person would then take on the responsibility of deciding what to do during each session, and what and how the learner should practice between sessions.

4. A language school or adult education institution near the adult's home or work might offer the best way for him to learn. The instructor and perhaps other members of the group would decide what to do during each group session, and would suggest what and how the learner should practice between sessions.

Misconceptions

Before we proceed, let me try to prevent certain misconceptions. First, the four types of planners (or four types of learning projects) are based on who or what *plans*

80

(directs, controls, influences, governs, manages, guides) the detailed content and learning activities from one learning episode to the next. We are not looking at who provides the subject matter. We are classifying the sources of the plans and decisions, not the sources of subject matter or the methods of learning.

Second, only the majority of the planning, not 100%, must be provided by the learner, object, person, or group in order to apply that label. A learning project is not necessarily mixed just because a *few* episodes are directed by an object, a few others by a person, and a few others by a group or by the learner himself.

Third, we do not call an episode or project self-planned just because the learner himself *chooses* the object, person, or group. If he then relies heavily on that object, person, or group for planning most of his learning episodes, the project is clearly not self-planned.

Other classification schemes

While developing this method of classifying learning projects, I found the thinking of several other persons very stimulating. Cyril O. Houle at the University of Chicago has developed a list of about 11 program-planning situations. Coolie Verner (1962), Donald Blackburn (1967), and Clark Moustakas (1968) have also classified learning methods or situations.

PREPARATORY STEPS Choosing the planner for a learning project is not always a simple or single step. Sometimes the initial choice will be reexamined several times during the project. Also, the learner may have to deal with several related questions and subquestions, and make several detailed decisions.

Four sequences of preparatory steps can be distinguished. The first sequence begins with a decision to gain certain knowledge and skill. The learner then chooses the most appropriate type of planner, and the particular planner. He may carefully review the various possibilities open to him, or he may simply choose an obvious planner or the first one that comes to his mind.

A second possibility is to choose the planner *before* determining the desired knowledge and skill. The person may read a great deal, for example, and usually decide what to read next rather than how to gain certain specific information. Or a man or woman may decide to learn *something* through one television series or another, and only then select the particular series (and thus the particular knowledge and skill). Some adults seem to be habitual course-takers or discussion group members: each September they decide to take another course or join another group that year, and then they look around for the most suitable one.

A third possibility is to choose the subject matter and the planner *simultaneously*.

81

This third method will usually be triggered by an announcement of a "package" of methods and subject matter. The most common example is a brochure, advertisement, or other announcement of a course or discussion group. When the adult becomes enthusiastic about the knowledge and skill mentioned in such an announcement, he is simultaneously choosing a particular instructor to guide his learning. An announcement of a particular television series could begin an object-planned project. Similarly, an advertisement by a guitar teacher or dancing school could begin a project planned by a teacher in a one-to-one relationship. A review of a particular book could trigger a brief self-planned project.

The fourth possibility is that the learner is required or forced to use a certain planner. He does not really have any choice. The requirements might come from his employer, who sends him to a workshop or conference. Or they might be set by a credit-granting educational institution: "If you want credit for this course, you must attend the particular group."

THE LEARNER'S CONSIDERATIONS

What factors does the learner consider when choosing a planner?

Efficiency is often his most important criterion: What is the fastest, easiest, cheapest way for me to learn the knowledge and skill that I want? The answer will depend on certain characteristics of the subject matter, on how the particular person learns best, and on what is available (and at what cost in terms of money and time). Many learners are quite accurate in their estimates of these factors. Many of the influential factors will be considered consciously, while others will be unconscious.

In addition, almost every learner will be swayed by considerations and forces other than efficiency. We all have our preferences for certain ways of learning, as Blackburn (1967) has demonstrated. Our previous experiences, successful or negative, with each type of planner will certainly influence our preferences, as will the advice and reactions of our acquaintances.

The choice of planner will also be influenced by one's emotions and personality characteristics. Each of us feels comfortable or happy in certain situations, but not in others. For some, a medium-sized discussion group is very pleasant; others shudder at the thought of being in such a group. Considering one's probable emotional reactions to certain types of planners is an intelligent and rational act. It makes sense for a learner to try to predict how much negative or positive feeling a certain planner will produce in him, as well as the efficiency involved. The shortest route is not always the most scenic and enjoyable.

BETTER HELP AND COMPETENCE

Choosing a planner may be a complex and difficult task. Any one of the preparatory steps involved in this decision could be troublesome. For example, the learner may

82

have little idea of the best way to learn French, or may not know what planners are available. He may have little idea of the costs and benefits of a language lab or a French tutor. As he becomes aware of his need for such information and advice, he may seek assistance from some friend who recently learned French, from his daughter's high school French teacher, or from a library book.

Most learners will want information, advice, and encouragement at this stage, and will then reflect on the alternatives and choose whichever planner seems best to them. Some learners, though, probably want to be told authoritatively which planner to use, and do not want to bother estimating all the costs and benefits of several possibilities.

It may be possible for us to provide much better help for adult learners while they are choosing a planner. It might also be possible to help them develop their own competence at handling this decision.

In addition to "goal-setting consultants" to help with the preparatory steps discussed in the previous chapter, we also need "strategy consultants." Such advisers could help the learner choose one sort of planner or plan his overall strategy. If the learner decides that self-planning is most appropriate, the strategy adviser (especially if he is a subject matter expert) could continue to advise him whenever he has difficulty making the detailed day-to-day decisions.

Both goal-setting consultants and strategy consultants would have to have a great deal of knowledge and skill in the field of adult learning. They could gain this through reading, interviewing, observation, self-analysis, and practice. Consultants could be made available by various institutions, and perhaps some could also be in private practice.

An example
To make some of this discussion seem more real, let us imagine one particular learner approaching one particular consultant. The learner has already decided that he wants to achieve two learning goals: (1) improve his ability to speak effectively and easily before an audience; (2) learn to read some elementary Spanish phrases for use while driving through a Spanish-speaking country.

The consultant decides that his first task is to help the learner become familiar with the various ways in which he can learn in general. He gives the learner a set of printed materials that describe the common methods of learning. These materials describe the characteristics of each method, the sort of objectives for which each is appropriate, and the sort of person who enjoys each method or learns best from it.

The learner then responds to a self-administered questionnaire that helps him discover his own characteristics, his general preferences in methods of learning, and his preconceptions and preferences in methods for his two specific learning goals.

Next he discusses with the consultant the best ways of achieving his learning objectives. The consultant tries to discover any characteristics of this particular learner and his situation that make the normal or standard sequence of learning activities for learning the given knowledge and skill inappropriate. The helper also makes certain that the learner believes that the planner they choose (or the general strategy or sequence of learning activities) is best for his goals. The learner must be confident that his learning activities will lead efficiently to his learning goals.

As a result of this counseling process, the person may decide to attend a course on public speaking, and to learn Spanish phrases at home from a booklet that provides simple Spanish for tourists (if he can find such a booklet). With the consultant's help, the adult then plans a brief strategy for discovering the most appropriate public speaking course close to his home or office, and for discovering the best Spanish booklet for his needs. In short, after choosing one *type* of planner, he proceeds to choose a *particular* planner for each project.

In order to choose the course, the learner might consult a directory of available courses in his city, or he might visit an adult education counseling service. To choose the Spanish booklet, he might consult a librarian in a public library, or a clerk in a bookstore.

FURTHER RESEARCH The process of choosing a planner for each learning project is an important decision-making process in adult learning. Further research is needed to answer several questions. What factors and characteristics do adults consider while choosing a planner? How careful and appropriate are their choices? How can we improve the effectiveness of their decision-making? That is, how can we help men and women become more competent at choosing a planner for each learning project? And how can we provide better help for them?

8 How common and important is each type of planner?

Some findings from our 1970 survey were reported in Chapter 3. We turn now to the findings concerning the type of planner chosen for each learning project.

WHICH TYPE OF PLANNER DO PEOPLE CHOOSE? The 66 adults interviewed in the 1970 survey conducted 538 learning projects during the 12 months before the interview. Table 8, which presents the percentages of learning projects that fell into the four different categories of planner, indicates who was primarily responsible for the detailed day-to-day planning in each project.

Two-thirds of all the projects were planned by the learner himself. All but three of the interviewees conducted at least one self-planned project. The mean number of self-planned projects per person was 5.8, as shown in Table 9. Almost half the interviewees conducted at least one project that was planned by a group or its leader. Almost the same number conducted at least one project planned by another person in a one-to-one relationship (Table 9). These two types of planners together, though, were responsible for only one-fifth of all the projects, as can be seen in Table 8. Both tables indicate that projects with mixed planning were fairly significant, but nonhuman planners were fairly rare.

The findings for the two youth groups are fairly similar to the adult pattern. The most common planner is the learner himself. Second is a group or its leader-instructor. Apparently, as an individual moves from the age of 10 to adulthood, the proportion of self-planned projects increases, and his reliance on a group decreases. The figures are provided in Table 10.

ADDITIONAL FINDINGS Several additional findings emerged from our 1970 survey. First, we divided the adult projects planned by a group or its leader-instructor into two categories. The interviewees classified most of their group-planned learning projects in the following way: "This group was sponsored by an educational institution, or it had an instructor or leader or speaker who was assigned to that group or was paid for this task." About one-fifth of the group-planned projects, though, were in the other category: "It was just a group of equals meeting outside of any organized or institutional framework, and taking turns planning their own learning activities."

Table 8 / On What Types of Planners Do Adults Rely?

Primary planner	Percentage of projects
The learner himself	68
A group or its leader-instructor	12
One person in a one-to-one situation	8
A nonhuman resource	3
Mixed (that is, no dominant type of planner)	9

Table 9 / Frequency of Various Types of Planners

Type of planner	Number of adult interviewees ($N = 66$) with at least one project	Their mean number of projects using the given type of planner
The learner himself	63	5.8
A group or its leader-instructor	32	1.9
One person in a one-to-one situation	31	1.4
A nonhuman resource	8	2.0
Mixed (that is, no dominant type of planner)	26	1.9

Adult learning projects planned by another person in a one-to-one situation were also divided into two classifications. In the majority of these projects, the person who served as planner "was paid to do so [paid by the learner or by someone else], or was doing so because this was a definite responsibility for him, or part of his job." On the other hand, in two-fifths of the projects, the planner was helping "primarily because he was a friend or relative." A few of the friends and relatives happened to be trained or professional instructors in the subject matter, but were chosen primarily because of the personal relationship.

Some additional findings are based on supplementary analyses of the adult data. When the figures for the four types of planners are combined in various ways, some interesting percentages emerge.

Table 10 / On What Types of Planners Do Children and Adolescents Rely?

Primary planner	For 16-year-olds, the percentage of projects	For 10-year-olds, the percentage of projects
The learner himself	46	41
A group or its leader-instructor	29	33
One person in a one-to-one situation	12	8
A nonhuman resource	3	0
Mixed (that is, no dominant type of planner)	10	18

Note. – Learning projects that were motivated primarily or partially for credit are not included in this table.

One of these percentages is based on Table 8. Approximately two-thirds (68%) of all learning projects are planned by the learner himself. Only one-third are planned by someone other than the learner, that is, by an "external" planner.

In a second analysis, we determined how many learning projects were professionally planned, rather than planned by the learner himself or by some amateur planner. To be more precise, we were interested in the proportion of projects planned by a paid person (or a person who was doing this as part of his job or responsibility as a volunteer in some agency), sponsored by an institution, or pursued for credit. Only one-fifth (19%) of the 538 projects fell into this category. The other 81% were planned by the learner himself, by a friend or relative, or by a group of peers unrelated to an institution. The detailed calculations are presented in Table 11.

Finally, it is interesting to note the relatively small number of projects in which the learner had little influence on the detailed procedures and content. In these projects, the planner did not seriously take into account the characteristics, needs, problems, and questions of each particular learner. Even if all projects planned by a group (or its leader or instructor) or a nonhuman resource fit here, the total is still only 16% of all projects. A very high proportion (84%) of learning projects are marked by individualized planning. That is, the planning is designed with a particular learner in mind.

Table 11 / Number of Learning Projects Planned by the Learner or an Amateur Compared to Professionally Planned Projects

Projects planned by the learner or by an amateur	Self-planned	368
	A person who is a friend or relative (and not a trained instructor)	11
	Groups that were equals, outside of any institutional framework	12
Total		391[a]
Projects planned by a paid or professional person, sponsored by an institution, or pursued for credit	A person who is a paid instructor, or helping as part of his job	24
	A person who is a friend or relative, but also happens to be a trained instructor	4
	A group sponsored by an institution and/or using an instructor or leader paid for this task	50
	A nonhuman resource	16
Total		94[b]

Note. – The total number of projects was 485, because 53 of the 538 learning projects were excluded from these calculations: 50 projects which had no dominant planner, and 3 projects in which the person responsible for the planning in a one-to-one situation was not classified further.
[a] This total is 81% of 485.   [b] This total is 19% of 485.

OTHER SURVEYS   Several other studies have also been interested in how many adult learning efforts rely on a group or institution, and how many are self-planned. These studies include Blackburn (1967, 1968), Harold Huston's doctoral dissertation (in progress), Johnstone and Rivera (1965), Litchfield (1965), Parker and Paisley (1966), Shorey (1969), and Yadao (1968).

Johnstone and Rivera treated self-planned learning projects merely as a residual category. In some subject matter areas (technical arts and hobbies, gardening, and home improvement skills), they found that at least 80% of all learning projects were self-planned. They stated that "the incidence of self-education throughout the adult population is much greater than we had anticipated [p. 37]." Blackburn (1967) was so impressed by the frequency of individual methods that he made the following recommendation: "Additional attention by educators should be devoted to designing and facilitating appealing educational experiences which adults can undertake through individual methods of study [pp. 207-208]."

None of the earlier studies, however, found as much self-planned learning as our survey discovered. Our 1970 survey indicates that most adults conduct several major learning efforts a year, and plan most of their learning themselves.

Several factors account for the differences between this survey and the earlier ones. Basically, the earlier studies uncovered only the learning efforts that the person could recall fairly quickly and easily. It is probably easier to recall a course or conference or discussion group than it is to recall most self-planned learning efforts. Consequently, many self-planned projects remained undetected in previous studies.

To reduce this error, we probed intensively for all of the person's learning projects. In our interviews, we used long lists of subject matter and learning methods to stimulate recall. Instead of asking a single blunt question, we tried several different ways of asking the person to recall additional projects. Each learner was interviewed intensively: mailed questionnaires, or interviewing the learner's spouse instead of the learner himself, did not seem appropriate to us. A two-hour interview was devoted exclusively to discovering all the person's projects during the preceding year, and gathering certain basic data about these projects.

Further surveys, using larger samples as suggested in Chapter 3, are needed to develop a complete and accurate picture of the relative frequency and importance of each type of planner. Despite our intensive efforts, the interviewers feel that in some interviews we failed to uncover all of the learning projects. Perhaps self-planned learning is even more common than our figures indicate.

The field of comparative adult education might benefit from a survey of learning projects in several regions of the world. Youth learning in various countries can perhaps best be compared by focusing on institutions – schools and colleges. With adults, though, only a small portion of their total learning occurs in an educational institution. Consequently, comparative adult education could focus on the adult's learning efforts in various countries, including all four types of planner.

COMPARING THE FOUR TYPES OF PLANNERS Our 1970 survey also differed from earlier studies by questioning the person intensively about the duration of each project, and by asking him to rate its importance on three criteria. The data from these questions are presented in Table 12, which enables us to compare the four types of planners.

In the top row, it is evident that self-planned and mixed projects are typically of much longer duration than the other three types. Common sense might suggest that a self-planned project would tend to be much shorter than a commitment to attending a group. According to the data, however, the opposite is true.

The second row shows the responses to the following question: "Please think for a moment about how much knowledge, information, and understanding you gained as a result of this one learning project – or think about how much your skills and habits improved – or how much your attitudes or sensitivity changed." Again, contrary to what would be expected, the amount of change or learning in a group is less than in a self-planned project. Also, the interviewees estimated that they learn about as much in each self-planned project as in a project planned by an object or person.

The second question about the importance of each learning project was this: "How

Table 12 / Duration and Importance for Each Type of Planner

Measure	Self	Group or its leader	Person in one-to-one	Nonhuman resource	Mixed
Number of hours per project	119	47	63	33	141
	94	35	20	19	63
Magnitude of change, or of	7.0	5.4	7.0	7.5	6.9
new knowledge and skill	7.1	5.0	10	7.5	7.1
Magnitude of enthusiasm	7.2	6.0	7.4	5.9	7.3
about having the new	7.0	5.5	10	5.0	7.5
knowledge and skill					
Magnitude of the benefits	5.5	3.9	4.6	4.6	6.6
to other people of the	5.0	5.0	5.0	5.0	6.2
learner's new knowledge					
and skill					

Note. – In each cell, the upper figure is the mean (the "average" person), and the figure below it is the median (the person in the middle, or the "typical" person). These calculations are based on individuals, not on the total number of learning projects. That is, the mean of the measure in each cell was first found *for each individual*; then the mean and median of these means were calculated. In the three measures of importance, 10 was the highest possible point on the scale and 0 was the lowest.

The four credit projects are not included in this table.

enthusiastic have you been about having this new knowledge and skill?" Although the differences are not great, people seemed a little more enthusiastic about the knowledge and skill gained through self-planned and person-planned projects than that gained from a nonhuman resource or a group.

The third question asked about the usefulness or importance of the learning project to other people in the world: "Let's set aside your own benefits for a moment, and look at any benefits for *other* people. Your new knowledge and skill might have been of some benefit to your family, your friends and relatives, your boss, your company or organization, your field, or even to people who live in other places." The bottom row in Table 11 does not indicate any clear or marked differences in this regard among the various types of planners, except that mixed planning tends to be high.

A summary of Table 11 might be useful at this point. In general, self-planned and mixed projects tend to be higher in duration and importance than other types of learning projects. That is, if a learner does not turn over the planning responsibility to a single person, group, or object, he spends more time at the learning and considers it more significant. Projects that rely on a group or object tend to be fairly low on most of the measures.

For the youth groups, no consistent differences in duration are evident. However, the group and self-planned projects tend to be rated especially high in importance.

9 Self-planned learning

We are now at the point where the person has decided to begin learning and has chosen a planner. Two chapters are now devoted to self-planned learning because it is so common and important. This chapter describes the present picture, and the following chapter suggests ways of improving self-planned learning. Subsequent chapters describe learning projects planned by someone other than the learner himself.

Over the years, several educators have discussed various learning efforts that are somewhat similar to self-planned learning projects, but not identical. They have labeled their phenomena in various ways: self-education, self-instruction, self-teaching, individual learning, independent study, self-directed learning, self-study. While engaged in such efforts to learn, individuals have been called autonomous learners, self-propelled learners, self-teachers, and autodidacts.

Throughout history, and throughout the world, self-planned learning has been common and important (Grattan, 1955; Houle, 1961, pp. 10-12; Kidd, 1959, pp. 9, 46-47; Kulich, 1970). As mentioned previously, 68% of all projects in our 1970 survey were self-planned and, in addition, most of the mixed projects (another 9% of all projects) were partially self-planned.

Why is self-planned learning so popular? Why does the learner usually handle the detailed planning himself, instead of turning to someone else? Even though he may go to various sources for suggestions on the details of what and how to learn, why does he retain the primary responsibility himself? Several reasons may account for this.

1. The learner may believe that he would actually lose time in the long run by turning the responsibility for planning over to someone else.
2. He may be confident that planning the learning episodes for the particular knowledge and skill he desires will be easy, and that the content will be readily available.
3. The learner may not be able to see past the next two or three learning episodes. He may not be sure how much longer he will continue the learning project, and

may think that the direction or subject matter will change soon. Consequently, he does not want to commit himself for a long period of time to a particular object, person, or group. He does not want to give up the possibility of shifting the subject matter significantly or frequently.

4. Using oneself as a planner avoids any difficulty in locating, selecting, and using the planner. The learner knows that he himself is available, whereas the other three types of planners may not be available in his community at the time he wants to begin the learning project. The learner may not want to bother investigating and choosing some other planner. He may be shy or reluctant to approach other people or an institution. The learner himself as a planner is always available at any time of the day or night, without an appointment or schedule, and without cost.

5. The learner may be reluctant to let others direct his learning project in case their procedures produce in him some inappropriate beliefs, attitudes, habits, or techniques.

6. The learner may be highly skilled at locating printed materials, and at quickly selecting and grasping their relevant ideas. Consequently he feels no need for another person or group to present the subject matter to him. He may also want to be free to read and reread any portion of a book, for example, in any order he wishes. Consequently he feels he would be frustrated by the relatively inflexible sequence imposed by other sorts of nonhuman resources.

7. The learner often has greater insight than anyone else into his own capacities, preferred methods, goals, needs, pace, and emotional blocks to learning.

8. The learner may expect to discover, invent, or synthesize the knowledge and skill because no one else has yet done so. The desired knowledge and skill may be unique: no one else is trying to obtain it. This is true of certain political decisions, research questions, and personal problems, for example.

9. In order to deal with a certain problem, the learner may want to gather a variety of possible solutions from several sources before selecting the best solution.

10. The learner may be especially likely to choose self-planning if he is self-reliant, independent, and autonomous.

11. He may expect to feel especially proud or pleased if he successfully plans his own learning, or he may hope to impress others.

WHAT STEPS DOES THE LEARNER TAKE? In order to gain the desired knowledge and skill, the learner or someone else must make many detailed decisions and arrangements. Because each of these is preparation for a successful learning episode, we call them *preparatory steps*. In a self-planned learning project, by definition, the learner himself is responsible for most of these day-to-day decisions and arrangements, especially the decisions about what and how to learn in each episode.

Some preparatory steps are necessary for making the basic decision about whether and what to learn; others are necessary for choosing the planner. These two clusters of steps have already been discussed in Chapters 6 and 7. To a large extent, these steps are performed near the beginning of the learning project. Throughout the project, though, the learner may occasionally reexamine or modify his earlier decision.

In this chapter, we leave the early comprehensive steps and move on to the day-to-day steps. These detailed steps are the "executive" steps: the specific decisions and arrangements, from one learning episode to the next, necessary for completing the project successfully. The policy or legislative steps have already been taken: the comprehensive goal and the planner have already been chosen. Now the detailed plans for implementation are required. Each learning episode must be planned.

The list

Several years ago, I began trying to develop a list of preparatory steps that the learner sometimes takes in a self-planned learning project. An early list, developed from exploratory interviews and a variety of literature, was tested in 40 intensive interviews (Tough, 1967), and additional tasks were suggested by the learners. These new tasks were then tested with 42 part-time graduate students who had done an independent study project. Through further thought and interviewing, Heather Knoepfli contributed a great deal to the present list.

The preparatory steps performed by the self-planner can be viewed at several levels of comprehensiveness. At a macroscopic level, the learner directs the general flow of the entire learning process. In order to do so, he frequently reflects on the current situation, decides the next detailed strategy and content, and evaluates the effectiveness of his choices. At the other extreme, he performs hundreds of tiny particular actions while planning and arranging the learning project.

The following list of possible preparatory steps is somewhere between the two extremes. It contains 13 clusters of steps, each of which is fairly general, common, and important. The list has been based on experience and interviews as well as on logical analysis.

1. Deciding what detailed knowledge and skill to learn. As part of this step, the learner might try to detect specific errors in his current knowledge, or specific weaknesses in his current skill or style.
2. Deciding the specific activities, methods, resources, or equipment for learning. As part of this preparatory step, the person could study his own particular needs,

or decide the criteria to be used in selecting a particular resource. He could also gather information on the advantages, weaknesses, accessibility, level, and suitability of certain resources or activities. He might glance at several books or articles, perhaps in a library or bookstore, before selecting the most appropriate. He might decide what sort of person could provide the needed subject matter, and then try to locate the particular person who would be most suitable. As part of deciding whether to use a certain activity or resource, the learner might try it out for a short time.

3. Deciding where to learn. The learner may select a quiet, comfortable place that will be free of interruptions, or he may need a place in which certain facilities, equipment, or resources will be available.

4. Setting specific deadlines or intermediate targets.

5. Deciding when to begin a learning episode.

6. Deciding the pace at which to proceed during a learning episode.

7. Estimating the current level of his knowledge and skill, or his progress in gaining the desired knowledge and skill.

8. Detecting any factor that has been blocking or hindering his learning, or discovering inefficient aspects of the current procedures.

9. Obtaining the desired resources or equipment, or reaching the desired place or resource. As part of this step, the person may spend time traveling, trying to find a certain book in a library, ordering a book or other particular resource, obtaining permission to use certain facilities, or arranging to see a certain individual.

10. Preparing or adapting a room (or certain resources, furniture, or equipment) for learning, or arranging certain other physical conditions in preparation for learning. This step could include installing an air-conditioner or soundproofing a den, or putting a film or tape into a projector or recorder.

11. Saving or obtaining the money necessary for the use of certain human or nonhuman resources – perhaps for buying a book, renting equipment, or paying for lessons.

12. Finding time for the learning. This step can involve reducing or reorganizing the time spent at work, family activities, or recreation. The learner may have to ask his employer or wife to reduce the other demands on his time, or ask someone to take over some of his usual responsibilities for a while.

13. Taking certain steps to increase the motivation for certain learning episodes. The learner might want added motivation to increase the frequency or pace of his learning episodes, or to increase his pleasure, effort, or concentration during them. Possible substeps are (a) dealing with lack of motivation for achieving the

action or learning goal; (b) increasing one's pleasure in the learning situation, or one's interest in the learning activities or subject matter; (c) dealing with the feeling that the current strategy or particular resources will not be effective in achieving the desired knowledge and skill; (d) dealing with lack of confidence in one's capacity to learn, or with doubts about one's likely success in the learning project; (e) overcoming feelings of frustration and anger caused by difficulties; and (f) telling someone about one's delight.

HOW COMPETENT IS THE PLANNING? Our list indicates that planning a learning project can be a complex and delicate task. Many of the decisions and arrangements are difficult, for the learner is operating in a field (or level) of knowledge and skill that is new to him.

There is a wide range in the ability of adult learners to plan and arrange their own learning. Some are inept at planning and guiding any sort of learning project. Many are fairly successful in most of their self-planned learning projects. Some highly competent adults plan a remarkable variety of successful learning projects.

Only rarely will a learner sit down alone at the beginning of a learning project and plan his detailed strategy for the entire project. For, in a field that is new to him, how can he know what books are most useful? In learning a new skill, how can he know what components to practice, or in what sequence? How can he predict the emotional blocks and other problems that will arise later in the project?

In short, at the beginning of a project, the learner usually lacks the information and competence to plan the entire learning project. But he can obtain the information and develop the competence. He may seek advice about strategy, activities, resources, equipment, and even pace from various individuals and printed materials. After evaluating the information and suggestions, he decides his detailed subject matter and strategy for the first few learning episodes. As he proceeds, he may modify his strategy.

With the available evidence, it is difficult to estimate how much time the learner spends at planning. In one study on self-planning, an estimate of 21 hours per project was obtained (see Table 5 in Tough, 1967). In our 1970 survey, the learners spent a mean of 7 hours at planning each self-planned project; the median, though, was only 2 hours.

Estimating competence and success

Learners are often concerned about how well they are guiding their own learning. They seek feedback and confirmation of their success by comparing, for example, their level of performance or knowledge to that of others. One man's evidence for his self-mastery of a field was his ability to talk intelligently with experts in the field,

96

and to ask them several meaningful questions. Another man claimed he had successfully mastered Toynbee while a hospital patient by citing the fact that several doctors began spending their coffee hour in his room to discuss his previous day's reading. Other learners may measure their success by the amount they learn, or by their own enthusiasm and satisfaction.

A few studies have used test scores or outside observers to assess the learner's planning. Examples of these are Bivens, Campbell, and Terry, 1963; Newman, 1957; Ault, cited on page 407 in Olson, 1959; Ryan, 1965; Tough, 1967, pp. 74-75. In these studies, learners who planned their own efforts were at least as efficient and successful as other learners.

AMOUNT OF HELP WITH THE PLANNING   It is possible to imagine an adult deciding all of the detailed day-to-day content and strategy for a learning project without any help whatsoever from any other person or resource. He would choose his books and other subject matter resources, and make various plans and arrangements, without obtaining any information or advice. He would base his decisions on the information he already possessed, rather than seeking any new information from an outside source. He would rely on outside resources for actually providing the subject matter itself, of course, but not for his preparatory steps.

We have not yet found an actual example of this imaginary picture. It seems clear that few if any learners decide their detailed content and strategy without help. On the contrary, during a self-planned project, the typical adult obtains an astonishing amount of help from a large number of individuals and other resources.

During some of the open-ended exploratory interviews for a previous study (Tough, 1967), I was impressed by the way in which some adults organized their account of their self-planned projects. They recalled and described such projects by means of the individuals and other resources that had helped them. Their narrative revolved around their experiences with first one resource and then another. Several of these helpers and books had a great impact on the learner's progress. It became evident that the learner's relationship to his social and physical environment is extremely important in his efforts to plan a learning project.

Despite this forewarning, I was surprised by some of the findings of the study itself. The 40 interviewees, in 40 self-planned learning projects, obtained definite help from a total of 424 individuals. This is a sharp contrast with some classrooms, in which the 40 learners receive most of their help from only one individual. All 40 learners in this study definitely received help from at least 4 individuals, through direct contact and interaction. The average learner obtained help from 10 individuals, and a few learners from more than 20. Several other measures, too, demonstrated the great importance of help in self-planned projects (Tough, 1966, 1967). All of this help concerned the planning and directing of the project; resources that merely presented subject matter were not included.

Such helpers – friends, colleagues, acquaintances, family members, subject matter experts, sales persons, and librarians – do not *control* the learning project. Although the learner receives advice, information, encouragement, and subject matter from several individuals, he makes the decisions himself.

The learner himself retains the primary responsibility for planning and guiding a self-planned project. However, he does not operate in isolation from other persons, objects, and groups. Instead, he seeks and obtains a very large amount of advice and encouragement. In addition, though, he is likely to feel the need for even more help than he actually obtains. The resources help the learner with a variety of preparatory steps: deciding his learning activities, obtaining other resources, dealing with lack of motivation, estimating his level of learning, and so on. The help with the planning (and with the subject matter) comes from many varied resources, not just from one or two individuals or objects.

HOW DOES THE LEARNER SEEK HELP? Certain chronological sequences of events are fairly common in the process of seeking help. Ray Devlin, for example, while a graduate assistant at the Ontario Institute for Studies in Education, identified five steps in the help-seeking process: (1) the learner develops a general awareness of the need for help; (2) the learner becomes fairly specific about just what he needs; (3) he selects a particular resource, perhaps after seeking advice about this decision; (4) he decides how to approach the individual or obtain the resource; (5) he takes that action.

The help-seeking process is not always rational and straightforward. Sometimes, for instance, it is best for the learner to take a certain step without thinking about it too much. One woman, for example, on impulse, went to a store to buy a guitar. She did not reread her consumers magazine article about guitars, and did not consider how expensive a guitar would be. If she *had* taken these rational steps, she might never have found the courage to proceed with the purchase.

Often a learner receives *unanticipated* help from some resource. He may seek one sort of help, and obtain several others in addition. Sometimes he does not even seek the resource in the first place: he may happen to notice a book on a coffee table, or may bump into some relevant person. As soon as he sees the resource, though, or when he becomes familiar with it, he realizes that it can help with a certain step.

Sometimes a learner will approach a certain individual or organization because he hopes for some sort of help, but does not really know what. His primary intention may be to find out what sorts of help this resource can provide. Or he may realize that

98

just describing a problem or necessary decision to someone else can be helpful.

The choice of a particular resource, too, may be based primarily on emotional or nonrational considerations. Using a list of 50 items, for example, Mairi Macdonald's doctoral study (1968) found that the least important reasons for choosing a particular helper were his expertise, his education, his relevant experience, and the recommendations of others. Instead, the helper was chosen because the learner expected to feel comfortable and relaxed with him. The learner predicted he would be able to talk freely and easily with this helper, would not feel awkward or embarrassed, and would not feel he was imposing on the helper or irritating him.

Needed research

One of our ultimate goals is to design and provide more effective help for adult learners. In order to do this, we must first understand how help fits into a learning project. In particular, we must understand the sequence of events, feelings, decisions, reasons, and perceptions that result in a learner seeking or receiving help from a particular resource. The entire process is important: becoming aware of needing certain help; having certain feelings and perceptions about that need; deciding how and where to seek help; succeeding or failing to obtain the desired resource or help.

Within this overall process, many specific questions arise. What experiences during self-planned learning make the person aware of his need for help? What specific help does he seek, and with what tasks and difficulties? How do learners feel about needing help during a self-planned project? How much time do learners spend deciding about help? How difficult are these decisions? How accurately do learners diagnose what steps require help, and what resources can provide it? Do some learners try to estimate the optimum amount of help, thus avoiding any wasted time from seeking too much or too little? Do learners typically get enough help, or are they often frustrated?

WHAT RESOURCES DOES THE LEARNER USE? During a self-planned project, the learner usually finds that his interaction with several individuals and objects is relevant to his planning and arranging. Friends may offer information or suggestions. His wife may encourage him to speed up his pace, and to feel more confident about his likely success. A television program may stimulate him to pursue additional aspects of the topic. Several books may suggest additional resources or activities for further learning.

Most of these interactions with the environment will facilitate his learning, but one or two may be neutral or may even hurt his progress or motivation. We will use the term *particular resource* (or just *resource*) to refer to each individual and object with which the learner has some contact that affects the learning project. A list of particular resources for any one project would be very detailed and would include every specific person and object that affected the learning.

Up to this point, we have discussed resources that help the learner decide whether and what to learn, choose the planner, and make day-to-day decisions about detailed strategy and content. All of these are preparatory steps. Now we will turn to resources that provide subject matter. For purposes of analysis and research, it is often useful to distinguish when a resource is helping with planning and when it is providing content or subject matter. But in actual practice, the same book or conversation may provide both sorts of help. It may, for example, present the knowledge (or demonstrate the skill) and simultaneously increase the learner's motivation or suggest some other activity for further learning.

Human resources
In self-planned learning, almost every learner uses at least 4 or 5 human resources. Many use 10 or even 20. In most projects the majority of these helpers are friends and acquaintances, colleagues, members of the learner's family, and neighbors.

Certain other persons, as part of their occupation, have a responsibility for helping adult learners. These people include certain doctors, nurses, pharmacists, lawyers, judges, executives, supervisors, religious leaders, professors, extension agents, community development workers, counselors, sales persons, librarians, consultants, professional athletes, social workers, and instructors. A learner may approach such a person because he is an expert in the desired subject matter, because he has been trained to help adult learners, or because of certain personal qualities.

In addition, many persons have a message that they want to communicate. These persons include authors, advertisers, technical specialists and engineers (regarding one product), poets, film-makers, television writers and producers, and artists. The adult learner may, as part of his learning project, read or watch their message.

Some learning projects rely on an astounding number of human resources. A political, military, or industrial leader, for example, may rely on a large network of people responsible for collecting, evaluating, and summarizing information for him. They may gather the information through investigation, research, espionage, or reading. They may test the information by experience, discussion, computer simulation, or pilot programs.

Sometimes contact with a fellow learner, too, is valuable. This interaction may greatly influence the person's goals, attitudes, basic conceptions, motivation, and specific directions.

Several researchers have studied the extent to which learners receive help and information from various types of persons. Examples are Hoeflin (1950), Jahns

(1967), Sharma (1967), and Tough (1967). It seems likely that almost every adult is capable of providing some sort of help with some learning projects. Every adult is a potential helper as well as a learner.

Nonhuman resources

The learner may also obtain various sorts of help from a large number of nonhuman resources. Almost all learners use several nonhuman resources in addition to at least four or five human resources. One man preparing for his new job as a national education director, for example, obtained definite help from 39 books and pamphlets (through 5 libraries), 2 advertisements, 8 helpers, and 1 guided tour – a total of 55 particular resources.

As this example demonstrates, printed materials are especially common. Books, monographs, professional and technical journals, popular magazines, newspapers, bibliographies, workbooks, self-improvement books, and duplicated documents are examples of printed resources. Platt (1966, Chapter 1) has speculated on the growing importance of microbooks. Programmed instruction and computer-assisted instruction are also becoming more common and sophisticated. Journals are experimenting with new formats and services.

A learner may already own various printed resources that are relevant. Dictionaries, encyclopedias, home repair manuals, and books on child care are often bought for future learning projects, not current ones.

Reviewing the achievements of magazines since 1900, Peterson (1964) found that "for millions of Americans, the magazine was an inexpensive instructor in daily living. It counseled them on rearing children, on marital and financial problems, on getting along with one another. It told them how to furnish and decorate their homes. how to tend their gardens, how to prepare food nutritiously and inexpensively [p. 450]."

A lecture delivered more than 130 years ago (Channing, 1838) foresaw the great potential of printed materials in self-planned learning. "One of the very interesting features of our times is the multiplication of books, and their distribution through all conditions of society. At a small expense, a man can now possess himself of the most precious treasures of English literature. Books, once confined to a few by their costliness, are now accessible to the multitude. . . . The results must be, a deliberateness and independence of judgment, and a thoroughness and extent of information, unknown in former times. The diffusion of these silent teachers, books, through the whole community, is to work greater effects than artillery, machinery, and legislation [p. 24]."

Other important nonhuman resources at the present time are television, radio, films, displays, exhibits, recordings, language laboratories, and training and simulation devices.

The learner may also look at finished products (if he hopes to make one himself). Or he may learn by observing his human or physical environment, perhaps after trying to manipulate it, and by reflecting on his observations. Here his resource is a natural event or phenomenon, such as an emotional reaction or a group process, rather than a person or product, that is presenting certain words or pictures to him. Researchers discover new and original knowledge in this way. Many other learners, too, during at least some of their learning episodes, simply observe people or natural events, or reflect on their previous experiences.

In addition, the learner may manufacture some resource for himself. One fascinating example of this is the "behavior graph" studied by Schwitzgebel (1964) and Kolb, Winter, and Berlew (1968). The learner makes a graph on which he then records the behavior he is trying to change. After each day or session, he may record how many cigarettes he smoked, sundaes he ate, daydreams he had, or errors he made. He may keep track of his weight, speed, exercises, or progress toward other goals.

In any self-planned learning project, the array of human and nonhuman resources is impressive. Reflecting on all of a person's learning for an entire year, or even a lifetime, points up even more the very large variety of resources that one learner uses in our society. Such reflection also makes it clear that no single individual, object, or institution aids more than a small portion of a person's learning during his lifetime.

Needed research

Much more research is needed about resources. Is it possible to develop an exhaustive list of all types of resources? Which types of resources are especially common and useful in self-planned learning projects? How many particular resources are used in each learning project? What characteristics of the subject matter, the learner, and the resources influence his choice? What difference does his choice make?

In order to tackle these questions, researchers will have to (1) develop a single set of mutually exclusive types of resources, or (2) develop and use a list of several variable characteristics. The first approach would develop a set of categories ("types of resources") into which all particular resources could be classified. Researchers could use such gross categories as a person, a book, and a real-life phenomenon, or could develop a fairly detailed classification scheme. It is unlikely, though, that all researchers will agree on a single scheme.

The second approach would develop several continua to describe the major variable characteristics of particular resources. Perhaps some variables would apply either to persons or objects, but not to both. With a person, for example, we might be interested in the extent to which providing help to the learner is part of his job, how intimate or remote the relationship is, how much the person knows about the subject matter, the extent of his experience and skill in helping adult learners, and the extent to which he was approached as an individual rather than as a representative or employee of some institution. We might also be interested in his age, sex, level of education, occupation, geographical proximity, and intention.

Either approach would benefit from trying to understand how the *learner* perceives the resources. Does he choose the type of resource before selecting a particular resource? What characteristics of resources are in his mind when he chooses them? His perceptions could influence the type of list that we develop.

The situation in which help is usually received could also be studied. How much time does the typical learner spend alone with no resource? To what extent does he receive his human help in a one-to-one situation, in a small group, in a large group, through a third person, by mail, and by telephone? Within what context, program, or institution (if any) are certain of the resources located?

10 Improving self-planned learning

What can we do to facilitate and improve self-planned learning? As a first step toward answering the question, this chapter presents some empirical data on what goes wrong during the help-seeking process. Then the chapter examines various ways of improving the learner's competence at planning his own learning, and of providing better help for him.

GETTING HELP IS OFTEN DIFFICULT
Many persons would welcome more and better help with their self-planned learning. They often experience difficulties in obtaining some of the help they do receive. They cannot perform all the necessary preparatory steps unaided, yet they fail to obtain all of the help that they seek or want. Few men and women have special training in planning a learning project. In addition, if the learner is operating in a subject matter area that is quite new to him, he will be unfamiliar with the structure of the subject, the best sequence for learning it, and the resources available.

Many things can go wrong during his attempts to get help. He may encounter difficulties and frustration at any point in his efforts to obtain help, and these problems may seriously affect his feelings and efficiency.

The impact of these difficulties in obtaining help became very clear to one researcher during 16 interviews. Vida Stanius, during a study of the difficulties that arise in the help-seeking process, noted the following: "The negative effects [of difficulties with help] can be picked out from the interviews – frustration, anger, confusion, procrastination, diminished enthusiasm, lack of motivation, and a vow never to go to a particular helper again. Several delays in a project were mentioned, and one suspension. Sometimes the person questions the quality of the learning because of the other negative aspects he experiences throughout the project. When something goes wrong with getting help, this can snowball into several other difficulties."

WHAT GOES WRONG?
There are several ways to study the question of what goes wrong. After deciding to use the various stages of the help-seeking process as a framework, we distinguished six stages or phases that the learner may go through in order to obtain appropriate advice, information, encouragement, or other help. Table 13 presents, in the left-hand

column, the six chronological stages. Any particular difficulty in the help-seeking process can be fitted into this framework.

Most of the difficulties occur *between* two adjacent stages. That is, the learner achieves one stage successfully but fails to achieve the next one. The right-hand column of the table summarizes the difficulties that may occur at each point in the chronological framework. Only the seventh difficulty (G) occurs *during* a particular stage; the others are defined as a failure to reach the next stage.

Table 13 helps us to see the points in the help-seeking process at which problems, breakdowns, and failures occur. The right-hand column provides a framework for the discussion on the next few pages.

In our small study of what goes wrong in the help-seeking process, Vida Stanius interviewed 16 adults intensively. Each adult described his difficulties in obtaining the help he needed during one self-planned learning project. The stage at which each difficulty occurred, and the frequency and impact of that difficulty, were recorded.

The most frequent and serious locus of difficulties in Table 13 was F, with G a close second. That is, the greatest difficulties usually occurred during contact with the person, book, or other resource, rather than earlier in the process. Certain persons would not or could not give the required help, and certain printed materials were useless. Even when beneficial help was received from certain resources, much of it cost the learner a great deal of time, money, effort, or frustration. The least troublesome points in the right-hand column were A and B.

From the standpoint of efficiency in any learning project, there will be an optimum amount of help for each of the preparatory steps. Many learners seek and receive that optimum amount. When difficulties do occur, they usually occur in the direction of seeking or obtaining too little help. We must also note the possibility, though, of a learner seeking and obtaining far too much help (because of his incompetence at estimating the optimum amount of help, perhaps, or because of his emotional or personality characteristics).

A. Unaware of needing help

In almost every self-planned learning project, the person does become aware of needing help. Some learners, though, expect to get along with just printed materials. They may experience considerable difficulty and frustration before realizing their need for a *human* helper.

B. Uncertain about which steps needs help

A few learners give little thought to their learning procedures. After interviewing one woman, for example, Stanius reported that "she was quite vague about the sorts of

Table 13 / A Framework for Studying What Goes Wrong During the Help-Seeking Process

Six stages in the help-seeking process	The difficulties and breakdowns that occur
	A. The learner does not develop even a general vague awareness of any need for help.
Stage 1: The learner becomes aware of needing help, although the awareness is vague and general.	
	B. He does not know, clearly and accurately, which of his specific preparatory steps would benefit greatly from help.
Stage 2: He becomes clear on the preparatory step with which help is needed, and/or on just what sort of help is needed.	
	C. He believes he does not know how or where to seek the desired help.
Stage 3: He knows or decides how to seek that help, or from what type of resource or what particular resource to seek it.	
	D. He knows how to get help, yet he does not take action.
Stage 4: He actually seeks the help or resource.	
	E. He tries without success to reach a particular resource.
Stage 5: He receives, reaches, or makes contact with a particular resource.	
	F. During his contact with that resource, certain characteristics of the resource, situation, or learner result in his failure to actually obtain the desired help.
Stage 6: He gets the desired help from that particular resource.	G. He does obtain the desired help, but only at great cost in time, money, effort, or frustration.

help she needed. She later felt that this hampered her learning and that she would have saved much time and effort if she had been more thoughtful sooner." In addition, the subject matter area may be so new or technical for the learner that he cannot figure out just what help he needs, or even what preparatory step to take next. A third problem occurs when a learner reaches stage 4 or 5 before completing stage 2 successfully. He may seek help blindly because he is lazy, dependent, or completely confused.

C. Uncertain how or where to get help

In some learning projects, the person is unable to decide what procedure to follow in order to obtain the needed help. He does not know a particular resource that is likely to be useful. Stanius interviewed several adults who knew the sort of person they needed, or the sort of knowledge such a person should have, but who were unable to think of a particular individual. They were clear about their needs, but could not think of an acquaintance who fitted those requirements. We do not know whether such a person was, in fact, readily available to the learner. The point is, though, that the learner was not *aware* of such an individual, and consequently could not move on to stage 4 in the help-seeking process.

Some learning projects probably shift direction or end prematurely because of difficulty in deciding how to obtain the subject matter or other help. The person wants to learn something, but the lack of appropriate help and resources (or his inability to find them) reduces his actual learning.

Rieger and Anderson (1968) asked adults to identify skills or areas of knowledge in their everyday activity about which it had been particularly difficult to obtain useful and reliable information. About 25% of the sample listed one or more subjects. It is interesting that urban residents and those with a high educational level were especially likely to report difficulty. The common areas listed were financial matters, community and national affairs, consumer information, and occupational problems and practices.

To illustrate the variety of information that can be difficult to obtain, I decided to recall examples of my own difficulties. I was able to list several topics on which I encountered great difficulty in finding accurate, helpful, relatively unbiased information. Yet I could clearly specify my needs, was strongly motivated to learn, and was willing to spend some money. My list includes the following areas of knowledge and skill: a printer's procedures and requirements; how to operate a movie projector; finding an out-of-print book; yearbook layout; various types of insurance; building a bookcase; finding an apartment in Chicago's Hyde Park area; moving procedures and movers; differences between American and Canadian banking systems; income tax during dual-status years; appropriate exercise; storing and preparing food; life style and basic problems in India; savings institutions; family budget procedures; finding a publisher.

D. No action

Although he is clear about his needs and how to satisfy them, the learner may still hesitate to actually seek that help. This may seem rather surprising before one looks at the learner's perceptions and characteristics.

One woman failed to realize that her project was a very difficult one. The interviewer felt she also failed to seek advice because she was self-reliant, stubborn, and afraid of criticism. Another woman mentioned three examples of not seeking help because she was lazy, she hesitated to bother people for help, and she felt people would not be interested in her project. Other learners may be shy, may feel that requesting assistance is childish and inappropriate, or may feel that a great deal of effort would be required in getting help.

Some learners hesitate to seek help because of their bad experiences in the past. After being rebuffed once or twice, or after several resources turn out to be a waste of time, the learner may refuse to seek further help. There are many anecdotes about such situations. Two of my favorite involve acquaintances of mine who were about 35 at the time of the respective incidents. One of these men asked a professor in a Spanish department for advice on which materials to use for learning vocabulary. My friend was shaken up by the reply: he was too *old* to learn Spanish. The other acquaintance decided to learn to play the piano. At his first (and last) lesson, though, the teacher gave him a book with a childish cover that referred to "tiny tunes for little fingers."

E. Unable to reach the resource

Even if he does take some action to obtain a specific resource, a learner may be blocked. One woman reported that her learning was hampered by wasted time, frustration, and inability to find a certain reference book – all because she could not reach a certain individual.

It would be interesting to study which sorts of resources are especially difficult to obtain, and to determine just what the difficulties are.

F. Difficulties during contact with the resource

Our data indicate that most learners experience some difficulty in getting help from at least one or two particular resources during their contact with those resources. All but one of the 16 interviewees in our small study reported this problem, and several

108

reported two or three examples of it. The learner obtains or reaches the desired resources, but fails to get the specific help he needs from at least one of them. What goes wrong?

Sometimes the learner simply chooses the wrong resource. In a sense, he has gone astray at stage 3, but this does not become evident to him until his contact with the resource. The learner may choose a convenient person or close friend, rather than the person with the best ability to help. Just as a young child may seek most help from his parents, an adult may habitually turn to the same neighbor or friend whenever he needs help. One member of our research team, Ray Devlin, hypothesized that some adults never think of turning to a remote helper because throughout childhood they received almost all of their help from nearby peers, teachers, and parents.

Some individuals who are approached for help simply do not have the information that the learner needs, or they lack the capacity to give the desired help. Some are impatient with the learner and prefer to take over the whole project themselves. Some are unwilling to help the learner, or are not interested in him or his subject matter. Some individuals are insensitive to the learner's real needs, and provide the same sort of advice or information in response to all requests. A helper may be so far above the learner's level of knowledge that he cannot communicate effectively. Some other possibilities are suggested in Appendix C, which deals with the relationship between helper and learner.

Sometimes the difficulties seem to reside in the situation rather than in the helper or the learner. For example, too many learners may simultaneously be seeking help from the same person. Or the learner and helper may be unable to communicate easily and accurately because they come from different cultural backgrounds.

Many learners realize that they themselves are at fault – not the situation or the resource. The learner may fail to communicate his needs clearly and accurately. He may not ask the right questions. He may be such a novice that he does not know what he really wants from the helper. The learner may be tense when he is with the helper, may be a little fearful of him, or may try very hard to please him. A learner may hesitate to accept suggestions and information because of such irrelevant factors as the helper's age, background, appearance, or status. For no apparent reason, the learner may dislike or distrust the helper.

In some helping situations, the learner assumes that the helper will take all of the initiative and responsibility, and will do all the work. The learner believes he can just sit back and receive all the necessary advice and content he needs without effort. Such a learner may fail to express his real needs and to evaluate what he hears.

We have just seen that many things can and do go wrong during the learner's contact with a potential helper. What is the ultimate effect of these difficulties? The answer is somewhat surprising and contradictory. Delays, discouragement, wasted time, and a reduction of motivation are common results. But, instead of quitting, most interviewees in our study became even more persistent in seeking the needed help. Some of them tried other helpers who proved to be satisfactory. Often a learner's motivation and effort will actually increase as the result of someone's indifference.

Printed resources, too, can fail to provide the expected sorts of help. Adults report that they are sometimes frustrated by printed materials that are out-of-date, too advanced, too elementary, or vague and ambiguous. Some learners report that materials actually available at any given time in a library or bookstore are inadequate.

G. Excessively costly help

In many learning projects the person succeeds in obtaining the desired help, but feels it was hardly worth the large amount of time, money, effort, or frustration that it cost him. In our study, for example, the interviewer reported that one man "almost gave up buying a new car because 85% of the salesmen he contacted were not helpful: he felt he wasted too much time going to all these people with only frustration as the result."

WHAT CAN WE DO ABOUT THESE DIFFICULTIES? If these difficulties could be greatly reduced, self-planned learning could proceed with far less effort, time, and frustration. The preparatory steps could be performed more effectively and efficiently, with better decisions and arrangements. The learning activities could be better suited to the individual learner's needs and level.

Basically, there are two ways to reduce the difficulties that occur during the help-seeking process. The ideal solution, though, may be a combination of both. One way is to increase the learner's *competence* at performing most of the preparatory steps without help – and at obtaining appropriate help when he does need it. The other way is to provide much better *help* for the adult during his efforts to plan and learn. The next section discusses the first way, and the remainder of the chapter discusses the second.

DEVELOPING COMPETENCE AT PLANNING Though many adults are already fairly competent at planning and conducting their own learning projects, a large proportion of adults are capable of dramatic improvement in their competence at self-planned learning. A new level of competence can lead, in turn, to more efficient and successful learning. The learner will also become more confident, and more willing to tackle difficult learning projects.

Helping people develop in these ways is an exciting frontier in human learning. What could be more important than helping people of all ages develop skill in

110

planning and conducting their own learning? At present, we do not know how to do this very well. We have not yet tried in any comprehensive way to help people become better learners and planners.

What competence is needed?

Just what types of competence are needed to make a self-planned learning project successful? Clearly it is important for every adult – and every younger person, too – to have a reasonably good ability to choose the subject matter and the planner, as was pointed out in Chapters 6 and 7. If the person decides to direct the learning project himself, he needs several further sorts of competence.

The self-planner must be competent in knowing which preparatory step to perform next. Instead of deciding to let some object, person, or group perform most of these preparatory steps, he has decided to perform them himself. This will require skill in diagnosing his current problems and needs, and in deciding just which preparatory steps to perform at any given time.

He also needs competence in actually performing those preparatory steps. In one learning project or another he will probably have to perform each one of the 13 steps we listed, some of which require a great deal of competence. In order to decide the learning activities, for example, the self-planner must be familiar with certain general principles of learning and behavior change, and with his own style of effective learning. In order to change certain habitual behavior, he may need skill in establishing some feedback mechanism for measuring his day-to-day performance. He might benefit from greater skill in finding appropriate resources in a library or bookstore, using reference books and bibliographic tools, and finding appropriate human help.

The more competent he is at performing each of the preparatory steps, the less help he will need. But almost every learner does seek and obtain at least some help. Many difficulties can arise during these efforts to obtain help, as we saw earlier in this chapter. Consequently, the learner can benefit greatly from being competent in each stage of the help-seeking process.

At the very early stages, for example, he must be able to diagnose fairly precisely and accurately just what help he needs. He must figure out which preparatory steps could be performed much more efficiently with help, and what the optimum (most efficient) amount of help would be. Then he must choose an appropriate resource for providing the help, and must successfully reach or obtain that resource. During contact with the resource, the learner must be competent at gaining the desired help.

Eventually the learner should be able to analyze and plan the entire learning process in any project, taking whatever actions are needed to maintain the successful flow of learning. Whenever necessary, he should be able to evaluate his progress and efficiency, diagnose difficulties, seek appropriate help, and plan the next steps. In short, he should always be "on top of the whole situation," comfortably and competently in control, seeking advice whenever necessary, but never relying too heavily on that advice.

Competence at actually doing the learning, not only at planning and arranging it, is also necessary. In almost any learning situation, the learner needs certain minimum skills in listening, taking notes, reading, memorizing, or performing some other learning activity. Such learning skills or "study habits" may be especially important when professional assistance is not readily available.

The increased efficiency that can result from a mastery of high-speed reading techniques is particularly impressive. Thousands of adolescents and adults have gained skills in previewing material at thousands of words per minute, in setting clear goals, and then in gaining the desired knowledge in a minimum of time. Selecting and using a variety of paces and techniques, a person can read an easy book in 20 minutes, a weekly newsmagazine in 10, a newspaper in 4. Learning through reading becomes a very effective and rapid process. Perhaps even more important, the person's confidence increases along with his competence: he no longer hesitates to tackle any book or topic, no matter how formidable.

Feelings and attitudes about self-planning
In the first interviews I conducted about self-planned learning, I was surprised at the typical attitudes of people toward their own self-planned learning (Tough, 1967, pp. 39-40, 75, 77). When I stated at the beginning of the interview that I was interested in the person's recent learning, the initial response was often a self-deprecating remark. The person's initial perception seemed to be that he had not done any learning at all during the past year, and any learning he had done was unimportant or of low quality. Many said their learning was very strange or offbeat – not at all like that of other people.

Although these initial self-deprecating comments were sincere, they were very unrealistic. By the end of each interview it was evident that the person had learned a great deal, had spent a large amount of time at learning, and had used a variety of methods. His actual learning had been much greater and better than his initial attitude suggested.

As we come to understand these attitudes, we will probably be able to help learners develop a more accurate image of their learning. More and more people will realize that self-planned learning projects are a common, natural, and important activity of many persons.

112

The competent self-planner is realistic about the potential power of self-planned learning, and about his own limits. He is aware of the total pattern of his own self-planned learning, and is confident about his ability to plan and conduct such learning successfully. He is never stopped from initiating a learning project because of a false notion that it will be a threatening, unpleasant, frustrating chore.

Methods

Several methods could help a person to improve his competence at self-planning. A new center or self-education bureau might be useful. A counselor, perhaps using a questionnaire, could help the person analyze his skills and weaknesses in planning. With this procedure, the person could decide just what additional planning and learning skills he wants to develop. The counselor could also help him choose an appropriate strategy for gaining these skills. In addition, this center or counselor might help learners with their ongoing learning projects. Such help could increase the learner's skill in planning along with his other knowledge and skill.

Parents, libraries, clubs, and employers could all play some role in developing competence at planning. Adult education institutions might sponsor a group program devoted to developing this skill.

A book on how to plan for learning could help the reader understand the tasks, problems, and feelings that a learner faces, and suggest steps he can take to deal with these. It could contain questionnaires or other methods for diagnosing one's own weaknesses in planning and learning, and for setting corresponding objectives.

Various books on how to study are already available, and some of them are excellent for full-time students or for adults returning to the classroom. But few if any of these books try to develop skills as a *planner*, and few of them deal with learning projects outside of academic educational institutions. Instead, they emphasize *learning* skills, such as how to concentrate and improve your memory, make notes, improve reading speed and writing style, and prepare for examinations. These skills are important, but they are not enough.

Schools and colleges also develop skill in passing courses rather than in conceiving, refining, planning, and guiding one's own learning projects. They deal primarily with a learning situation in which an instructor rather than the learner himself is responsible for most of the objectives, planning, requirements, and even resources. The learner's task, in this case, is to learn the subject matter chosen by the instructor.

Even within this context, though, efforts to help students increase their learning competence are becoming increasingly important. Courses in effective reading and effective writing are common, and courses in study habits or "learning how to learn" are developing.

113

The importance of these efforts has been demonstrated by a study in the United Kingdom (Jahoda & Thomas, 1965). The authors concluded that "one of the most surprising findings of our studies is that most students are almost unaware of how they learn. At best they have a sort of undeveloped folklore of fetishes and home remedies to which they have become too closely wedded because it has 'succeeded so far.' It would appear that quite large increases in the effectiveness of university education are possible through fairly simple improvements in the students' basic skills [p. 55]." They recommend that "emphasis should be put upon encouraging students to become increasingly aware of how they learn and to question, experiment with, and thus develop the effectiveness of a wide range of learning skills [p. 55]."

If educators in schools and colleges really want to prepare their students for a lifetime of larning, they should certainly think more about how to develop self-planning skills. Adolescents and college students already conduct many self-planned learning projects outside of their educational institution, as we saw in Chapter 8. Though few educators and schools even notice or care about such learning projects, the student's out-of-school learning may prepare him better for adult learning than his in-school experiences do.

Adult education programs and advanced graduate programs could also make a major contribution toward increasing competence in self-planned learning. At present they may do just the opposite: they may increase the person's tendency or need to rely on someone else.

We need several innovative pilot programs that are oriented toward developing the learner's competence at self-planning. Penetrating, meaningful evaluations of these pioneer programs will provide information useful for improving them. Several research projects, and some attention to theorizing, will build up a body of knowledge to serve as a foundation. These various activities will interact, each one stimulating and contributing to the others.

This further work will result in a much larger number of highly competent learners – learners with excellent ability in diagnosing, planning, and arranging their learning; learners able to obtain appropriate help with a minimum of time and effort; learners who foresee the potential difficulties in obtaining help, but strive to learn none-theless – learners willing to surmount all sorts of obstacles with the ease and good humor of crosscountry runners.

BETTER HELP WITH THE PLANNING

The ideal learner accepts the world of resources as it is, and learns in spite of his difficulties in obtaining help. This characteristic should not stop us, however, from trying to change that world in order to make his learning efforts more efficient and pleasant. The possibility of developing better help with the day-to-day preparatory

114

steps is examined in this section.

It is interesting to speculate on adult learning in the future. What major changes will occur in adult learning, and in various forms of adult education, during the next 20 or 30 years? Some important changes will occur in what people learn, why they learn, and the total amount they learn. Changes in the help available for the adult learner will probably be even more significant. Human help with the major decisions about learning will be more available, effective, and individualized. Hardware and nonhuman resources will increasingly be tailored to the individual, or at least flexible enough to meet his needs.

Clearly adult learners need greatly improved help in various aspects of planning learning projects. Inadequate help results in countless wasted hours, inappropriate projects, and inefficient methods. Because of the lack of available help, the person may not even start the learning project in the first place. Yet, without learning, how can he deal effectively with his job, home, family, recreational activities, and finances?

The development of better help should be based on the characteristics and needs of the adult learner. We must ensure that the help suits *his* plans and needs and schedule as much as possible, rather than insisting that he accept a prestructured body of subject matter learned through a predetermined sequence of methods and activities.

The specific help that could be provided

The preparatory steps that face the self-planner provide one basis for thinking about better help. The 13 preparatory steps involved in planning and arranging learning episodes were listed in the previous chapter. (The preparatory steps for deciding what to learn, and some possibilities for better help with these early steps, were discussed in Chapter 6.) The 13 day-to-day preparatory steps are summarized in the left-hand column of Table 14, and the right-hand column presents some reflections on the help that is needed with each step.

A comprehensive source of help for the self-planner should be capable of helping with most of the 13 steps. If it cannot help with one or two, it should at least be able to help the learner find that assistance somewhere else. Table 14 indicates which steps will probably require the most help.

The self-planner will not require a massive amount of help. By definition, he assumes the primary responsibility for steps 1 and 2. In addition, the typical self-planner performs most of the preparatory steps by himself, seeking help with two or three that he finds especially troublesome. As he becomes more competent at planning and arranging his learning, he will need even less help.

Table 14 / Some Reflections on the Help Needed with Each Preparatory Step

Summary of the 13 preparatory steps	Some reflections on each step
1. Deciding detailed knowledge and skill.	Often a difficult but crucial decision. The most effective resource will usually be a subject matter expert, or a nonhuman resource dealing with the given subject matter. By definition, the self-planner makes this decision in the majority of episodes.
2. Deciding activities, materials, resources, and equipment for learning.	Probably the most important task in this list, and often the most difficult. By definition, the self-planner assumes the primary responsibility for these decisions. The best helpers (and the writers of the most helpful materials) will usually be expert in the subject matter and/or in the principles of learning. A librarian can help with decisions on nonhuman resources. Decisions must be highly appropriate for *this* particular learner.
3. Deciding where to learn.	Usually a brief, easy decision, unless it is difficult to find the desired equipment or facilities.
4. Setting specific deadlines or intermediate goals.	The best help may be simply suggesting this step and pointing out its advantages. This help can be provided by human or nonhuman resources.
5. Deciding when to learn.	Usually an easy decision.
6. Deciding the pace.	Rarely causes much difficulty.
7. Estimating level or progress.	This step is sometimes troublesome for the self-planner. Help can be human or nonhuman. It can range all the way from unconsciously showing the learner a higher level than he has yet reached (as in skiing), to sophisticated measurements of his current level or progress.
8. Detecting blocks and inefficiencies.	Often the learner can perform this step best. If not, a highly skilled diagnostician may be needed. The best help will be provided by a human rather than a nonhuman resource.

Table 14 – Continued

Summary of the 13 preparatory steps	Some reflections on each step
9. Obtaining or reaching resources or equipment.	Often requires only time and aggressiveness, not skill. A helper can smooth the way, however, or can even perform this step entirely, thus saving the learner a great deal of time and frustration. Most help will be human.
10. Preparing a room or other physical conditions.	Rarely difficult. Almost all help will be human.
11. Obtaining money.	Not much a helper can do, except lend or give the money.
12. Finding time for the learning.	A resource can offer advice. A human helper can take on some of the learner's time-consuming responsibilities.
13. Increasing motivation or dealing with motivational blocks.	Sometimes this step is necessary to avoid quitting. A skilled diagnostician familiar with the psychology of learning and motivation can sometimes be crucially important. Even forcing or berating the learner can occasionally be helpful. Help can be human or nonhuman.

Who will provide the better help?

To some extent, almost everyone may provide the improved help. Already the self-planner receives a great deal of help from his friends, relatives, and co-workers. In the future, perhaps most of these acquaintances will provide even better help because of certain training they receive. Thurman White (1965) has suggested that in the future one sort of skill required of each college graduate will be skill in helping others learn. One goal of parent education can be greater skill in helping children learn. Supervisory and management training can try to develop competence in helping subordinates learn appropriate knowledge and skill.

In addition, more comprehensive or sophisticated types of help might be provided by a variety of agencies. Libraries of all types – public, university, school, and special – are certainly logical centers for such help if they improve the variety and quality of their human and nonhuman help. Some new sort of learning consultant, helper, counselor, guide, or tutor might be trained. New bureaus to help adult learners might be set up by city governments, boards of education, the YMCA, or other voluntary agencies. Organizations might provide help for their employees or members, and educational institutions for their staff and students. Many of these agencies already help people learn, but their help could become much more individualized and useful for the self-planner.

Department stores or manufacturers might provide learning advisers for those who want to begin a certain hobby or consider some major purchase. Book stores, college residences, and hospitals are other possible locations for learning consultants. An association or union of those in a certain profession or occupation might provide learning advisers for their members.

Providing effective individualized help, both human and nonhuman, is also a responsibility of various government departments that is just as appropriate as group instruction and mass media instruction. Individualized help for adult learners is not necessarily more expensive than mass or group instruction if (1) we become more efficient than we are now at providing it, (2) it is provided only for appropriate individuals and subject matter, and (3) one looks at actual results, not just the number of persons who are reached.

In his chapter on the "autonomous" adult learner, Miller (1964) suggested that adult learners might benefit from a lounge or club. They could interact with other learners, and feel less isolated or strange as self-planners. Another possible format is a group of learners meeting to discuss their self-planned learning. They could help one another clarify goals, decide strategy, find resources, and increase motivation. One crucial aspect of effective help is the relationship between helper and learner. The significant variables in this relationship are discussed in Appendix C, which outlines a way of describing accurately the relationship between a human helper and the learner during a self-planned learning project. The last portion of the appendix describes some strong motivations for amateur teaching.

Table 5 indicated that nonhuman resources, too, can be helpful with some preparatory steps. These objects might include a book, computer, television program, or recording. A nonhuman resource can sometimes provide highly individualized help. One example is a 12-page booklet by Knowles (1961), which is designed for anyone who wants to improve his leadership skill. It helps him with preparatory steps 1 and 2. The booklet helps the reader list the leadership competencies (skills, attitudes, insight, and knowledge) that he wants to possess, rate his present level in each, and then develop an individual set of goals. For each of 15 different goals that the person might have, the booklet recommends the relevant pages in several different books.

118

Until now, this chapter has focused on planning and arranging the learning, not on the highly deliberate learning episodes. For the rest of this chapter, we will turn our attention to the learning itself. The learning episodes can include a variety of activities and methods, such as reading, watching television, reflecting, and practicing. The learner can also observe a natural phenomenon or someone displaying his desired skill.

Print

Reading printed material is an especially important learning activity in many self-planned learning projects. All 40 projects described in *Learning Without a Teacher*, for example, used some printed materials.

If he has reasonable skills in getting what he wants from printed sources, a learner finds that books and other printed materials provide a highly efficient and flexible way to learn. He can read the sections in whatever sequence he pleases, omit the irrelevant portions, and reread the difficult sections.

As more and more adults learn to scan print at thousands of words per minute, books may prove to be too slow and cumbersome. Instead, someone may invent a machine for displaying a continuous vertical scroll. The speed and direction of the scroll could be controlled by two foot pedals. A separate analytical table of contents could be displayed beside the machine. Access to printed words on a television screen or a similar screen may also become more common.

To deal with the flood of new knowledge and information, various systems using abstracts and key words are being developed. An individual may establish a profile of his interests, occupational specialities, and desired areas of information. These key words or subject matter areas are then used by an agency to determine which abstracts or news items to send him, thus weeding out much of the irrelevant material before it even reaches the learner. Even when he does receive the material, it may be in the form of abstracts (summaries) rather than complete articles in a journal or newspaper. Using the telephone or a reply postcard, the learner can then order a more detailed version of any item he judges to be especially relevant for him. Cheaper or faster ways of getting the desired materials into the learner's hands will eventually be developed – perhaps a combination of television transmission and cheaper photocopying methods. One-hour delivery by car or motorcycle is another possibility.

The days of disseminating stock quotations, career opportunities, and information on expensive consumer purchases (houses for sale, product information) indiscriminately to a mass audience may be ending. Instead, the person who wants to check the value of his stocks, seek a new job, or buy a house or television set will convey his request to some central agency or bureau that will quickly provide him

119

with the detailed information he needs.

Programmed instruction and computer-assisted instruction are also new ways of learning. By taking the learner through a subject step by step, with frequent testing, they help him learn efficiently. The sequence of steps is largely predetermined, though the use of a computer permits a fairly sophisticated sort of branching. These methods are sometimes called "individualized instruction" because they let the learner proceed at his own pace, unlike the classroom situation in which 20 or 40 students learn identical subject matter at an identical pace. Programmed instruction and computer-assisted instruction provide opportunities for highly efficient learning of certain subject matter that could not be learned nearly so efficiently 10 or 20 years ago. Incidentally, having just a few of the learning episodes controlled by a set of printed materials or a computer does not change the entire learning project from self-planned to object-planned. New forms of self-instructional workbooks may combine some of the principles of programmed instruction with characteristics that will help the person himself choose appropriate branches or paths, and help him apply his learning to practical situations. Highly sophisticated printed simulation materials provide additional new opportunities for learning that are far more effective than just reading about the topic.

Individually selected films and television programs
Although some new forms of printed materials are being developed, the self-planned learner's basic reliance on print is not new. One or two other ways of learning, however, provide dramatic (but relatively untapped) potential for self-planned learning.

One of these potential new ways of learning is the provision of *individually selected* films or television programs in the home or office. We all recognize that watching a film or television program is a highly effective way to learn, combining the gripping quality of ever changing color pictures and other visual stimuli with spoken words, music, and sound effects. So far, though, this powerful learning resource has not really been made available for self-planned learning. Films are almost never viewed by one person alone in his home or office, and at any given time the typical television set offers a choice of only a dozen programs. Because the adults in one viewing area may be conducting learning projects on a hundred thousand topics in any one week, only a small proportion of these persons will find a highly relevant program on television.

Giving the learner access to thousands of films or programs, so that he can choose one or more that are directly related to his current learning project, will be a major innovation. The film or videotape he selects might then be transmitted individually to

120

his home or office at whatever time he chooses, or the film or videotape might be delivered to him by truck or car within an hour or two of his request. Television sets with attached videotape players are already available, as are individual viewers for movies using foolproof cartridges. Presumably, in the future, the learner will be able to stop the film or videotape at any time in order to study a single picture in detail. He should also be able to replay any portion he wishes, control the speed within certain limits, and locate any particular portion quickly (Ely, 1970). A summary of the various systems that are being developed has been provided by *Time* (August 10, 1970).

In 1968, Ithiel de Sola Pool pointed out the likelihood of this shift in television from a mass medium to an individualized or interactive medium. He announced boldly that "we are at the beginning of an era in which the preferred communications devices need no longer have the quality of mass communications. Increasingly, communications devices will be adapted to individualized use by the consumer where and when he wants, on his own [p. 87]." An executive quoted by *Time* (October 10, 1969) called the new form of TV "personalized television," and stated that "mass programming will no longer completely satisfy the customer."

Already some public libraries lend films as well as records and printed materials. A brochure from a public library in a Toronto suburb, for example, points out that "films are ideal for home use because many families have their own projectors. The subject range represented is tremendous: films for pure fun are combined with travel films and information reels on cooking, sewing, drafting, electricity, woodwork, etc. There is something for all age and interest groups. Drop in at your nearest library branch and take home a film tonight!"

Television and print might be combined more frequently in the future. When a person watches a news story on television, for example, he might be able to obtain background information or more detailed printed information on news items of particular interest to him. These correlated printed materials could be mailed or delivered, or could be transmitted immediately by means of the television set itself and a photocopy attachment, or over telephone or teletype lines. In an interview for the January-February 1969 issue of *Think*, John Diebold predicted that reading "will be increasingly integrated with electronic technologies – and eventually even with biochemical fields. This integration is already beginning."

Experts
Enormous untapped potential can be found in another method of learning: talking with an outstanding expert in the field of knowledge or skill. Many experts, researchers, theorists, political leaders, athletes, professors, and others are willing to

speak to groups. They might also be willing to answer questions for an individual for half an hour, on the phone or in person, perhaps for a large or a small fee. They might criticize the learner's present style, assumptions, or procedures. Many learners and employers would be willing to pay up to $50 or even more for a high-impact talk with a certain outstanding expert. Perhaps such an arrangement will become increasingly common and acceptable during the next few decades.

Travel

Travel is another powerful way to learn. While traveling, though, the tourist is often plagued by lack of complete up-to-date information on the opportunities available to him. Also, many travel booklets and bus tours are aimed at a mass audience of typical travelers, and ignore the variety of special interests and learning projects that travelers have. Perhaps students could serve as individual guides to answer the tourist's questions about the particular city or country, and to show him the aspects that are especially relevant to the tourist's personal interest. Tours of factories, homes, schools, farms, and villages could also be provided.

Information centers

A significant source of information in the United Kingdom is the neighborhood information center (Kahn, 1966). Without going far from home, a person can obtain information and advice on a variety of problems. These centers are especially useful when a person is uncertain of his rights and opportunities under various government policies. If the neighborhood information center cannot answer his question, he is referred to some other agency for the appropriate information or help.

Miscellaneous

Several other new and improved methods of learning already provide (or soon will provide) opportunities for learning that were not available 10 or 20 years ago. Videotape recorders enable the beginning teacher or salesman to observe his own performance. Encounter groups provide a variety of affective and interpersonal learning experiences for couples and families, as well as for the occupations and other clientele served by T-groups since the early 1950s. New simulation materials and equipment provide realistic but risk-free practice for increasingly complex skills and judgments. Language laboratories provide an effective but inexpensive way for the individual to learn a foreign language. Perhaps the Geoscope described by Buckminster Fuller (1962) or flexible computer diagrams will be able to display certain phenomena and principles that cannot be effectively or accurately portrayed by film.

122

HELPING THE LEARNER CHOOSE HIS LEARNING RESOURCES A dramatic gain in the effectiveness of self-planned learning projects will come from an increase in the number and effectiveness of printed materials, individually selected films and videotapes, accessible experts, and individualized travel opportunities. Such inventions can and probably will be produced with relatively little cost and technological difficulty. After becoming generally accepted, and when produced and distributed on a large scale, the cost to the individual learner (or his employer) will be quite reasonable.

These new methods of learning are not sufficient, however. They will not be used much unless parallel social inventions also occur. There is a crucial need for one or more corresponding devices or processes to help the potential learner discover and select the resources he needs. The availability of thousands of books, films, and experts is irrelevant to the learner unless he has a fairly quick way of selecting the ones most appropriate for his current learning project. In short, we must develop some parallel improvements in step 2 (Table 14).

I can see two basic ways to handle this function. One possibility is a liaison person who acts as a link between the learner and the wealth of available resources. He would do his best to understand the learner's current needs and level, and would then select the most appropriate resources for that learner. He might even order or deliver the resources himself, thus saving the learner this step. This liaison person would be thoroughly familiar with all available information retrieval systems, catalogs, bibliographic tools, and other resources. Consequently, the learner would not have to spend any time coming to understand this overwhelming array of information systems and resources.

The other possibility is to produce a variety of indexes, reviews, lists, bibliographies, and other printed tools for the learner himself. These ways of locating appropriate *printed* resources already exist. Many adults (and many students in schools and colleges emphasizing individual and independent work) are already highly skilled in their use. We need similar or better means of access to available films, videotape recordings, experts, and travel opportunities. The annotations in such lists might provide evaluations of the resource and estimates of the most appropriate audiences for it, as well as factual information about its content and level. For the beginning learner in each field or topic, a booklet might be produced to describe the various branches and subfields that he could learn about if he wants to proceed past the introductory level, and to describe the best resources available for each branch or topic.

We should probably try to develop both of these possibilities, not just one. In some subject matter areas, a particular learner could probably operate effectively himself if good indexes or lists were available; in others he would feel hopelessly lost. It is possible, too, that the liaison person would sometimes send the learner a detailed description of several suitable possibilities, leaving the final selection to him.

Computers

As computers become less expensive and easier to use, they may play an increasing role in helping learners find appropriate resources. The experts polled by Bjerrum (1969) predicted that, by the year 2000, computers will become as common as telephones or televisions in homes, will be used for instruction at home, and will cost less than 1% of their present price.

One example of the use of a computer was demonstrated at the University of Western Ontario in 1969 and 1970 (North & Forgie, 1970). The learners were Canadian volunteers preparing for service in West Africa. They used the computer to select appropriate materials from the varied collection. By typing key words, they received a list (including abstracts) of the relevant videotapes, films, slide sets, audiotapes, books, and vertical files. All of these materials were available and used in the same room as the computer terminals. The busy, varied, concentrated, effective learning going on in one room was the visitor's main impression.

11 When a nonhuman resource serves as planner

The most efficient way to learn certain knowledge and skill is to rely on a carefully designed program, set of materials, or other nonhuman resource. This object will then determine the detailed content and procedures for each learning session. Instead of making frequent decisions about what and how to learn in the next episode, as in a self-planned project, the learner can follow the path set by the program or object.

Relatively few learning projects have an object as the planner, according to our 1970 survey. It is much more common for the learner to handle the day-to-day planning himself, to rely on a group or its leader, or to rely on a person in a one-to-one situation.

SOME EXAMPLES OF NONHUMAN PLANNERS In some learning projects, the plans are provided by a special kind of book. In learning to type, for example, a person may follow the sequence of content and practice exercises presented by a teach-yourself-typing book. Someone who wants to learn French or introductory psychology might seek the orderly progression and exercises provided by a textbook. Several books present an effective sequence of explanations and practice exercises for those who want to increase their reading speed. Some persons rely on a guided or packaged reading program in which they read a set of books in a certain order. In each of these examples, the learner lets a book (or a set of books) determine the detailed sequence of content, exercises, and other learning activities.

Various types of programmed instruction are now available to provide even more detailed control over the learning activities, and to provide frequent feedback and reinforcement. Programmed materials are available for persons who want to learn bridge, science, algebra, basic English, parliamentary procedure, grammar, and a wide variety of other subject matter. Some programs are in book form, either scrambled or with frames; others require a teaching machine of one sort or another. With programmed instruction, the learner usually sets his own pace and learns the material thoroughly, though with many programs he cannot control the sequence, skip material, or backtrack.

Some courses, library centers, schools, and colleges now rely primarily on

125

programmed instruction for both credit and noncredit learning. Part of the subject matter may be presented by supplementary audiovisual devices; in certain training and stimulation devices the audiovisual portion is even more important than the printed portion. In addition, reference materials and a teacher for answering specific questions or dealing with difficulties may be provided.

Computers are increasingly being combined with programmed instructional materials. The computer can present "printed" material (or even audio and visual material), evaluate responses, and use the learner's response history for choosing particular branches or sequences of material. Several experimenters are working toward a dialogue program that Atkinson (1968) hopes will "provide the richest possible student-system interaction where the student is free to construct natural-language responses, ask questions in an unrestricted mode, and in general exercise almost complete control over the sequence of learning events [p. 226]."

For learning to read (and type), some children and adults have used a "talking typewriter." When the learner hits a letter on the keyboard, this machine repeats the letter aloud and simultaneously types it. By requiring the learner to type letters in a cerain order, the machine can teach him to spell certain words.

In many correspondence courses, the day-to-day plans are provided by the materials sent to the learner. He follows the sequence of reading, questions, and assignments spelled out in each lesson. Feedback usually comes by mail from a distant marker, not from the materials themselves as in most programmed instruction.

For learning a language or certain other subject matter, the person may follow a series of phonograph records or tape recordings, perhaps accompanied by a filmstrip. Language records have been common for some time, and a wide array of lectures and other spoken material is also available on records and tapes.

A more sophisticated format for language learning is the language laboratory, which is essentially a series of tape recordings, sometimes combined with printed materials. The learner may be able to repeat each word or phrase after the voice on the tape, and then replay his own pronunciation to compare it with the model.

In a few object-planned projects, two learners work together. One early form of this, described by Roalman (1963), combined programmed instruction and studying with a friend. A question-and-answer book is provided for a pair of learners. The two partners take turns reading and answering the questions, or they can work out the answers together. A more recent program, designed to improve communication between husband and wife, is called "INTIMACY: An encounter program for couples." It uses audio tapes, booklets, and other materials to help bring a husband and wife into meaningful interaction with each other.

Some effective learning projects rely on a series of television programs, videotape recordings, or motion pictures. A learner interested in a certain topic might spend many hours watching such a series. He might watch a series of television documentaries on the future of mankind or on the various geographical regions of the world, for example. He might take a credit course in sociology or English literature through television or films.

Several decades ago, some schools experimented with learning projects in which the plans were provided by a set of printed materials. One example of these experiments was the Dalton Plan, introduced into the school system of Dalton, Massachusetts, about 1920. For a given topic, the student would receive a set of mimeographed content and instructions, including the questions and exercises for each day. Some current experiments in schools also emphasize nonhuman planners, but the planner is usually a set of programmed instruction materials or a package of audiovisual materials.

SOME CHARACTERISTICS OF AN OBJECT AS THE PLANNER

A large investment of time and money is required to develop a good program or a new piece of hardware. This initial cost rules out nonhuman resources as planners for learning unique or rare subject matter. For financial reasons, a program will be developed only if hundreds or thousands of individuals will be learning that knowledge and skill in the near future. In recent years, however, a much greater willingness to invest in developing such programs has been evident. Important progress has been made in developing new or refined programs and hardware. New occupations in programming and designing hardware for programmed instruction have developed.

Because of the enormous amount of time and money spent on developing a program, it may be the most efficient guide in a learning project. No single person, including the learner himself, could plan a better sequence of learning activities in the particular field.

Television programs and other nonhuman resources can bring to the learner the expertise, personality, and teaching style of experts and good teachers in any field. The learner does not have to travel or spend much money for his contact with these individuals.

A series of printed materials, recordings, or television programs may provide the quickest route for gaining certain types of knowledge and skill, such as a technical skill or cognitive subject matter that is detailed (step-by-step), specific, and clearly defined. Examples are physical fitness, a foreign language, and effective reading. A nonhuman planner is also suitable for skills and bodies of knowledge that are relatively standard; that is, the knowledge and its boundaries are generally accepted, or the skill is performed in the same way by everyone. Individual opinions and styles are not important in these areas, and there may be a single sequence of learning activities that is highly efficient for most learners.

With a nonhuman planner, the decisions about what and how to learn can usually be combined (in a single resource or package) with the actual presentation of the subject matter. That is, the planner provides the subject matter as well as the plans.

Human qualities

It is obvious that there are differences between a nonhuman and a human planner. On the positive side, an object never becomes impatient with the learner. It never laughs at his mistakes or makes a scornful or damaging remark. Also, the learner who relies on a nonhuman resource for the planning is not likely to feel any obligation to it. He is not trying to please the planner, and can modify or reject its suggestions, or quit, without hurting the planner's feelings. On the negative side, an object does not provide the companionship, human interaction, and human warmth that some learners want.

Flexibility

How flexible for the learner is a nonhuman planner? Again, there is both a positive and a negative side. On the positive side, some objects leave the learner free to set his own pace, or to decide when to learn. Also, certain materials and programs are always available to the learner at any time of the day or night. The learner, therefore, does not have to fit his project into someone else's schedule or make an appointment. Some of the materials can be carried around (if purchased or borrowed) and used anywhere. Others can be kept in the home or at work, and some are available in a library carrel. The learner can listen to a television or radio series in a variety of locations, even in a hotel or cottage. In programmed instruction, branching can provide some flexibility in the sequence of learning activities; some programs even permit the learner to control the sequence.

On the negative side, an object is not as flexible as a person, even with branching and other mechanisms for handling a certain range of individual differences. Also, the learner may not want to master a complete, predetermined body of subject matter or set of skills, and he may not want to proceed in a predetermined sequence. Instead, he may be motivated by a question or by a responsibility or problem that he wants to handle successfully. Even a sequence that seems appropriate at first may turn out to be unsuitable if the person's interests shift.

12 Learning projects planned by a person in a one-to-one relationship

Learning can proceed very effectively when guided by the appropriate person interacting with the learner in a one-to-one situation. For certain subject matter and learners, if the right person can be found to serve as planner, this is clearly the most efficient way to learn.

Learning to drive a car is an example of this dyadic relationship. Most of us, when we want to learn this skill, ask some other person to teach us. We expect him to give us the required information, and to tell us just what to learn during each session (left-hand turns, backing up, parking), and how to do so. Throughout these lessons, we expect him to point out any errors and weaknesses, and to suggest specific ways of improving.

A project planned by one person in a one-to-one relationship is also useful for gaining certain athletic skills. The golf pro or the ski instructor is usually available for private lessons, or for semi-private lessons with two or three learners together. The most advanced track and field star, skating champion, swimmer, or other athlete may regard his coach as the planner of his learning (training) episodes. Other learners interested in acquiring athletic skills *wish* they had access to an expert; examples from our studies include a man learning to play squash and a woman learning tennis.

Music lessons provide another common example of learning that is planned by another person. In order to play the piano or guitar, a young person or adult may be glad to put himself in the hands of a competent teacher. This instructor will demonstrate certain skills and styles, decide which weaknesses and skills to work on next, and tell the learner what to practice at home between lessons. During the lessons themselves, the teacher will also decide most of the topics and activities.

Preparation for certain occupations, too, is usually planned by a single person in a one-to-one situation. This planner may be more competent than the learner himself if he has already performed successfully in the occupation and knows just what knowledge and skills are necessary. He can also provide much of the subject matter himself, recommend additional learning activities, and even test whether the learner has achieved the desired level. In some forms of internship and apprenticeship, the learner is attached to one practitioner in his field. For example, a teacher-in-training is assigned to practice in one particular teacher's classroom, an auto mechanic works in a garage under the supervision of an expert mechanic, and a novice T-group leader ("co-trainer") works with a highly skilled leader.

Learning projects planned in a one-to-one situation are common in many other areas of knowledge and skill. These include lessons in dancing and sewing, learning a foreign language, counseling and rehabilitation, and learning from a management consultant.

SOME VARIABLES   In some dyadic relationships, the instructor or teacher will provide most of the subject matter himself. That is, he will present the knowledge orally and demonstrate the skill for the learner. In other projects, the coach or tutor or other planner will not present much of the subject matter himself. Instead, he will recommend certain reading, exercises, practice, and other learning activities, perhaps based on his diagnosis of the learner's current level and weaknesses.

Projects planned by someone in a one-to-one relationship with the learner vary in another way. In some relationships the learner can definitely influence the learning objectives, detailed content, and learning activities. In others, though, he feels compelled to follow the teacher's instructions without question or complaint, believing he has no power to influence the activities. The latter situation may occur with an especially rigid teacher, or with a teacher much older than the learner or clearly superior to him in the particular subject matter area. A learner does not feel very free to suggest alternative needs and activities if he is studying the cello with a great master, for example.

The majority of planners in a one-to-one relationship are professional or expert helpers, as was pointed out in Chapter 8. Our 1970 survey also found, though, that the number of planners who are friends or relatives of the learner is also quite significant.

Learners who choose a professional planner are probably attracted by his expertise. Those who choose a friend or relative may be choosing the easiest and cheapest planner. When learning to drive a car, many persons prefer a driving school instructor to a parent or spouse, because of the relaxed interpersonal relationships (Hagstrom, 1965).

Our 1970 survey found that the typical pattern is one learner with one planner. However, in a few learning projects, one or two other learners are present.

SOME ADVANTAGES   There are many advantages in having a learning project planned by a single person in a one-to-one relationship. These advantages help us understand why many learners are attracted to this type of project.

1. By having a person direct his learning efforts, the learner benefits from having the person's expertise adapted to him as a unique individual and to his particular learning project. The planner can modify the procedures and content whenever desirable, after diagnosing the learner's current level of knowledge and skill, and his current weaknesses and errors. In the one-to-one situation, the planner can come to understand the particular learner (and his unique goals, problems, and weaknesses) faster and better than he could in a group situation.

2. The learner can obtain immediate responses to his questions, difficulties, fears, doubts, and concerns.

3. The learner's errors (in understanding, style, posture, behavior, responses, and so on) can be immediately detected and corrected before they become habitual. The learner can practice with an expert (in learning a foreign language, for example, or in role-playing in order to practice salesmanship, counseling, tutoring, or consulting).

4. The planner may also provide the actual resources and facilities that are needed, or arrange for them to be available.

5. A person as planner is very flexible in the proportion of the knowledge and skill that he himself presents to the learner: in any one session, it can range from zero to 100%.

6. Despite first appearances, this type of planner may actually be less expensive than an object or a group if there are few learners. It may even be less expensive (measured in money or time) with a large number of learners if the efficiency of their learning (and the amount of appropriate knowledge and skill they learn) is much greater than with any other sort of planner. The cost can sometimes be cut to a third without greatly affecting efficiency by having the planner deal with three learners simultaneously.

THE NEGATIVE SIDE Our 1970 survey found that individual learning projects planned by an appropriate person are not as common as self-planned learning projects or group-planned projects. The advantages listed in the previous section seem convincing, yet it is not very common for a learner to turn over the planning to another person in a one-to-one relationship.

It is difficult to determine the negative characteristics that account for this lack of interest. Sometimes the cost may appear prohibitive to the learner. But even if the help is free, the learner may be reluctant to consume so many hours of the other person's time.

131

The person who plans the project for the learner will probably perform certain actions, make certain decisions, and follow certain procedures. The molar level of the planner's behavior is probably the most significant portion of what he does. That is, the molar or comprehensive level of his behavior and the overall process he follows probably have a greater impact on the learning than any particular decision he makes about the detailed content and strategy. He can probably afford to make a few mistakes in his choice of particular methods of learning if his overall pattern or style of teaching and helping is effective.

In order to understand this process better, it is useful to select several clusters of activities from the total process. Although the process is fairly continuous, it can be divided into several clusters for purposes of analysis. It is possible to distinguish six types of things that the planner does. These are presented here in approximate chronological order.

1. At an early stage in the learning project, the planner usually verifies that he and the learner agree on the learning objectives. The planner may help the learner discover and clarify the knowledge and skill he wants to gain, decide whether its attainment is realistic, and suggest certain modifications in the objectives.

2. The planner may be aware of several routes (learning activities, resources, or sequences) by which some learners can obtain the desired knowledge and skill. Some people successfully learn to type by starting right in typing essays or personal letters, for example, whereas other people learn successfully by beginning with detailed exercises such as j u j u j u j m j m j m. The planner may also try to "dream up," as creatively and flexibly as possible, additional possibilities for learning. The range and number of routes vary from one sort of subject matter to another. Familiarity with these various routes is an especially common sort of expertise provided by planners.

   Even before he has much information about the learner, the planner may be aware of the relative effectiveness of the various routes. That is, he knows the most effective way to achieve the given goal for the typical or average learner, the second best way, and so on. His criterion is probably something like this: by which route will a learner be most certain to achieve the desired outcome, but with a minimum of time (both his and mine) and money? With a highly motivated learner and readily accessible subject matter, there may be very little difference between the efficiency of the best two or three routes.

3. Before choosing or recommending one particular route, the planner tries to discover the factors that will influence the relative effectiveness of the various possible routes. He may have to ask questions or even administer tests in order to obtain some of this information; other factors will be evident without much

132

effort. Certain characteristics of the learner will probably be included in the factors that influence the choice of route. These characteristics include the learner's motivation, current level, ability to learn, emotional or physiological blocks to learning, and confidence. Certain physical factors, such as the accessibility of certain equipment or resources, may also be influential.

A few planners seem oblivious to most of these factors. They do not really know and understand each particular learner, they suggest methods of learning that are inefficient, or their actions and comments actually do more harm than good (in affecting the learner's self-concept or future ability to learn, for instance).

The planner also takes into account his own personality, skills, needs, feelings, and competence. How comfortable and effective would he be as the planner, and possibly the provider of content, for each of the various possible routes? He will not let these factors override the others, but he will not ignore them either.

4. At the beginning of most learning projects, the learner will have some idea of how to learn the desired knowledge and skill. He will be surprised if the planner suggests a radical departure from these preconceptions. If he wants to learn to type, for example, he will probably be disturbed if the planner hands him a novel to read and some arithmetic problems to do. Consequently, the planner will probably try to discover the learner's expectations about the learning activities and resources. He will then reinforce the expectations that are suitable, will point out the weaknesses in other expectations, and will suggest alternative or additional activities.

   Because of the planner's greater experience or skill in choosing appropriate ways to learn the given subject matter, the learner will usually accept his suggestions. At the same time, though, the planner will probably explain the reasons for each of his recommendations, and will emphasize the causal relationship between his recommended learning activities and the desired outcomes. As a result, the learner will follow the recommended route because he believes it will lead efficiently to his goal, and will not feel it is just the planner's whim or unthinking recommendation.

5. Throughout the learning project, the planner will notice or try to discover the learner's activities, progress, and difficulties. He may also notice additional factors that influence the effectiveness of various possible activities. Whenever it seems desirable, the planner will modify the route originally chosen, and may even suggest some entirely different route. In general, he oversees and monitors the entire process of learning.

   The most important action that the planner takes is to seek feedback. He realistically assesses just how effective his suggested activities are proving to be in actual practice. If the learner is not gaining the desired knowledge and skill quickly and efficiently, another procedure is recommended.

If the planner accurately obtains feedback on the effectiveness of his suggestions, he will probably avoid some of the worst pitfalls that trap so many teachers. He will not choose learning activities primarily for his own benefit and needs, rather than for the needs of the learner. He will not merely plan activities without regard to outcomes. He will see the folly of recommendations based on a fond but unrealistic hope that they will result eventually in certain changes in behavior.

6. In addition to recommending certain activities for the learner to perform, the planner may himself perform certain actions. He may provide materials or other resources, remove some physical distraction, provide orally some of the desired knowledge, or demonstrate part of the skill.

In the next chapter, we will see that the leader of a learning group may follow a similar process. A helper in a self-planned learning project may also follow parts of this process.

13 A group or its leader as planner

Sometimes the learner chooses a group, or the instructor or leader in a group, to plan his learning efforts. He wants the leader or other members of the group to make most of the decisions about what and how he should learn during each learning episode.

In many groups, one individual does the bulk of the planning, and may also present most of the subject matter. He or she may be called a teacher, instructor, professor, leader, resource person, trainer, helper, program planner, planning committee chairman, group worker, therapist, scoutmaster, or minister. He may emerge naturally as the leader or major resource person in the group, or he may be assigned this task as a definite responsibility. If it is a definite assignment for him, he may be paid or a volunteer, his responsibility for leading learning groups may be full-time or part-time, and he may be professionally trained or relatively inexperienced.

During most meetings of the group, the leader or some other member will decide what content should be presented. He will present that content, choose a film or speaker or other technique for presenting it, or suggest a topic for discussion. Unless the learner happens to be on the planning committee for the group, he will rarely be responsible for these decisions about content and learning activities. He may occasionally make a suggestion or have a turn at planning or leading one session, but certainly will not be responsible for the majority of the decisions throughout the total series of group sessions.

Some additional learning episodes may occur outside the group sessions. Here the learner may assume more responsibility for deciding what to practice or read, and how to proceed. Often, however, he will follow the suggestions of the leader or someone else in the group when choosing his reading and practice exercises. If the leader of a parent education group asks everyone to read a certain chapter for the next meeting, for example, most learners will do so.

A wide range of groups may be open to learners, especially in a large city. Some groups will contain only four or five members, others several hundred. Some groups provide credit toward a certificate or degree, but most do not. Some groups emphasize discussions, others rely on lectures or films, and still others emphasize experiential learning through role-playing or a discussion of feelings. Some groups meet once a month for 10 months, but others are compressed into a conference format, which includes one-day institutes, weekend workshops, three-day meetings of a professional association or research field, and six-week short courses. The subject matter available in groups, meetings, and conferences is even more varied than the format: effective reading, sewing, sports, investing, human relationships, the United Nations, new teaching methods, recent research in adult education, infant care, foreign languages, woodworking, and psychology, to name just a few.

In a certain group, some members may be relying on the group (or its leader) as their planner, and others may not. For example, one person might use the group as merely one learning activity within a much larger *self-planned* project. Almost one-quarter of the learners described in *Learning Without a Teacher* (Tough, 1967) used a group as one small part of their total learning strategy. In some learning groups, it is also possible to find someone who is not conducting a learning project at all. For him, the desire to gain and retain certain knowledge and skill is not an especially important reason for attending the group.

An enormous amount of literature and research has dealt with learning in groups. Social psychologists have described group processes and other aspects of groups in general. The vast research literature on teaching methods describes learning in classrooms or in other group programs provided by educational institutions, as does much of the literature in adult education. In addition, much has been written on group discussion, and on how to lead a discussion group. More recent is the increasing amount of literature regarding encounter groups and other group techniques of the human potential movement. There is no need to summarize these bodies of literature here, because they are readily available to the reader.

ATTRACTIVE CHARACTERISTICS OF LEARNING GROUPS

Relying on a group as planner is fairly common. In our 1970 survey, for instance, the average person conducted one group learning project during the preceding year. What reasons do learners have for turning the responsibility for planning over to a group or a group leader? In short, what are the attractive characteristics of learning in a group?

1. Learning in a group, with the planning done by the leader or other group members, may be a highly efficient route for a given learning project. This is especially likely if several other learners want the same knowledge and skill (and thus make the formation of a group quite feasible), or if the knowledge and skill and level of an available group happen to fit the particular learner's needs.
2. The learner can have access to an expert instructor at much less cost than private sessions would entail. He can also see a relevant film, hear an outstanding

speaker, or see an expensive demonstration at low cost, because the total cost is spread over several learners.

3. A learner may choose a group because of the positive emotional benefits. Learning in the company of several others can generate and maintain a high level of enthusiasm and motivation. No one can really understand and share the learner's joy of achievement except those who are currently going through the same learning stages. The learner's realization that some of the other learners are doing better than he is may spur him on.

4. Between group sessions, because he faces another meeting of the group soon, the learner may be motivated to complete the practice exercises, reading, or other learning episodes that have been suggested. Also, he will be motivated to keep up a certain pace instead of putting off his learning until later. These two types of motivation will be strengthened specifically by (a) the fact that the group meets each week or so; (b) not wanting to displease or disappoint the instructor; (c) the example or reactions of other learners; and (d) a commitment to completing the course or series of sessions, perhaps because of having paid a fee.

5. The learner may feel better about his learning when he realizes that other learners, too, have problems, difficulties, and frustrations. The slow progress or low level of others may encourage him or cheer him up about his own progress and level. He will no longer feel inferior or inadequate or "just a beginner."

6. The members of a group can help one another in various ways. In a group, for example, a learner can practice a musical instrument, try role-playing, receive criticism and feedback, receive answers to his questions, and hear reactions to his opinions. Some of the interaction can be in one-to-one situations. It is almost impossible to learn without a few group sessions in certain areas, such as public speaking, understanding group processes and one's own behavior in a group, and becoming an effective group member or leader.

7. A group provides the maximum range of values, beliefs, attitudes, and views to stimulate the learner to examine and perhaps change his own.

8. The learner may just assume that learning in a group is the best way, or the only way, to learn. He may have blind faith in its effectiveness: a course may seem to be a magic cure, a guarantee of success.

9. If the learner is facing a certain problem or responsibility, he may want to learn in the company of others who face a similar situation.

10. If the learner has firm convictions about the topic, if he feels anxious about it, or if it deals with values or issues, he may want an opportunity to state his own 'views and to interact with others.

137

11. Some people prefer the anonymity of a large group to an intimate one-to-one relationship with an instructor.
12. The instructor or other group members may provide appropriate resources and facilities for the learner, or arrange for them to be available.
13. Attending any group, not just one designed for learning, can be a pleasant and stimulating experience. A group provides companionship, the stimulation of meeting new people, and the enjoyment of a social situation. Some learners add to their enjoyment by attending with a close friend or relative.
14. The learner may gain some prestige or status by joining a certain group or attending a certain institution.
15. Some entrepreneurs who have developed a unique set of learning activities may guard them closely; consequently, the learner must attend one of their courses or workshops if he wants those learning activities.

NEGATIVE CHARACTERISTICS OF LEARNING IN GROUPS

Although the average adult learner uses a group for one learning project a year, he relies on some other planner for his other seven projects. What are the negative characteristics of groups and group leaders that make the learner hesitate to rely on them?

1. The learner may not be able to find a group nearby with a convenient meeting time and an appropriate starting date.
2. The learner may not want to feel tied down to a set time each week.
3. He may simply want to gain enough knowledge to satisfy his curiosity, or enough skill to handle a specific responsibility, instead of learning a wider body of subject matter.
4. The learner may be unwilling or unable to leave his home for learning, or may hesitate to spend much time and effort traveling to a group. Our 1970 survey found that travel time (and other time spent at planning and arrangements) constitutes about one-eighth of the total time spent at the typical group learning project.
5. The adult's efficiency in learning through a group will rarely be as great as it would if the same instructor were used in a one-to-one situation.
6. Using a group may require a large commitment of money (registration fee) or time before the learner is certain that he wants to spend that much on the particular project or program.
7. Unless he happens to find a group that fits his own goals and level, the learner may find that the content and procedures are not precisely what he wants or needs. Consequently, a large portion of his time during the group session may be wasted. Also, he may want to gain the knowledge and skill at a much faster or

slower pace than the group.

8. A group is usually a relatively inefficient way of learning a long sequence of detailed, well-established facts or skills.
9. In a group, only a small fraction of the total time can be spent listening to any one learner, or dealing with his unique concerns, difficulties, and feelings.
10. The learner may not want to let others see his ignorance, errors, or poor performance.
11. The learner may fear that he will encounter an instructor or group leader who is incompetent or insensitive. Custom and habit are more likely to influence an instructor in a group than in a one-to-one situation. In addition, a group leader may not be influenced primarily by the needs and hopes of the learners. Instead, he may be influenced by his perceptions or stereotypes of what a good teacher (professor, instructor, discussion leader) does when in the spotlight, or he may be influenced by his own needs, by tradition, or by the perceived demands of the institution. Too few teachers seek feedback concerning their own behavior and effectiveness at helping learners. When asked to outline their objectives, many teachers describe their own behavior or activities instead of the learners' final knowledge and skill.

A VARIETY OF FORMATS Several different formats are found in learning groups. We will now examine nine of these.

A group with an instructor

When we think of a learning group, we often picture 20 or 30 persons meeting in a room with one instructor who is an expert in the knowledge and skill that the people want to learn. He is responsible for planning most meetings of the group and for presenting the subject matter. This is the most effective format for certain learners and certain subjects.

The instructor of a group is, in a sense, the planner of many learning projects. He probably goes through a process similar to that of the planner who operates in a one-to-one situation, as described in the previous chapter.

A crucial early step is to obtain agreement on the learning objectives. In some groups, the learners come because they want to gain the knowledge and skill that the instructor outlined clearly in the publicity for the course, workshop, or other program. In other groups, the instructor distributes a duplicated sheet of tentative objectives, and then asks the learners to compare their objectives with the sheet; the instructor and the learners can then negotiate some agreement. Another possible role for the instructor is merely to help the learners in the group discover and clarify their own objectives; he will help them learn whatever they wish.

The instructor will then perform several of the functions described in the previous chapter, following many of the same principles. In the group learning situation, the instructor may try to provide alternative methods of learning for different members of the group. For example, he may occasionally establish three simultaneous discussion groups on three different aspects of the topic. Or he may give the learners a choice of two simultaneous learning activities, such as a film and a speaker. In addition, he may urge the learners to skip the sessions that are not especially relevant to them.

We may expect far too much of an instructor. Diagnosing the needs and problems of all the learners in a group, selecting and managing appropriate learning activities, and generally carrying through the entire process of teaching and helping is almost a superhuman responsibility. Few individuals have the skill, insight, and energy to perform all of these functions for a large learning group. Perhaps we need to experiment with a team of teachers with differentiated functions, or with co-teachers, or with new learning formats that place less responsibility on a single instructor.

Answering questions

Another possible format for a group is to have an expert who speaks only in response to questions asked by the members. Although he is the main source of content during the group session, he does not prepare a speech beforehand.

In my own experience, I can recall only one example of this format. It was a single, two-hour session that occurred during a series of evening sessions for expectant parents at a Chicago hospital. As we entered the lecture hall for this particular session, we realized from the presence and excitement of several nurses that the session would be something special. When the 20 or 30 expectant parents were assembled, a very competent and likable pediatrician entered, told us he would be glad to try answering any question at all that we had, and then settled back to wait for the first question. Because the group had similar concerns and questions, each person found that the majority of the questions and answers were relevant and interesting. All in all, the session, which entailed little time at program-planning beforehand, was very lively and enjoyable.

Discussing identical printed material

In another format, all members of the group read the same printed materials for each meeting and then discuss the subject matter they have read. One or two discussion leaders are responsible for focusing the discussion, but not for presenting any subject matter. The meeting is devoted to clarifying the author's meaning, reacting to his

140

points, discussing the implications, and so on.

This format has become increasingly popular in recent years. A great deal of money and effort has been invested in developing a small number of packaged discussion programs on a variety of topics. Sometimes the materials that everyone reads are portions of certain great books. Other materials deal with world affairs, art, primitive cultures, and child care.

The subject matter resides within the group itself

In some groups, very few printed materials or resource persons are used. Instead, the group focuses on the current feelings and processes within the group itself. The subject matter consists primarily of the feelings, behavior, and statements of the learners themselves during the session. The leader or trainer is not so much a planner as a catalyst, facilitator, and mirror.

Various names are applied to groups that follow this format: T-group, encounter group, sensitivity training group, human relations training group. The rapid expansion of these groups during the past two decades has been one of the most dramatic events in the field of adult learning.

Tapes for encounter groups

In a similar format, a nonhuman resource is substituted for the group leader. This nonhuman resource is a set of prerecorded audiotape instructions for guiding small groups through certain human relations exercises. These tapes make it possible for a small group, without a trained professional leader, to gain the benefits of certain encounter experiences. These experiences are designed to help each member of the group express his real feelings, accept the feelings of others, and understand himself better. Exploratory studies (Berzon & Solomon, 1964) indicated that these "self-directed therapeutic groups" could be effective and safe, and subsequent testing and research have largely confirmed this. One study (Berzon, Reisel, & Davis, 1969) concluded that, for the future, "particular promise seems to exist in the development of custom programs. For instance, there might be a program written specially for children, or for families, or for parties to a negotiation – labor, foreign power, or civil rights. Programs could be developed for any given group of people who have a special problem or concern in common [p. 85]."

Group help for self-planned learning

Another format is not really group-planned learning at all. Instead, several individuals who are conducting self-planned projects meet occasionally to stimulate and help one another. Their projects may fall within the same broad area, or may be quite diverse.

141

At the meetings of the group, there is no subject matter. Instead, the sessions focus on the self-planned learning project of one member at a time. The purpose is to give him encouragement, stimulation, suggestions, and other help.

An unstructured conference
In an unstructured conference, very little planning occurs beforehand because no sessions are scheduled. Instead of attending preplanned presentations of subject matter, the participants learn through informal discussions in pairs and groups that form spontaneously. One example of an unstructured conference consisted of about 70 persons interested in student mental health and counseling in colleges and universities.

Despite the rarity of this format, it is a very interesting notion and could perhaps be used much more widely. The basic idea is very simple: bring together 20 or more persons with a similar concern or responsibility. Do not plan any speeches, discussion topics, or scheduled group discussions, but let the participants do as they wish for two or three days.

Some of the learners will spend most of their time in conversations. If a learner wants to find an individual who shares a certain concern, or if he wants to try forming a small group to deal with a specific topic, he can post a notice on the bulletin board. If someone wants to deliver a speech, he can announce its time and place on the bulletin board. Depending on the emotional climate and the area of common concern, learners might gain far more from this format than from a more structured conference.

A large conference or professional meeting
Most professional associations hold an annual meeting, which members attend to hear research reports and other presentations by members of the organization or by outside speakers. Before the meeting, the program is usually planned by a small committee composed of members, subject matter experts, and, occasionally, professional program planners.

This format is common, important, and effective. Many researchers, top executives, and professional persons receive a great deal of stimulation and subject matter at conferences and annual meetings.

Autonomous groups
Autonomous groups are very common and important, but have rarely been studied by researchers and discussed in the literature. Consequently, the rest of this chapter will be devoted to this particular format.

AUTONOMOUS LEARNING GROUPS

In some small and medium-sized groups that meet frequently, the members themselves plan the group learning sessions. The entire group, or a small committee or even a single member selected by the group, is responsible for planning each session. Instead of relying on an outsider or a set of materials to guide its learning, the group itself accepts the responsibility for planning.

Because their learning activities are not determined by an outside expert or organization, these learning groups are often called *autonomous*. Some women's groups, hobby groups, historical societies, and book review groups use this format. It is also used by some service clubs, church groups, and small voluntary associations.

These groups vary in their relationships with the outside world. Some are entirely self-contained. To use Kempfer's (1955) phrase, they are "independent and self-governing, with no outside allegiance or relationship [p. 231]." Some use a church or other institution merely as a meeting place, but most meet in homes or restaurants. Some write for program suggestions or reading materials, and some invite speakers or use films occasionally.

Some autonomous groups (depending on one's definition) are affiliated with similar groups or with a larger organization (such as a national or international association, a church, a central clearing house, or a state or provincial organization), although the group's program is not greatly influenced by that organization. In many groups, the relationship with the outside environment will increase, decrease, or otherwise change over the years.

Widespread and diverse

The range and diversity of autonomous learning groups is surprising. Many bible study groups, investment clubs, current affair groups, Alcoholics Anonymous chapters, book review clubs, local consumer associations, literary and philosophical groups, local historical societies, science clubs, conservation and nature groups, and rock-collecting clubs could be included. Groups also are formed to learn about cross-country motorcycle riding, collecting buttons, and casting soldiers.

Benjamin Franklin kept his Junto alive for 30 years. Van Doren (1938) pointed out that Franklin "seems to have borrowed the scheme of the Junto in part from Cotton Mather, who in Boston had originated neighborhood benefit societies [p. 75]." The Junto members answered a set of questions at each meeting, and raised questions in turn for the others to discuss. Every three months each member was to "produce and read an essay of his own writing, on any subject he pleased [p. 76]."

Describing the period 1826-1840 in the United States, Ewbank (1969) has stated that "lyceums popped up like mushrooms throughout almost every state in the Union, and in a few places abroad [p. 1]." These were voluntary self-education groups in

143

which the members themselves planned their educational programs. Often they took turns presenting a subject in which they were especially interested, or leading a discussion on some current issue. For other meetings they brought in a speaker who was especially knowledgeable on some topic. Ewbank concludes that at present the free university, the community schools, the seminars on race relations, and similar groups reflect the learning patterns that were common in the lyceum movement.

In New Zealand in the late 1920s, James Shelley began experimenting with a "box" scheme for "tutorless groups." This scheme consisted of sending boxes of materials to small groups of learners. Each box contained printed materials, books, and even phonograph records. The members would read the materials before gathering together to discuss them, and no human instructor was required.

A similar scheme of assistance for discussion groups in the Australian state of Victoria received an important impetus in 1947, when the Council of Adult Education was established in Melbourne. The council now provides boxes of materials for more than 400 discussion groups in Melbourne and in the rural parts of the state. The groups meet in private homes, usually monthly or fortnightly. Each month a group can choose any one of several hundred novels and nonfiction books described in a catalog issued by the council, and can borrow a box of materials for that book. The box contains 15 copies of the book, 15 copies of commentary and supplementary information, a discussion guide, and about 10 additional reference books. The questions for discussion are arranged in increasing order of difficulty. According to Wesson (1966), new groups rely heavily on the discussion questions. The typical group uses one box a month. The group is encouraged to comment on each box or book, and many of these comments are printed in a quarterly newsletter that goes to all groups.

In the United States, Mowrer, in *The New Group Therapy* (1964), has drawn attention to "the spontaneous appearance of a wide variety of special groups and associations, inspired and operated largely by *laymen*, whose main objective is to provide restorative experiences which scores of people have sought, but failed to find, at the hands of would-be professional healers, religious and secular alike [p. iii]." Mowrer states that most of the groups in this "lay group-therapy movement" do not seek or even want professional leadership by clergymen, psychiatrists, psychologists, or social workers.

In a textbook in adult education, Kempfer (1955) devoted an entire chapter to the topic "Working With Unorganized Autonomous Groups." This chapter provides examples of some specific ways in which adult educators can assist autonomous groups.

Autonomous learning groups exist for almost all ages. In our exploratory interviewing in Toronto, for example, we found a naturalist club of 12-year-old boys in which each boy had an area of specialty (birds, astronomy, or whatever). At the other end of the age scale was an 85-year-old woman responsible for a weekly meeting of about 10 women to hear speakers on the United Nations and other international topics.

Survey findings

In our 1970 survey, we wanted a rough measure of the number of autonomous groups. Consequently, for each group project, we asked the interviewee whether his group fitted either of the following categories: (1) "this group was sponsored by an educational institution, or it had an instructor or leader or speaker who was assigned to that group or was paid for this task," or (2) "it was just a group of equals meeting outside of any organized or institutional framework, and taking turns planning their own learning activities." The second type is a crude lay definition of an autonomous group or democratic peer group. About 20% of all group-directed projects (including credit projects) were of this type. If our findings apply to the general population, about one adult out of five is a member of an autonomous learning group.

Women's groups

One pioneering study of women's groups, a widespread form of learning group, was conducted by Heather Knoepfli while a Ph.D. student at the Ontario Institute for Studies in Education. It is reported in her dissertation (Knoepfli, 1971).

Because of her special interest in how women's groups originate, Knoepfli included only those that began completely independently of other organizations. The typical pattern was for one woman to become concerned about some problem or issue, or to become aware of some useful function that an autonomous learning group could perform – for her and for others. She then discussed her ideas with one or two other women, made several tentative plans and decisions for the formation of a group, and called the first meeting.

The founder of an autonomous learning group is both a learner and an adult education program planner. We already know something about the program-planning process followed by the professional adult educator and even the self-planner. Knoepfli's study fills a logical gap in our knowledge by describing the process followed by the founders of autonomous learning groups.

When interviewed by Knoepfli, the founders recalled a variety of reasons for forming a group. For many founders, the major reason was to increase their own motivation to learn: they needed an impetus or stimulus to learn. A second major reason was a desire to use or apply the knowledge and skill. This second reason was also very important in our study of why adults learn (see Chapter 5).

The groups studied by Heather Knoepfli covered a wide range of subject matter. Their purpose was to learn about investing (one group was called The Fortune Cookies), the Bible, French, history, contemporary literature, current events, women's liberation, writing, yoga, painting, urban living, and psychological theories.

In many women's groups, the members take turns presenting reports or topics. A few groups rely on outside resource persons for most sessions, and a few hire an outside expert or teacher for the entire year. Other groups rely exclusively on group discussion for the input of subject matter.

Most of the women's groups meet each month or so, usually for two hours, in a member's home. Half the groups in the study did not have a formal leadership structure, others appointed an executive committee, and a few appointed a single leader.

The future

As we become more and more aware of the frequency and importance of autonomous groups, perhaps we will develop more effective ways of helping them plan and conduct their learning. New types of organizations and consultants might be developed to encourage and facilitate the formation of a wide range of autonomous groups for all ages. Booklets or handbooks as well as human assistance could be provided when such groups want help in planning their learning activities.

As with self-planned learning, we must first understand how the learning proceeds in its natural form. Only then will we be ready to fit our help into that natural process without disrupting it.

14 Practical implications for institutions and instructors

The starting point for discussion in previous chapters was the *person*. We described what, why, and how he learns. On the basis of this empirical data, we pointed out (especially in Chapters 6 and 10) the better help and new services that he needs. Throughout, the learner himself was the major focus.

In this chapter, our focus shifts to the *institution*. Certain implications and suggestions for educational institutions arise from our empirical data. If our general picture of adult and out-of-school youth learning is accurate, then major changes are needed in various institutions of education. These institutions include secondary schools, colleges, universities, professional schools, graduate schools, manpower training programs in businesss and industry, and military training colleges. In short, this chapter suggests changes for any educational institution or program that operates primarily by providing courses and classes. Because of the changes that probably occur in youth learning between the ages of 10 and 16 (see Chapter 3), this chapter will not try to suggest implications for education below the secondary school level.

The suggestions are presented as a series of gradual steps, with the easiest steps first. Each step arises from the specific data presented in the previous chapters, and from the general picture they provide of adult learning (and out-of-school youth learning). If an educational institution takes this picture seriously, how can it change to help learners more effectively?

My own classroom teaching in various educational institutions has certainly been influenced recently by the contents of this book. My teaching in elementary school, junior high school, secondary school, graduate school, and adult classes has been reasonably successful by the usual standards. But I have become increasingly dissatisfied with my earlier teaching as our picture of noninstitutional learning efforts developed. As I reflect on the motivation and methods of learners in real life, my previous assumptions, procedures, feelings, and attitudes as a teacher seem strangely distorted and ineffective.

The suggestions in this chapter have arisen directly from our data and our general picture. Some of them are not completely original, however, in that they have already been suggested by some educational reformers. In addition, some institutions are

147

already experimenting with helping the learner to operate more independently by conducting individual projects in learning resource centers and other settings.

1. PROVIDE NEW HELP

Without changing their current programs, educational institutions could experiment with providing new sorts of help. Several specific suggestions have been presented in Chapters 6, 7, and 10. The help might be provided for the institution's present learners, or for certain learners it is not currently serving.

2. HELP TEACHERS LEARN

Educational institutions do very little to facilitate the learning of their own staff members. Like any adult, the teacher is sometimes a learner. It is useful to examine his behavior as a learner – when, why, what, and how he learns – as well as his behavior as an instructor. For his doctoral dissertation at the Ontario Institute for Studies in Education, Jim Fair is interviewing teachers about their learning projects. Some of his preliminary work is presented in a recently published article (Fair, 1970).

Most teachers and professors conduct several learning projects each year. Some of their efforts to learn require only 10 or 12 hours; others require several hundred hours, as was pointed out in Chapter 3. Some of their learning is for credit, but most of it is not. They learn in a group, from reading, from conversations with their colleagues, and in self-planned learning projects.

What do instructors learn? One common and obvious thing to learn is the subject matter that they are going to teach. They also learn about teaching methods in general, or about a particular new teaching method. Sometimes they learn about a particular student who is especially difficult or intelligent, or about their students in general (adolescents, disadvantaged, immigrants). Some teachers read about the future of education. Some work at a specific weakness or problem. Many try to improve their teaching by seeking various forms of feedback.

Intentional learning by administrators and teachers at all levels of the educational system is an essential component of innovation and reform. The adult education program planner may also learn in order to do a better job. For example, he may gather information about the needs of the particular audience he wants to serve.

3. EMPHASIZE THREE OBJECTIVES

Many schools and colleges claim that they teach their students how to learn, and prepare them for a lifetime of adult learning. They should state these objectives more precisely, do everything possible to encourage and help their students attain them, and measure the extent to which their graduates exhibit these behaviors several years after leaving.

These objectives can be stated in behavioral terms as follows.

1. As a result of his experiences in this educational institution, the student will tend to initiate a learning project when facing a major problem or task, and when experiencing strong puzzlement or curiosity. He will use learning as one step in achieving certain action goals in his home and family, in his leisure activities, and on the job.
2. The student will realize that learning projects are common, natural, and useful. He will be aware that people learn for a variety of reasons, that most learning is not for credit, and that each type of planner is appropriate in certain circumstances. He will not regard any reason for learning, or any type of planner, as strange or inferior. He will not believe that learning with a professional teacher in an educational institution is the only way to learn, and will not feel guilty when he chooses other formats for learning.
3. The student will become much more competent at discovering and setting his personal life goals and learning goals, at choosing the planner for his learning project, at conducting his own self-planned projects, at defining the desired help and getting it from a person or group, at learning from nonhuman resources, and at evaluating his progress and efficiency in a learning project.

Incidentally, some agency might develop a test of the person's competence at learning, and issue a certificate to successful learners. Such a test might assess the learner's skill at setting learning goals, at reading aggressively and effectively, at planning his own learning, and at getting necessary help.

In his book relating individual learning and self-renewing societies, John Gardner (1964) expresses the third objective very well. He says, "Education at its best will develop the individual's inner resources to the point where he can learn (and will *want* to learn) on his own. It will equip him to cope with unforeseen challenges and to survive as a versatile individual in an unpredictable world. Individuals so educated will keep the society itself flexible, adaptive and innovative [p. 26]."

Other writers, too, have touched on these three objectives. Roby Kidd (1959), for example, has noted that a common purpose of education is to produce "a continuing, 'inner-directed,' self-operating learner [p. 47]."

In a major work on andragogy, Knowles (1970) has pointed out that "education is not yet perceived as a lifelong process, so that we are still taught in our youth what we ought to know rather than how to keep finding out." Hence the need for "helping individuals to develop the attitude that learning is a lifelong process and to acquire the skills of self-directed learning [p. 23]."

Arnold Toynbee (1968), the distinguished British historian, has declared that "the pupil should transform himself into a self-teacher, and the teacher should transform

149

himself first into a stimulator and then into a consultant. . . . The initiative should be transferred to the student himself [p. xxiv] ."

Suggesting a university course called "Learning to Learn," Jahoda and Thomas (1965) said that "the purpose of this course would be to encourage the students to think of themselves as autonomous people, i.e. as self-organizing systems responsible for their own learning, who can view the facilities offered by the university (e.g. lectures, projects, work periods, programmed texts, teaching machines, seminars, tutorials, laboratory facilities, library, research staff, etc.) as opportunities to be used for pursuing self-defined ends."

Schools and colleges can foster all three objectives without making major changes in the curriculum or in the organization of the institution.

4. HELP THE INSTRUCTOR FEEL EQUAL Educational institutions should encourage the instructor to feel equal to the students. He will not be an effective helper if he feels superior or inferior as a person. The instructor may have greater knowledge in one subject matter area than most of the learners, and he may have greater skill in helping people learn that subject matter. At the same time, though, he may realize that some of the learners in the group are clearly superior to him in certain other ways.

For example, a few learners may be older or stronger than the instructor. Some may have traveled more widely or held a greater variety of jobs. A few may have had more experience than the instructor with certain subject matter being discussed. One or two may have more poise or confidence, greater speaking or teaching skill, or a higher income or social class. If the teaching occurs within a company or the armed forces, some learners may hold a higher rank or position in the organizational hierarchy than the instructor does.

If the instructor feels that he and the learners are equal as persons, his feelings and behavior will be influenced in certain ways.

First, he will not feel or act as though he is on a pedestal – superior in all ways to all the learners. Instead, he will comfortably accept the fact that there are differences in status on various dimensions between him and certain learners. He will realize "the importance of respecting the person-to-person parity which exists between teacher and students," to use McClusky's phrase (1964, p. 166). He will not feel the need or urge to show off, bluff, pretend to know all the answers, or pretend to be superior in all ways. He is unlikely to act in an overly authoritarian, dictatorial, or arrogant manner. If the learner's expectations tend to force him onto a pedestal, he will resist or discuss their expectations.

Second, the instructor's feelings of equality with the learners will probably lead to his interest in establishing friendly relationships with them. He will enjoy talking

150

with them, before and after the group sessions as well as during the sessions. Their conversations will deal not only with the subject matter of the course or workshop, but also with many other things they have in common – family, housing, cars, hobbies, travel, problems, interests. He expects to learn from them, just as they learn from him.

Third, the equality may be reflected in the seating arrangement. In the traditional arrangement, the class faces the instructor because it does not really matter whether the learners can see and hear one another. The basic assumption is that the instructor knows all the answers, and will be the only one with much experience and knowledge to contribute to the group. When the instructor is aware of the wealth of experience and knowledge among the learners, though, he will probably arrange the seating so they can see and hear one another. In addition, he will probably make some effort to help them become well acquainted.

Fourth, the instructor may be eager to have the learners assume certain responsibilities in planning the learning activities. If he accepts their competence and experience, he will realize that the specific content and learning activities can be made even more appropriate as a result of their suggestions.

Fifth, the teacher may emphasize that any superiority he has is strictly limited to the one area of expertise, as suggested by Geer (1968). He may clearly expect some reciprocal help, and thus be a learner or receiver as well as a helper. He may not call himself a teacher. He may let the learners take much of the initiative in asking questions and setting directions.

Sixth, if the instructor realizes that he is approximately equal to the learners in his group, he will probably not experience the difficulties and embarrassment that sometimes arise because an instructor is inferior in some ways to some of his students. If the instructor accepts equality between teacher and learner as a normal occurrence in adult groups, if he has sufficient competence in teaching the central subject matter, and if he has a pleasant, friendly manner, he is unlikely to encounter resistance. Instead, he will probably be accepted readily by the learners despite his youth, lack of experience, lower rank, or whatever.

5. INCREASE THE STUDENT'S CHOICE OF HOW HE LEARNS

Increasing the student's freedom of choice with regard to how he learns is a fairly easy step for most instructors and professors to take. Even if they refuse to let the student decide *what* to learn, they can at least leave him free to choose his own methods.

The instructor might announce, for example, that each student in his class or course must learn certain knowledge and skill by a certain date. The instructor defines the scope and level of the knowledge and skill fairly precisely, and gives some idea of how the students will be tested. He suggests several methods and resources, but gives the students complete freedom in their choice of which ones to use. The resources might include certain pages in the textbook, certain reference books and other printed materials, a few students who already have the knowledge and skill, programmed instruction, parents, phonograph records or tape recordings, two or three meetings of a discussion group, and the instructor himself. The test or examination will not be biased toward any one way of learning.

This arrangement is probably not suitable for all courses and subject matter, or even for all students. But instructors in schools and colleges might well experiment with several variations in some of their courses or topics. Each of these variations would break away from the traditional classroom stereotype of a single instructor being responsible for the entire sequence of events: setting the objectives for a group of 20 to 100 students, motivating them, orally providing the subject matter to the group, prescribing other learning activities, and evaluating the learning.

Giving the student more choice in how he learns has several advantages. It develops his competence in choosing methods, resources, and strategies. He will not come to believe that all learning occurs under the control of a professional instructor within a large educational institution. Instead of spending time "just getting something done" or gaining certain knowledge and skill to be retained for just a few hours or one day, he will spend a greater proportion of time at learning episodes. Also, this arrangement clearly emphasizes learning objectives, and thus breaks the tendency to think only about activities and exercises rather than outcomes.

Several analyses of what many students actually experience in classrooms have successfully captured certain negative aspects. These analyses include Philip Jackson's *The Teacher and the Machine* (1968), George Leonard's discouraging description of what you may find when you visit your child's classroom (1968, pp. 106-109 and 117), Jerry Farber's article (1968) on "The Student as Nigger," and Carl Roger's article (1968) on graduate education in psychology. Giving students greater freedom in deciding how to learn might improve the quality of the interaction between teacher and learner.

I have found that students with freedom in how to learn are very creative in their choice of methods. In addition to reading, they may discuss the subject matter with one or two fellow students, may visit or observe someone or something, and may even interview some people or do a small research project. In addition, the instructor might facilitate the formation of small groups, structured or relatively unstructured, with or without the instructor present. The instructor might also identify programmed instruction materials and other resources developed for the "individualization of instruction," which usually refers to an object-planned learning project in which the student sets his own pace. Field work and laboratory experiences might also be provided for the students who are interested.

Help as well as freedom

It is necessary to increase the amount of effective help as well as the freedom for the individual student. Some students, for certain topics, will need help in choosing appropriate methods and resources. The student may even need help at first, from the instructor or a small group or a how-to-study guide, in learning how to go about planning an appropriate strategy. The instructor or group will also have to deal with students' initial reactions to increased freedom; resistance, frustration, anger, and puzzlement are common at first.

Preparation for a career

Professional education and preparation for certain other careers might be improved by giving students a greater choice of how to learn. This could be done within each course or subject, perhaps in blocks of two or four weeks, or for an entire curriculum that ordinarily requires somewhere between two and five years. For example, the professional school could announce precisely what knowledge and skill are required to receive a degree or certificate for the given occupation or profession. It could also suggest various resources, probably including lecture courses and correspondence courses, and could provide some of these. The student could then gain the required knowledge and skill in whatever way he wished, at home or at one or more educational institutions, in a shorter time than usual or spread over many years. When he felt ready, he would present himself for the written examinations and practical tests established by the educational institution or professional school.

Preparing for a demanding career in this way has several advantages. It is probably more efficient for certain learners who can learn faster on their own than they can in highly structured courses. Even more important, it enables the student to develop a high degree of competence in planning and conducting his own learning with the subject matter and reference tools of his chosen profession. This skill, in a rapidly changing world or occupation, is almost as important as the basic minimum knowledge and skill. A lawyer, doctor, professor, architect, or social worker who is not willing and able to continue learning soon becomes obsolete.

6. INCREASE THE STUDENT'S CHOICE OF WHAT HE LEARNS

What proportion of his time does the typical student spend learning subject matter (or performing learning activities) chosen by his instructors? To arrive at an answer, we would first have to add up all the hours that the student spends in class, at homework and assignments, in studying for tests and examinations, and at other activities necessary for passing a course or obtaining credit. From this total number of hours, we would then subtract the times during which the student was learning subject matter that he himself had chosen freely from a fairly wide range of possibilities.

It is difficult to generalize for all years from Grade 9 through to the final year of a Ph.D. program. My guess, though, is that the typical student spends at least 60% to 80% of his time learning subject matter chosen by someone else. I suggest that this percentage be reduced by increasing the proportion of subject matter that the student chooses without restriction. In fact, this trend is already evident at most levels in the educational system.

At the simplest level, the school or college can recognize that its students already learn a great deal completely outside the structure and requirements of the institution. As mentioned previously, our interviewers found that 10-year-old children and 16-year-old adolescents conduct a large number of out-of-school learning projects. The school or college should recognize, encourage, and assist this type of learning. A teacher, for example, can encourage students to continue learning about any topic discussed in class or raised in a film or on a field trip. The school or college might also help its students find resources for their out-of-school learning, and help them set additional learning goals. Indeed, the institution could even take some initiative in locating, listing, and perhaps developing additional out-of-school resources for its students. The institution might help parents become more conscious of their children's learning, and more competent at helping their children set goals and find learning resources throughout the city.

Students can also be given much more choice in what they learn within a single course or subject. At the beginning of the year or semester, the instructor could announce just what level of common knowledge and skill must be learned by all students, and tell them clearly how much additional time is to be devoted to knowledge and skill chosen by the individual student. For example, the instructor might define the proportion of the course devoted to free-choice subject matter in terms of percentage, hours, or number of assignments.

Even within assignments, the amount of freedom can vary. At the broadest level, the instructor can simply require that the student do some sort of essay or project on any subject whatsoever that has some connection with the course. Or the instructor can provide a varied list of topics or questions from which the student can choose. Another possibility is to assign a single topic or question, but to make it broad and flexible enough to allow the student to approach it in his own way.

The school or college that wants to let students devote even more time to freely chosen knowledge and skill may let certain students initiate and carry through a large

154

project. The institution can also let the students take an independent study course or individual reading course in place of a regular one.

When permitting a student to choose what he will learn, some institutions limit him to academic or approved topics. Some also limit his freedom by requiring a long-term commitment instead of giving him the freedom to shift direction frequently. For example, the student may have to outline his entire project before beginning, or he may have to obtain approval for a long list of books before reading the first one.

If some schools and colleges really give students complete freedom, without demanding that they obtain approval, they may find that many students will learn things other than established bodies of academic subject matter. Many students will focus on a problem or responsibility, and will gain the knowledge and skill for fairly immediate application; others will be motivated by curiosity or puzzlement about some question or phenomenon. If the student learns what he considers important, not just what society or his instructors consider important, his subject matter will probably be closely related to his real-life problems and interests. For example, a student may learn about himself, about various careers, about love and sex and the choice of a marriage partner, about getting along with other people, about drugs and smoking and alcohol, about social change and protest, about certain regions to which he hopes to travel in the near future, about certain personal problems, and about various other matters in which he is interested. As students increasingly learn such real-life subject matter, the distinction between in-school and out-of-school learning may become blurred.

Help as well as freedom

Most students will need a great deal of help in developing skill in choosing their learning goals. Such skill also involves the ability to determine one's own problems and interests. Some sort of counseling or personal assistance, with no evaluation or approval included, may be necessary for most students while they develop increasing competence at setting their own goals.

The institution will also have to make available a wider variety of learning opportunities. The freedom to learn whatever one wishes is rather a hollow freedom if there is no opportunity or resource available for learning the chosen subject matter. Consequently, the institution may have to provide additional printed materials for self-planned learning projects, additional programmed instruction and other resources for object-directed learning, and encounter groups or other group opportunities for certain subject matter. The institution might also foster the formation of small, spontaneous groups of individuals interested in learning the same thing.

155

Effects

Does it make sense to let children and adolescents decide for themselves what to learn? Will it work in actual practice? The answer is probably affirmative. Many schools and colleges have already had good experiences with this. Already a great deal of successful youth learning is self-initiated outside of educational institutions without any credit. Gardner Murphy (1958) has stated that observant teachers can readily notice in children "the reaching out, the sense of exploration, the insatiable curiosity, the urge to new experience, the delight in manipulation and the mastery of new media [p. 317]." After observing young children learning in the home and with their playmates, John Holt (1967) concluded "that children learn independently, not in bunches; that they learn out of interest and curiosity, not to please or appease the adults in power; and that they ought to be in control of their own learning, deciding for themselves what they want to learn and how they want to learn it [p. 185]." One other interesting piece of evidence comes from those who work with alcoholics and drug addicts: instead of urging or forcing the addict to reform, they wait until *he* is certain that he wants to change.

Two major benefits would result from giving the student complete freedom in choosing a larger proportion of the knowledge and skill that he learns. First, at least some of the subject matter he chooses will be more useful and interesting to him than the standard curriculum. Not only will he gain more appropriate knowledge and skill, but also he will probably do so more efficiently and with stronger motivation. Second, he will develop skill in setting his own learning goals, and in understanding his own needs and interests.

These two factors may, in turn, have a dramatic influence on his learning for the rest of his life. Because of the relevance, pleasure, and success of his learning as a full-time student, he may learn far more as an adult. In addition, the knowledge and skill that he decides to learn during adulthood will probably be much more appropriate for him.

It would be interesting to compare, 10 or 20 years later, students who attended traditional educational institutions and those whose education was marked by freedom and help in deciding what and how to learn. The amount of learning, the confidence and pleasure in learning, and the methods would probably be quite different in the two groups of adults.

7. EXPERIMENT WITH GROUP HELP FOR SELF-PLANNED LEARNING

Educational institutions should experiment with some of the group formats described in the previous chapter. In particular, they should experiment with effective group help for *self-planned* learning. This format consists of a group of students who are conducting self-planned learning projects and who help one another with setting

156

goals and planning for their individual learning projects.

My experience with this format began in 1967 when I started planning a university course called Psychological Development During Adulthood. Although this course was for academic credit, I wanted to make it as close to noncredit learning as possible. The instructions given to the students at the beginning of the course stated that "each member of the group will freely decide what knowledge and skill he or she wants to learn, and will go ahead and learn it individually, seeking help from the members of the group whenever appropriate. There will be no lectures, assignments, tests, examinations: such procedures are not very effective when each person is learning something different."

Each student was expected to fulfill two major requirements, but these were quite different from requirements in most courses. The first requirement was the following: "Decide what knowledge you want to learn at first. You are completely free to choose whatever you think will be most interesting or useful for you. Your decision can be to begin reading an entire book at first, or to cover the entire field of psychological development during adulthood. Or your decision can be to begin learning intensively about one or two aspects, such as intellectual development, motivation, emotion, or moral and religious development. Or your choice might be a problem to which you will apply whatever subject matter seems relevant. After this tentative initial decision, begin learning the knowledge you have chosen. Modify your objectives, desired knowledge, and strategy whenever appropriate. Do not hesitate to alter your goal or route greatly, even to the point of abandoning an inappropriate one. The whole point of this course is that you learn whatever *you* find most interesting or useful."

The other requirement was to help the other members of the group to learn. Each student was to feel some responsibility for helping others clarify the knowledge and skill that they wanted to gain, and for helping them select appropriate procedures and resources for doing so.

During the group sessions, either in the total group or in smaller subgroups, each student had several opportunities to describe what he wanted to learn, why, and how. The other members of the group, including the instructor, tried to figure out what sorts of help he would benefit from most, and decided how to provide that help. Sometimes a suggestion or a question about goals was made right in the group session. At other times a suggestion for some additional reading was jotted down and handed to the student. Often one or two students in the group would initiate a further conversation with the student after the group session.

This format differed from the typical university seminar in that the students did not present their findings or other subject matter to the group. The group did not

157

at any time discuss or listen to someone presenting subject matter, except as an incidental part of helping one learner with his own project.

This format is effective only if the students are strongly motivated to learn at least some aspect of the subject matter included within the scope of the "course."

During the summer of 1967, each student was clearly more capable than I was of deciding how much knowledge and skill he had learned, and how many hours he had spent on his individual learning projects. Consequently it was his responsibility to evaluate his own learning and to assign himself a grade. This grade was based completely on his self-planned learning, because there were no other requirements or activities as part of the course. I do not think any students "cheated," either consciously or unconsciously, in assigning a grade. Even if one or two students had marked themselves excessively high, though, I would not abandon the format if it proved highly effective for many of the other students.

A group of self-planners probably provides an effective format for other sorts of subject matter as well. Pearson (1967) describes a very similar format that he used in an undergraduate course on personality and in a graduate course on aging, dying, and death. Kolb, Winter, and Berlew (1968) describe a format in which each individual directs his own change project, but receives group help with goal-setting and other aspects. I have found the format fairly effective in two other graduate courses that I have taught recently: a course about individual adult learning, and a doctoral research seminar.

8. REDUCE THE EMPHASIS ON CREDIT

Some educators suggest or imply that all learning controlled by a professional instructor in an educational institution is good (and therefore a certificate or degree is a guarantee of good learning) – and that other sorts of learning are poor or nonexistent. Some want to extend the stamp of approval of the educational institution to the rest of the world: having won control of a major portion of the lives of children and adolescents, they want to control and give credit to all other learning as well. Some urge that compulsory schooling be extended to four-year-olds and to young adults.

In my opinion, shifts in the opposite direction would be more appropriate. The necessity and compulsion of schooling, and the emphasis on credit, should be reduced, not expanded. A variety of learning opportunities and resources (not just full-time classroom-centered instruction) should be made available. Learners of all ages should increasingly be left free to learn whatever, whenever, and however they wish. Their status and their employment opportunities should depend on their actual knowledge and skill and their relevant performance, not on where or how or when they gained that knowledge and skill. They should be judged by what they are, not by the pieces of paper they lack or hold.

As schools and colleges increase their students' freedom to choose what and how they learn, the emphasis on credit will decrease. Instead of frequently assessing the students' progress and level, the institution will emphasize the provision of resources and help for their learning. As a result, students will probably learn far more.

There are several ways in which a school or college can reduce the emphasis on credit. We will examine each possibility in turn.

A pass-fail distinction instead of a precise mark

If all the students in a class or course are expected to learn the same knowledge and skill, it is possible to measure fairly precisely just how much each student has learned. This, in turn, makes it possible to rank order the students or to assign each student a fairly precise grade or mark. The mark might be *A*, 78, or the first decile.

When students in a course are learning a wide variety of subject matter, though, it is more difficult to compare them. For example, if one student reads widely in the field and another student collects some original data in order to learn about a narrow portion of the field, who should be given the higher mark? When students have a great deal of freedom in what they learn, it is often better simply to decide whether each student has learned enough to pass the course or not. A student who has learned enough knowledge and skill (regardless of what it is) or who has spent enough time in learning efforts related to the course receives a grade of "pass." There are no further distinctions within this category. If a student spends little time at learning, or finishes with insufficient knowledge and skill, he receives a grade of "fail."

In some schools and colleges, the student and instructor cooperate in writing a short description of what the student learned. This statement is then recorded on the student's official record along with the "pass" grade.

Distinguishing the functions of helping and evaluating

The help that an instructor provides to the students in his course is often distorted and restricted by the fact that he is also the judge or evaluator of each student. The learners feel they must follow his advice and try to please him.

An alternative is to divide the helping and evaluating functions between two different instructors. One instructor then becomes a helper who is clearly "on the students' side." They can seek his help in meeting the external requirements without worrying about his opinion of their efforts and decisions. Some other instructor or institution then sets or at least marks the assignments and examinations.

If the examinations and assignments are narrow or biased, however, or if the marker is harsh, this situation may not be an improvement. But if the helper and evaluator cooperate, and if certain safeguards are provided, dividing the functions of helping and evaluating can potentially improve the learning.

When helping a graduate student as a member of his thesis committee, a faculty member has difficulty in divesting himself of his role as judge. He can, though, make it clear just which of his suggestions must be accepted in order for his eventual approval, and which suggestions may be rejected safely by the student after some thought. In addition, the thesis adviser can make it clear that his suggestions are not just a personal whim, but are designed to make the research project more important, valid, or efficient.

The learner assigns his own mark
In some courses and classes, it is most appropriate for each student to choose the most suitable procedure for determining his grade. Such a procedure is especially appropriate when much of the knowledge and skill learned by each student is different from what the other students are learning.

When given a choice of procedures, most students prefer to assign their own marks individually. That is, each student will decide his mark and then report it to the instructor's secretary or to some central office. The major criterion used by the student is usually the amount of knowledge and skill that he has learned, or the extent to which he has successfully applied that knowledge and skill. He may also take into account the amount of time that he has spent at the learning. In a group of self-planners, each learner may also take into account a less important criterion: the extent to which he has helped other students learn.

In one variation of this procedure, the student also submits his reasons for believing that the mark he has chosen is the most appropriate one. If the instructor feels the mark is not appropriate, he then discusses it with the student.

Another variation is for the student to set a target grade near the beginning of the course, instead of waiting until the end. The student then learns enough to feel that he has achieved his target grade.

Let us quickly dismiss two objections to procedures in which the learner assigns his own mark. One objection is that students will learn less if they are not being evaluated by an instructor. In actual practice, the opposite seems to be true – depending, of course, on the instructor's skill in establishing an appropriate group climate. The other objection is that a few students will give themselves a much higher mark than they deserve. Even if this does occur, I would hesitate to abandon or distort a procedure that is most beneficial for the largest number of students just because of a small number of "cheaters." In practice, the usual experience is that students mark themselves too low, not too high.

Reducing the proportion of credit learning

A school or college can also decrease the amount of credit learning required of its students. The institution might reduce the amount of compulsory knowledge and skill, the number of courses that the student must pass, or the proportion of his time spent at credit learning. The institution could either insist that the student learn *something*, without restricting or evaluating just how and what he learns, or the institution could leave him completely free to learn or not as he wishes.

The success of the "free universities" (Werdell, 1968) suggests that college students are quite eager to learn without credit. *Time* (June 6, 1969, p. 60) has described the 450 American free universities as·"academic utopias where students and teachers can pursue whatever subjects interest them without formal examinations, grades or degrees."

Jacobs (1969) has suggested that, in an ideal university, "there should be no courses, no credits, no degrees, no hours, damn few administrators [p. 14]." A school or college could refuse to provide any marks or credit whatsoever. Instead, assuming that people will be eager to learn many things for various other reasons, it would concentrate solely on providing help with that learning. If it screened its learners before agreeing to serve them, it would simply select those who could benefit most from the institution's help or who would put their learning to use in society.

In effect, the educational institution would say to its learners something like this: "We have some library resources, librarians, noncredit lecture series, seminars in which students take turns presenting papers, groups to help self-planned learning projects, and some staff members who are competent at helping learners set their goals and plan their strategy. If you think any of these resources would be beneficial to you in planning and conducting some learning projects, you are welcome to come and make use of them for a nominal fee."

Thurman White (1965) foresees a learning society in which people will be judged on whether they can learn or are learning, not on their past attainments in formal educational institutions. "The learning man will replace the knowing man as society's most valued and highly prized member. . . . Political candidates will run on their problem-solving ability. Employers will advertise for the most learnable applicants. Television will use prime time to show people as they study questions of common concern. . . . Mastery of the learning process will stop the aims of formal schooling. Teaching as the art of helping someone else in his effort to change himself (i.e., learn) will be a required proficiency of all college graduates [p. 2]."

Demonstrating one's knowledge and skill once, instead of passing courses

It will probably never be possible to eliminate credit entirely, for two reasons.

First, in most societies, it is considered essential for every member of the society to learn certain things, such as how to read, enough arithmetic to handle money, and something about the nation's history. If we ever realistically examined the minimum knowledge and skill that a society should require, it might turn out to be a surprisingly short list. There would probably be *some* required knowledge and skill, though, and consequently some sort of evidence of its achievement might be required of each individual.

Second, it is necessary for some associations or government departments to certify that certain individuals are competent to perform certain tasks or occupations. We care about the competence of our doctor, plumber, and accountant. Consequently, we want someone to verify their knowledge and skill before they work for us.

At present, both of these needs for credit are usually handled by providing courses and requiring people to pass them. It might make sense to experiment with another procedure for determining whether certain individuals have gained the necessary knowledge and skill. Instead of requiring them to take courses, we could point out to them some alternative ways of learning the knowledge and skill. Then, at least every month or two, we would provide some sort of examination for anyone who felt that he had reached the necessary level.

A child could learn to read and handle money in whatever way seemed most enjoyable or efficient to him. He might use a variety of methods and resources. He might occasionally seek help in establishing procedures for evaluating his own progress or level, or he might even ask some other person to evaluate his level privately for him. Then, when he was satisfied that he had reached the required minimum level, he would demonstrate this in some examination situation.

The person interested in entering a certain occupation, too, might seek some help in determining what knowledge and skill he is lacking. He would then gain that knowledge and skill, using whatever resources and institutions were most convenient and effective. He might obtain practical experience in a variety of situations, or perhaps only in a single situation. Before being allowed to become a full-time, unsupervised practitioner, he would have to demonstrate that he was ready to enter that occupation.

This procedure might not be appropriate for every occupation, but it could certainly increase the quality of those who enter certain occupations. The success of the experiment might hinge to a large extent on the nature of the examination situation. If the examinations are based only on two books or a few particular courses, then the person does not really have much choice in how and what he learns. Instead, the examination situation should test the person's competence in handling real-life problems, cases, or tasks. He might be observed during several weeks of actually performing on the job, for example. This would permit him to seek information and advice from various printed sources and colleagues, just as most competent practitioners do in actual practice. The examination situation might also test a person's basic understanding of the field, and a certain essential core of knowledge and skill.

Who should evaluate occupational competence?
It is evident by now that I believe that evaluating and helping a person are conflicting tasks. Educational institutions as well as individual instructors find themselves in the awkward position of evaluating the learning of the same individuals they are helping. The result has been to distort and reduce the effectiveness of educational institutions in promoting learning. In fact, they sometimes hinder significant learning instead of facilitating it.

My solution is simple. Schools and colleges should evaluate their students' level of knowledge and skill only when absolutely necessary, if ever. These evaluations should be used only for the internal purposes of that educational institution. They should not be released to prospective employers.

For many positions, the employer himself should assess the individual's capacity to perform the job. An employer should develop screening procedures that are fair, realistic, and reliable instead of simply insisting that the person hold a certain degree or secondary school certificate. The employer's procedures should test the person's competence in the knowledge and skill that are essential for his new job, not some peripheral learning. Or, as White suggested (1965), the employer might assess the candidate's learning ability, or the amount and success of his past noncredit learning, instead of his current level of knowledge and skill.

For occupations that are standard in many companies, or that are practiced individually by self-employed persons, the test of competence could be developed and administered by the professional association and/or government. For certain occupations and professions, these tests of competence might be repeated every five to ten years.

Some employers might well shift their emphasis from the initial screening to a trial period on the job. Surely the most effective way to tell whether someone is suitable for a particular job or company is to let him try it for a certain period. The trial period might be one week for a simple job, three months for a complex one. At the end of that time, employee and employer would decide whether the position should become permanent or not. This procedure might eliminate Peter's Corollary (1970), which states that "in time, every post tends to be occupied by an employee who is incompetent to carry out its duties [p. 8]."

163

9. DO NOT RELY ON A SINGLE INSTITUTION

Until recently, it has generally been assumed that each student's education during any given year will be provided entirely by a single school or college. In addition, it has always been recognized that certain attitudes and skills should be taught in the home. Children and adolescents take music lessons, swimming lessons, and ballet lessons from instructors outside the school system. Our 1970 survey indicated that some students spend a great deal of time at out-of-school learning projects. Nonetheless, most educators and parents assume that the school or college attended by the student is far more important in his learning than all the other resources put together.

Several chapters in this book have directed our attention to certain steps that learners take, and to the help they need with these steps. Instead of accepting an educational institution as our starting point, we began with the learner – his motivation, steps, and needs. It is no longer necessary to assume that a single educational institution will meet all the needs of a given learner. By focusing on the learner, we can see a variety of ways of meeting his needs through a variety of institutions.

Earlier in this chapter, I suggested that it is important to help each child and adolescent to develop certain attitudes toward various ways of learning, and to develop competence in setting his learning objectives and in planning his own learning. It is not necessary for him to attend a single institution in order to develop these attitudes and skills; instead, he can develop them through reading a how-to-learn book, through practice, through discussions with a competent learning consultant, and from his parents.

An even more important function of schools and colleges at the present time is to help learners in deciding what to learn, in planning that learning, and in obtaining the subject matter. The responsibility for providing subject matter is already shifting toward a variety of institutions, with the student no longer tied to a single institution. The student learns from field trips to museums and forests, in the public library, and even from certain television programs recommended by an instructor. Perhaps schools and colleges will eventually encourage learners to obtain much of their help and subject matter from resources outside the institution.

As we shift away from having each student attend a single school or college full-time, we may find that the student spends more and more of his time learning at home. Indeed, his study area at home, and his immediate neighborhood, may become his base for learning. Instead of traveling to a certain building or campus five days a week, he may learn at home, and may travel to a number of buildings and resources throughout the city.

All students could be provided with free transportation on the city's buses and

164

subways, and free admission to various museums and other educational buildings. Alternatively, each student could be issued an identification card and a certain number of educational coupons that he could use in place of money for these purposes. In addition, he might be allowed to buy whatever books or informational magazines he chooses up to a certain amount of money.

Neighborhood helpers

If the learner's base of operation shifts from the school or campus to his home, perhaps the instructors should move in the same direction. That is, professionally trained persons who are competent at stimulating and facilitating learning should be provided throughout each geographical area, not clustered in certain buildings.

Let us picture, for example, a typical one-block street in a typical city or suburb 15 years from now. One person, trained as a teacher, is paid by the local board of education to stimulate the 30 children and adolescents on that street and to help them learn whatever seems appropriate to each one. Much of the teacher's time is spent conversing with individual children. Some conversations take place in the teacher's home or on his front steps, some in the child's home, and some on the street. The teacher helps each child set certain learning objectives, and helps him plan how to achieve them. Sometimes the teacher suggests pairs or small groups of children who might get together for certain learning projects. The teacher has a few books, newspapers, and magazines to lend to children, but the learners obtain most of their printed resources from the public library and from people living on their street. Some field trips are organized for the younger children, occasionally including children of a similar age or with similar interests from a nearby street. For certain recreational and athletic activities, as well as for specialized workshops and laboratories, the children and adolescents travel to the building that used to be called "the school."

The teacher might also be responsible for helping any adults on the block who want help in planning their learning. In addition, the teacher might try to stimulate some adults to increase their learning or to see a wider variety of learning possibilities.

A similar arrangement might be useful in certain developing nations. Instead of establishing school buildings and liberal arts colleges, such countries might experiment with this neighborhood helper model, as Illich (1971) has suggested. Most helpers would be mature local adults. In addition, some experiments might try using overseas volunteers as neighborhood teachers. Anyone who wanted to learn about agriculture or health, or how to read or do simple arithmetic, would then approach this helper.

165

Small pilot projects

Experiments with a variety of educational alternatives are already being tried in actual practice. Most of these, however, occur within an educational institution or take the form of an experimental school or free university. That is, it is still assumed that a single institution will be predominantly important in a person's learning.

Perhaps we should also initiate some small pilot projects in which the learners use a variety of resources and locations, perhaps with a neighborhood helper to consult at certain stages in the planning. Although each project may be physically small, it should be complete and comprehensive in scope. That is, instead of merely modifying the present approach, we should try to initiate a completely fresh approach.

As these pilot projects teach us how to be more effective in stimulating and guiding learning, we might become ready to attempt a large-scale pilot project. The eventual result might be an astounding increase in the amount of appropriate knowledge and skill learned in our society, accompanied by a high degree of individual competence at planning and learning.

15 What needs to be done?

Though this book suggests a fresh approach to theory and practice in the field of adult learning, it is just one small step toward understanding and helping adult learners better. Our total understanding of adult learning remains far from complete, and our help for many learning projects is ineffective.

What needs to be done now? What are the next steps? What theorizing, empirical research, and pilot programs are most urgent? This chapter will list a few high-priority projects – action projects as well as theory, development projects as well as research.

SUGGESTIONS FROM EARLIER CHAPTERS

Several research and development projects have been suggested in previous chapters. Further surveys of the frequency and importance of learning projects were proposed in Chapter 3. The same surveys could collect additional data concerning each type of planner, as was suggested in Chapter 8. Needed studies of what and why people learn were outlined in Chapters 4 and 5. Some research and development projects dealing with two major decisions faced by all learners were suggested in Chapters 6 and 7.

Two major directions in which innovative practices for self-planned learning might move were suggested in Chapter 10. One involves better help and resources with both the planning and the actual learning. The other direction involves new ways of helping people become more competent as learners.

The need for further studies of autonomous learning groups was noted in Chapter 13.

Because adults carry on most of their learning outside of formal institutions, and because their helpers are found largely among their acquaintances, there is no organized corps of adult learners and no professional association of their helpers. A useful and revealing experiment might be to establish an association of learners and helpers to decide what new services to seek from governments, universities, public libraries, and corporations. A corporation, such as an insurance company or automobile manufacturer, might simultaneously experiment with an emphasis on complete and accurate learning, perhaps with the following slogan: "We help you *learn* about our products and services, and then *you* make the decisions."

Other specific suggestions for research and innovation are scattered throughout the book. In addition, the creative reader will himself think of further possibilities.

SOME PARTICULAR FIELDS Most of the research and development projects listed above are comprehensive in scope. They include, for example, the entire range of subject matter that people try to learn.

Many readers, though, are primarily interested in a single cluster of subject matter, a specific target population, or one type of institution. Such a reader can consider the implications of this book for theory and practice in his particular field. As he does this, a significant research or action project in that field may begin to take shape.

Most of the comprehensive projects listed earlier can also be conducted within one particular field. During its pilot stages, for example, an attempt to provide better help for adult learners could focus on one sort of subject matter, population, or institution.

To demonstrate the endless possibilities, let us select a few particular fields as examples.

1. Some important innovations might be initiated within the *human growth* cluster of subject matter. At present the human potential movement emphasizes techniques centered in groups and growth centers. Long-term help for self-planned learning has been relatively rare so far.

2. *Parent education* is a second area in which self-planned learning could be fostered and aided more than it is now. Although many books are available for the parent, he may also want help in evaluating his performance, in setting goals, and in applying successfully the suggested principles.

3. *Policy-making* is another area in which research and development projects in adult learning could be especially beneficial. As was pointed out in Chapter 3, politicians spend a great deal of time at learning. How can we help them learn more effectively, and face the entire range of views on an issue? How can high-level decision-makers – politicians, public servants, and top executives – be encouraged to study all the long-term, far-reaching consequences of each major decision?

4. *Schools and colleges* are changing rapidly, but additional improvements are clearly possible. Chapter 3 pointed out that children and adolescents initiate many learning projects outside of their required learning. Educational researchers, theorists, and innovators might study this out-of-school learning, and reflect on the implications for in-school learning. A series of specific steps that educational institutions might take was outlined in Chapter 14.

5. Learning related to *an occupation or profession* is common and significant in most societies. How do people learn a new occupation or job? What are the outstanding characteristics of the daily learning efforts of a lawyer, doctor, nurse, engineer, executive, architect, artist, musician, manager, foreman, writer, teacher, researcher? How can each person in an organization facilitate the learning of his subordinates and colleagues? How can a company foster effective learning projects among its managers? How do staff learning projects facilitate organizational development or change?

6. Further studies and experimentation may increase the effectiveness of our efforts to *reform or rehabilitate* certain individuals, including criminals, alcoholics, and drug addicts. Synanon and Alcoholics Anonymous have already adopted one basic principle of adult learning: dramatic improvement occurs only when the individual himself becomes highly committed to changing.

7. *Librarians and information specialists* are already experimenting with new forms of information storage and retrieval, including a liaison or intermediary person between the learner and the systems. As they study the needs of the adult learner, they may develop better help for his decisions about what and how to learn, as well as his decisions about specific resources.

8. As *social workers* come to regard their clients as potential learners, they may experiment with new ways of helping them set goals, plan learning, and actually learn.

9. *Counselors* have traditionally accepted much of the responsibility for planning and guiding a client's learning. They may increasingly try to help some clients become effective self-planners – dealing with their problems through reflection, reading, conversations with several individuals, and certain group experiences, rather than limiting their learning efforts to the counseling sessions.

A PERSONAL NOTE Many other directions could also be significant. I hope each reader will try to relate our approach and findings to his own field, to his own professional concerns and interests.

This is an open-ended book. It certainly does not present a complete and final picture of the adult's learning projects. Instead, it is designed to encourage a great deal of further exploration, for both new practices and better theory are needed in the field of adult learning.

My hope is that this book will stimulate people to undertake research in many directions, not just the ones listed in this chapter. Mankind will benefit from a wide range of efforts to understand and foster human learning.

**ADULT LEARNING
IN THE FUTURE**

What will all these research and development projects add up to? What might adult learning be like in 20 or 30 years?

First, the body of knowledge regarding human learning projects will be much more complete and accurate than it is at present. The comprehensive study of learning projects will be a well-defined field of research and theory, integrating the efforts of persons from various fields that are now widely separated.

Second, the man or woman of the future will have a high regard for deliberate learning efforts, and will perceive them as normal and significant. He will realize that each type of planner is effective and appropriate in certain circumstances. The adult learner of the future will be highly competent in deciding what to learn, and in planning and arranging his own learning. He will successfully diagnose and solve almost any problem or difficulty that arises. He will obtain appropriate help competently and quickly, but only when necessary.

There is another reason, too, for the speed and ease with which the adult learner of the future will obtain help. The help available to him will be greatly improved and readily available. New types of immediate, inexpensive help will be widespread. Helping individual learners will be regarded as an important responsibility of educational institutions, libraries, employers, professional associations, and sales persons.

All in all, in 20 or 30 years, the amount of appropriate knowledge and skill gained by the typical adult will be much higher than at present. His willingness to learn will also be stronger. Because of his competence at learning and the help that is available, he will select knowledge and skill that is especially relevant for his particular responsibilities and interests. He will learn the knowledge and skill efficiently, easily, and pleasantly – with a minimum of time, money, and frustration. Challenging, rewarding, effective, fun – the adult's learning projects will continue to be a significant and integral part of his total life.

Appendix A   Some borderline cases in defining learning projects

The definition of a learning project contained in Chapter 2 is fairly precise. Some specific questions and borderline cases may arise, however, either at the conceptual level or at the operational (interview) level. This appendix tries to clarify a few of these difficulties.

The learner is doubtful

Some series of episodes cannot be classified with assurance as learning projects because the learner is doubtful or uncertain about some aspect. Occasionally he cannot sort out his reasons for beginning a certain episode. He sees his reasons only dimly, or he cannot judge their relative strength with precision. Consequently, he is not sure whether the desire to gain and retain certain knowledge and skill was more than half of his total motivation. In addition, with a few series of learning episodes, interviewees cannot precisely recall the number of hours involved.

Probing and other efforts to help the interviewee sharpen his recall may cure some of these difficulties. If, however, there is still much doubt about whether a particular example meets the criteria, it is best to assume that it was not a learning project.

Brief episodes

Another difficulty arises when a person's learning effort consists of a large number of very brief episodes, as sometimes occurs when watching television newscasts or when reading newpapers and weekly magazines. Ordinarily we exclude such episodes because the knowledge and skill are not clear and definite in the person's mind beforehand. He knows only that he is "going to catch up (or keep up) with the news." He has little idea of what items will be included. (In wartime, or after an assassination or space flight, this may be different: he may turn to the news media because he knows they will concentrate on that topic.)

Sometimes, though, the person will encounter a certain topic in which he is particularly interested. At that moment his motivation changes from a vague general interest in the contents of the newscast or newspaper to a desire to learn about the specific item he has encountered. If this occurs enough times with a given topic, the total of all these three-minute episodes over six months might be seven hours. Consequently, to set some sort of minimum duration for an episode, we arbitrarily exclude any episode of less than 10 minutes.

This is not an essential part of the concept of a learning project. It is just a convenient rule for use in borderline cases found in interviews.

Levels of comprehensiveness

Learning projects occur at various levels of comprehensiveness, and shorter-term or specific learning projects may occur within broader ones.

Let us imagine a mother whose first child is having difficulty going to sleep. Between October 5 and November 23, she may spend many hours reading about children's sleep, discussing the problem with her husband and pediatrician, and deliberately learning occasionally through trial and error. Clearly this could be a learning project, but it might also be a portion of one or two larger learning projects. For example, she may have gone through a similar flurry of learning about sleep two months earlier, in July and August, and then felt no need for further learning during September. We could consider each of the two flurries of activity as a learning project, or we could consider them as a single learning project with a relatively quiet month in between. At an even more comprehensive level, the woman might consider these episodes and her efforts to learn about feeding and disciplining the child as a unified attempt to learn about raising that child. Two higher levels are also possible: a 20-year project of learning about raising all three of her children, and a 30-year project of trying to become a better mother-wife-person.

Which of these is "really" the learning project? Three answers are possible.

First, each of them is a learning project, because each fits our definition.

Second, if only one must be selected, we could be guided primarily by the woman's own perception of which series of learning episodes is clearly distinct, with a clearly discernible beginning.

Third, our research purposes and strategy might influence our decision. If he is trying to understand at the most comprehensive level how learning fits into a person's life, the researcher might study the broadest learning projects. Usually, though, it is more useful to select the smallest learning project that is clearly distinct in the person's mind, or that is marked by a clear flurry of activity after a relatively dormant period. When studying reasons for beginning a learning project, it is best to seek projects that have recently been initiated or "started from scratch" rather than revived or continued. An educator might be especially interested in certain subprojects within a larger course or educational program: an essay or leaderless discussion group within a college course, for example, or a series of 10 sessions planned by an outside resource person within the longer-term program of an autonomous learning group.

Preparatory steps

Before beginning a learning project, the person must decide what to learn. As part of this decision, he may try to become clearer about the problem or puzzle that is sparking the learning. He must also decide, at a comprehensive level, just how to go about the learning. Should he take a course, pay for private lessons, or plan the learning himself?

If he does decide to plan the learning himself, he must then make many decisions about how, when, and where to learn. He will also have to select the detailed subject matter, and he may set intermediate targets. In addition, he may have to arrange appropriate conditions for learning. For example, he may arrange a study area in his home.

In some episodes, the person's primary intent may be to deal with some of these decisions, arrangements, and other preparations for learning. We allow these preparatory episodes, up to a maximum of two hours, to count toward the minimum criterion of seven hours for a learning project.

172

Maintaining a capacity

Several months after completing a speed reading course, a person might devote certain episodes to *maintaining* the capacity to read rapidly. Someone who has learned a foreign language might select certain activities to help him maintain the vocabulary or fluency already gained. The jogger, after his first few weeks or months, may be primarily interested in maintaining his physical condition, not in improving it. Each of these examples should probably be included as a very deliberate learning episode, even though the main purpose is to maintain rather than gain something. The person is probably motivated by the fact that if he does not perform these episodes, his capacity or skill in the future will be less than if he does perform the episodes.

Doing one's best at the moment

Another type of borderline case occurs when a person tries to do his very best at a particular time. When playing a sport or game or musical instrument, for example, he may do everything possible at the time to play well. He may evaluate his own performance (or seek feedback from others) and try to detect weaknesses. He may try to apply some principles that he recently read about, or try some new technique.

When performing some responsibility, too, such as looking after children or leading a group, a person may try to perform to the best of his ability. He might also resolve to try harder to be more patient or cooperative while performing such a responsibility.

Such episodes meet our criteria only if more than half of the person's motivation is to increase his level of skill in order to perform even better in the future. If his motivation is primarily to *be* rather than to *become* a better person – to do a good job or play a good game today – then it does not meet our criteria.

The single strongest reason

Occasionally an interviewer finds that learning is the strongest *single* reason for an episode, even though it accounts for only 40% of the total motivation. The right-hand column of Table 1 in Chapter 2 provides an example. Though it may seem logical to count this as a learning episode, our criterion of "more than half" prevents this.

The example in Table 1 also points up the necessity for our criterion, and the flaw in looking at the *single* most important reason. The flaw is the assumption that we know just how to combine or divide the other reasons. Another interviewer might combine the third and fourth reasons in the table into a new single one called "pleasure, relaxation, escape, interest." For the women in the right-hand column, this would become their strongest reason. Consequently, the two interviewers would not agree on whether or not her strongest reason was to learn. Our criterion of "more than half" (instead of the *single* strongest reason) avoids this problem.

Appendix B   Influential factors

Adults vary greatly in how often they begin a learning project, and how much time they devote to learning. Some men and women conduct a large number of learning projects each year, and spend hundreds of hours doing so. What factors – past and present, internal and external, conscious and hidden – influence them to learn so much?

Other adults make little effort to learn. Why? What stops some individuals in key positions from trying to learn a great deal about an issue before making a major decision? Why do only a few citizens study peace, population, or pollution before voting on these matters or spreading their opinions to others? Why do accident-prone individuals not try to improve? Why do some intelligent adults shy away from learning about the past and future of man's life on earth? What blocks many parents from trying to improve their competence in raising children?

A large number of factors may form part of the answers to these questions. At present we can only speculate about which factors are especially influential. It will be many years before researchers are able to determine the relative importance of the entire array of factors.

Past experiences

Certain past experiences are probably among the most influential factors that determine how much time a person devotes to learning. Such factors might include (1) the extent to which the person's parents read and learned, (2) the amount of activity or achievement in his childhood home, (3) the use of vocabulary there, (4) the number of years he spent in school, (5) the characteristics and curriculum of those schools, (6) his satisfaction with his previous attempts to learn, and (7) his ordinal position among his siblings. Landsman (1969) suggests another factor: the frequency and intensity of positive experiences at all ages, especially during childhood. Houle's stimulating exploratory study (1961) suggests several other factors.

Childhood experiences have certainly influenced some men and women strongly. One young adult, for example, stated: "From my childhood I was taught the beauty and adventure of books, and the necessity to constantly seek out answers. I was encouraged rather than discouraged to ask *why* as I grew. I developed in an atmosphere of openness where subjects ranging from Thoreau to the current crisis in the news were discussed, not around me, but with me, encouraging me to participate in the discussion. I was taught, and subsequently learned, that there is so much to know and so little time in which to learn it."

174

Psychological characteristics

Many of the person's current personality or psychological characteristics will also influence the amount of time he spends at learning. If the person is outstanding in some of the following characteristics, for example, he will probably conduct more learning projects than most people: (1) level of mental ability; (2) energy level; (3) degree of initiative and aggressiveness in daily life; (4) degree of deliberateness and rationality in daily life; (5) amount of insight into himself; (6) amount of current knowledge and skill; (7) strength and number of interests; (8) positive perceptions regarding the pleasure, usefulness, and appropriateness of learning; (9) extent to which he is future-oriented, and willing to put forth effort in hopes of later gratification, rather than living essentially for the present (Kuhlen, 1963); (10) importance in his life of motivation for growth, expansion, achievement, creativity, self-actualization (compared to motivation from lower-level needs, anxiety, threat, deficiency, defensiveness and protection, attempts to satisfy the real or imagined demands of others); (11) past or anticipated residential mobility; (12) general readiness to change, and optimism about the future (Johnstone & Rivera, 1965); (13) amount of margin (a concept being developed by Howard McClusky), that is, the amount of energy, power, time, money, and other resources left over after the person deals with his current minimum tasks and routine demands; (14) strength of motivation for achievement (Parker & Paisley, 1966); (15) amount of enjoyment from using the mind; (16) amount of curiosity, and amount of pleasure from exploring new fields and phenomena; (17) clarity of life goals; (18) competence at setting learning goals; (19) extent to which his self-concept and self-assessment are clear and accurate rather than denied or distorted; (20) extent to which he perceives positive consequences in the development of new media and educational technology (Rees & Paisley, 1967); (21) extent to which he deals with a problem rather than its symptoms, understands the heart of a problem, realistically perceives his own role in causing a problem, and feels that he should accept at least partial responsibility for solving his problems.

The absence of most or all of the characteristics just listed will usually reduce the number of learning projects that a person begins. In addition, a person may be especially likely to make very few learning efforts if (1) his habitual reaction to new situations and requirements is negative, (2) he does not react positively to ambiguity, puzzlement, and unanswered questions, (3) he is fearful of failure, (4) he rarely returns to a task when interrupted, (5) he cannot clearly see the gap between his present self and his ideal self, and (6) he has not yet reached a high level of ability in thinking in a flexible and integrated manner.

Several other current characteristics of the individual must be understood before one can predict, with any assurance at all, the amount of his learning in any one year. These characteristics include (1) his concept of himself, (2) his high-priority, long-term goals, (3) his values, attitudes, and beliefs, and (4) his developmental tasks, role changes, transitions, personal crises. Several other influential factors became evident during the wide-ranging interviews described by Dow (1965).

Negative characteristics can have a positive influence on the amount of learning. Some persons may be driven to learning by their emotional problems, by their difficult or boring or unsatisfying marriage, by their search for a husband, by their troubled childhood, or by their frequent failures in life. Attending a course or reading extensively may provide satisfaction or social stimulation to those who lack a happy home life or a variety of other satisfying activities.

Other people
The amount a person learns is also influenced by various characteristics of the people around him. The customs and expectations of his circle of friends and relatives may be important, for example. These acquaintances may praise and support anyone who tries to learn, or may scoff and tease. They may themselves learn frequently – or rarely. The types of people with whom a person interacts may be affected by his age, sex, occupation, income level, and social class. Studying the factors that make some people readers and others nonreaders, Ennis (1965) found that many readers feel they live "in a book-rich and book conscious circle of family and friends [p. 24]." Many adult learners receive stimulation and support by being part of an enclave of learners (Houle, 1961). Jourard (1968) has suggested that the way to understand the person marked by "turned-on, fascinated, autonomous questing" is to study the significant people in his world as he perceives them. Researchers, too, are usually more productive if they work in a stimulating intellectual milieu, or have contact with colleague at meetings and by mail or phone.

Community and societal factors
Community or societal factors may also be important. Entire communities or societies may be oriented to learning much more than other communities and societies. Urban and suburban Californians, for example, may be more stimulated to learn than peasants in developing countries. The typical medical doctor or sales clerk in London and Boston may learn more now than his counterpart did 200 years ago; an even greater increase may occur in the next 200 years.

Sometimes a community or group is established specifically to promote learning. Universities and residential adult education centers are sometimes examples of this. Some recently established utopian ("intentional") communities have individual development as a major goal.

Other communities and situations marked by a great deal of free time lead to learning efforts by a few individuals, through reading or discussion. Examples are prisons, hospitals, concentration camps, remote military outposts, and certain occupations. Some people leave their ordinary surroundings, perhaps for a religious retreat or mountain cabin, in order to think or learn or write.

The geographical proximity of certain facilities and services may increase the adult's learning efforts. In particular, the availability and accessibility of libraries, bookstores, educational institutions, discussion groups, counseling, and other sources of help and materials may be influential.

Appendix C   Freedom, autonomy, and control: The relationship between helper and learner

During the past ten years or more, a large proportion of the literature on education has dealt with such concepts as freedom, control, authority, autonomy, and the role and functions of the teacher. In a major review of teaching methods research, for example, Wallen and Travers (1963) found that "the vast majority of the studies" revolved around the control or authority of the instructor. The authors declared: "The common denominator of these studies is that they all involve as a primary dimension authoritarianism as we define it, i.e., the degree to which some person or persons (in this case, the teacher) exercises control over the behavior of others (in this case, students) [p. 470]."

Much of the discussion about these concepts has been emotional or imprecise. The process of trying to sort out my own thinking about these concepts helped me see the usefulness of distinguishing four types of learning projects according to the primary locus of the control and responsibility for day-to-day planning: self, object, person, or group (see Chapter 7).

That process also led me to develop a set of more detailed variable characteristics for describing help. These variables are fairly clear and precise, though a few may be difficult to measure or estimate in particular helping situations. They can be applied to the relationship between a learner and any one of his helpers *within* any type of learning project. I find my thinking is much clearer when I replace such general concepts as autonomy, freedom, and control with more precise variables.

Let us start with the simplest situation: one learner receiving help with his self-planned learning project from one helper. These two persons interact face-to-face with no one else present, or perhaps they interact by mail or telephone. The helper might be a friend, acquaintance, colleague, teacher, salesman, librarian, supervisor, counselor, consultant, medical doctor, spouse, or parent.

Some variables

One variable is the extent to which the helper influenced the learner's decisions. How great an impact did the helper's information, advice, and encouragement have on the learner's decisions and other preparatory steps?

Within the total impact or influence of the helper, one can conceptually distinguish two types of influence. One type is providing information, advice (or suggestions or recommendations), and reasons that help the *learner* make the decision and understand the reasons for it. The helper provides detailed information about the various possibilities that are open, but lets the learner himself make the decisions. This is similar to the role of the consultant, who enables someone else to do something; the consultant does not himself make and implement decisions. The other sort of influence by a helper is a controlling, managing, and directing sort of influence. It is the extent to which he is "in charge" of the learning project – the extent to which he rules or governs it. This sort of help means that the learner gladly or reluctantly gives up some of his responsibility, control, autonomy, and perhaps initiative and freedom. The distinction between help and control is important, because it helps us realize that a learner can receive a great deal of help without giving up any of his control or responsibility.

In addition to considering the actual help or influence, one can note how much help the learner *wanted* from the helper. As the learner reflects back on his relationship with the helper, does he wish he had received much more or much less help than he actually did, or does he feel satisfied with the amount? Too little help may be the sign of a rather useless helper, or of one who is encouraging the learner to assume more responsibility for his own planning. More help than desired is often the sign of a helper who tried to control and dominate the learner's decisions and arrangements. Sometimes another clue is a dramatic increase over a period of time in the amount of help that the learner welcomes.

Another variable that can indicate an attempt to dominate the learner is the following: to what extent was the helper trying to influence the learner more (or less) than he actually did? In other words, does the learner feel that he had to resist the helper's attempts to influence his strategy and subject matter even more? At the opposite extreme, does the learner feel that he had to work hard at getting even the amount of help he did get?

In summary, we have three major variables that can help us study freedom, control, coercion, influence, autonomy, and authority in a helping relationship. We look first at the helper's actual influence. How great an impact does he have? We then note whether this is congruent with the amount of help that the learner wanted or welcomed. In addition, we note whether the learner felt a lack of congruity between the actual amount of help and the amount that the helper wanted to provide.

These variables may become clearer when put into the form of a diagram. Figure C1 presents each of the three variable characteristics as a vertical continuum. In Figure C1,

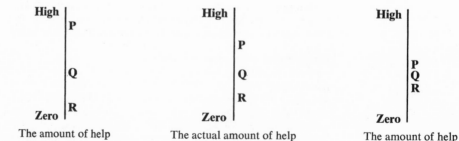

The amount of help that this helper apparently wanted to provide

The actual amount of help received from this helper

The amount of help that the learner wanted

Fig. C1 / Three helpers (P, Q, and R) on three continua.

178

Mr. P was overeager: he intended to influence the learner far more than the learner wanted; Mr. Q was just right: all three characteristics are congruent; and Mr. R was reluctant to help much.

One other characteristic of the help is especially relevant for studying control. For what *reasons* does the learner accept the helper's advice, suggestions, and decisions? Perhaps it is because he trusts the helper's judgment, or finds that the helper's enthusiasm for the recommended action is contagious. On the other hand, perhaps he follows the helper's advice in order to please or impress him, or because he feels some sort of obligation, or because he anticipates certain rewards or punishments from the helper.

Individualized help

Most human help in a one-to-one situation is highly individualized, but some is not. Human help in a group, and help from printed materials or computers, are usually less individualized than one-to-one human help.

Adults need individualized help particularly in self-planned learning. Indeed, by definition, the self-planner has decided to build his own sequence of learning activities, rather than follow a sequence of learning activities determined by a group, by programmed instruction, or by a series of recordings or television programs. Consequently, he will probably need individualized help, not just mass or prestructured sorts of help.

To be more specific, one can look at the extent to which the help is designed for this particular learner and learning project rather than for different learners and learning projects. Even when one learner and one helper interact face-to-face, the help may be so influenced by tradition, habit, previously established procedures or structures, pre-conceptions about the learner's needs, or the helper's own goals that it is in effect designed for someone other than this particular learner. Such a helper provides habitual or stereotyped help, not individualized help. He may not be sensitive to the characteristics, needs, learning goals, and perceptions of the person he is dealing with.

As a second but related variable, one can ask the following question: to what extent (in the learner's opinion) would he have been able to influence the helper's words or behavior if he had tried? In less precise words, how much control or influence did the learner have over the helper or other resource?

One can also note how satisfied the learner is with these two variables. To what extent does he wish the help was designed more specifically for his particular learning project? How much more influence over the helper's behavior and words would he have liked?

Possible uses for the set of variables

The last two sections have provided a set of characteristics that vary from one helping relationship to another. From the hundreds of characteristics in helping situations, we have selected a few that seem especially important when considering who dominates the helping relationship and how individualized it is.

Basically, then, the set of variable characteristics enables us to study or analyze various helping relationships in self-planned learning projects, and to describe those relationships. In addition to studying and describing a relationship, we could compare a variety of situations and helpers to detect some crucial differences among them. For example, we might compare the help in self-planned learning provided by a spouse, trained learning adviser, medical doctor, management consultant, piano teacher, judge, presidential adviser, professor, research assistant, travel agent, librarian, tutor, elementary school teacher, or instructor in independent study. We could also use the variables to compare the help in person-planned and group-planned learning projects with the help in self-planned projects. Rather than comparing two or more current helping relationships, we could try to describe trends over time by comparing "modern" help with earlier or traditional help.

Looking to the future, we could tentatively but precisely describe certain characteristics of ideal help. These characteristics could then be used in selecting and training helpers. Our advice to the helper might be something like this: give the learner approximately the amount and sorts of help he wants. If in doubt, give too little rather than too much help, because this may help him be more competent and confident in planning his next learning project. Do not try to decrease his control or unduly influence him. Give him accurate, detailed reasons for any recommendation you make.

We could also study which variables are important in the learner's choice of a helper, and in his satisfaction with the helpers he does choose. If the learner is dissatisfied with the helper, the variables could help us pinpoint just what went wrong.

Further research could study a variety of possible relationships among the variables themselves. Certain positions on certain continua, for example, may typically occur together. Researchers could also study the ways in which these variables influence the learner's behavior and perceptions – his success and efficiency in the learning project, his confidence and competence in future self-planned learning projects, his attitudes toward help, and his perceptions of himself as a learner.

Influential factors

No one position on a continuum will be best for all learners and all subject matter. Various characteristics of the learner and the content will influence the characteristics of ideal help. The influential characteristics of the learner probably include his age, occupation, income level, cultural background, place of residence (whether rural or urban, especially in developing nations), mobility, major personality characteristics, need for affiliation, attitudes towards schools and instructors, operating principles of learning, habitual style of learning, and competence at learning.

The influential characteristics of the desired knowledge and skill can best be summarized by a series of questions. How difficult is the subject matter for this learner? How large or threatening is the task of gaining the subject matter? How familiar is the learner with the subject matter? How close to the learner's self is it, and how much will it affect his self-concept and mental health? Is it completely original (no one has ever gained this knowledge before), or is it established knowledge? How many other persons are, in the learner's awareness, learning the same subject matter? What are his major reasons for wanting to gain it? How long does he want it to last? Is it for credit? How clearly has he defined just what he wants to learn, and why? What methods and help are objectively most efficient for gaining this subject matter?

Nonhuman resources

So far we have been talking primarily about human helpers. Some of the variables can also apply to the help received from nonhuman resources, such as a book, program, recording, or computer. By studying one particular resource or one type of resource in several learning projects, a general profile of its characteristics could be developed.

180

Preparatory steps

Our discussion up to this point has concerned the total helping situation – the total relationship throughout the learning project between the learner and one resource. It is also possible to apply the variables separately to each preparatory step, or to major clusters of preparatory steps. This procedure will enable us to produce much more precise descriptions and answers than the general approach, because important differences in the characteristics of the help may occur from one cluster of steps to another.

To the preparatory steps, we can add the function of providing subject matter, which is not a preparatory step because it occurs during a learning episode, not a planning episode. This addition will give a more complete picture of the types of help provided by any one resource.

A glimpse of what a profile of one helper might look like is provided by Table C1. It assumes that a scale from 0 to 100 has been developed for each variable, and that appropriate measuring procedures have been developed. Table C1 presents the empirical data that might result from interviewing a learner about the help he received from his major helper in a self-planned learning project.

Some personal characteristics of the helper

The personal characteristics of the helper may greatly influence the helping relationship, even if they are not especially conspicuous to the learner. These internal characteristics include his self-concept, perceptions, feelings, motivation, and thoughts.

It is not always easy, of course, to distinguish between the personal characteristics and overt behavior of the helper. Indeed, the two sorts of characteristics are interrelated. Several of the helper's internal characteristics, for example, will affect the variables listed earlier.

Some inner characteristics that mark the highly effective or highly desired helper are emerging from various studies. Carl Rogers, for instance, has written extensively about a small number of helper characteristics that are related to effective help for at least one broad class of emotional problems. An unpublished study by Stanley Searle, conducted at the Ontario Institute for Studies in Education in 1968, listed several characteristics of the most effective helpers in adult learning projects. Using a list of 169 variables printed on cards, he interviewed 20 adult learners intensively. In her doctoral thesis, Mairi Macdonald (1968) listed the characteristics of persons chosen as helpers by adults with a problem.

The ideal qualities of the helper will be affected somewhat by the preparatory steps that require the help, by certain characteristics of the desired knowledge and skill, and by the degree of self-direction that the learner desires. Nonetheless, a fairly consistent composite picture of the ideal helper emerges from the literature, and from other sources and experiences.

One cluster of characteristics might be summarized by saying that the ideal helper is warm and loving. He accepts and cares about the learner and about his project or problem, and takes it seriously. He is willing to spend time helping. He is approving, supportive, encouraging, and friendly. He regards the learner as an equal. As a result of these characteristics, the learner feels free to approach this ideal helper, and can talk freely and easily with him in a warm and relaxed atmosphere.

A second cluster of characteristics involves the helper's perceptions of the person's capacity as a self-planner. The ideal helper has confidence in the learner's ability to make

181

Table C1 / The Characteristics of One Helper

Variable	Deciding whether to begin	Choosing the director	Deciding detailed content and strategy	Diagnosing difficulties	Obtaining resources	Dealing with motivation	Actually receiving subject matter
Actual amount of help or control	30	20	30	20	0	10	20
Proportion that is *control*	0	0	0	0	0	0	0
Amount of help and control welcomed by the learner	30	20	30	10	10	10	30
To what extent was the helper trying to provide more or less than this?	0	0	0	10	–10	0	–10
Reasons for accepting help: ratio of "trust his judgment" to pleasing, impressing, obligation, consequences	90	100	90	100	–	100	100
Extent designed for this particular learner	100	100	90	100	–	100	90
Extent he could influence the helper	100	100	100	100	–	100	100
Learner's satisfaction with the two previous variables	100	100	100	100	–	100	100

appropriate plans and arrangements for his learning. The helper has a high regard for his skill as a self-planner, and does not want to take the decision-making control away from him.

Third, the ideal helper views his interaction with the learner as a dialogue, a true encounter in which he listens as well as talks. His help will be tailored to the needs, goals, and requests of this unique learner. The helper listens, understands, accepts, responds, helps. These perceptions of the interaction are in sharp contrast to those of "helpers" who want to control, command, manipulate, persuade, influence, and change the learner. Such helpers seem to view communication as "an inexhaustible monologue, addressed to everyone and no one in the form of 'mass communication' . . . a transcribed message from an anonymous answering service to whomever it may concern [Matson & Montagu, 1967, p. 6]." Gibb (1964) has described the person who molds, steers, controls, gives information, indoctrinates; such a person's orientation to the helping relationship is not marked by shared problem-solving, freedom, candor, interdependence, and mutual exploration. Such a helper perceives the learner as an object, and expects to do something *to* that object. He is not primarily interested in the other person as a person, and in his needs, wishes, and welfare.

Another cluster of internal characteristics involves the helper's reasons for helping. He may help because of his affection and concern for the learner. Or the helper may, in an open and positive way, expect to gain as much as he gives. Other sorts of motivation, too, are possible – pleasure from knowing he was helpful, satisfaction from seeing progress or from the learner's gratitude. It might be interesting to study the efforts and motives of the individual who is especially active at encouraging and advising learners in several areas of knowledge and skill.

Finally, the ideal helper is probably an open and growing person, not a closed, negative, static, defensive, fearful, or suspicious sort of person. He himself is frequently a learner, and seeks growth and new experiences. He probably tends to be spontaneous and authentic, and to feel free to behave as a unique person rather than in some stereotyped way.

Strong motivation for amateur teaching

Much of the teaching in our society is done by school teachers, college professors, and adult education instructors. Certain other professions, too, often include teaching as one major responsibility. For example, film and television producers, visual artists, writers, advertisers, editors, judges, lawyers, medical doctors, and clergymen may perceive teaching (imparting information or changing human behavior) as part of their job.

In addition, a great deal of "amateur" teaching occurs throughout our society. The term *amateur* is not used to suggest poor quality, but to indicate that the person is not paid for his teaching and is not doing it as a necessary part of his job.

Much amateur teaching is merely a response to a request for help from a learner. In this section, however, we will look at amateur teaching in which the teacher takes the initiative. He is strongly motivated to impart certain knowledge and skill, or to change the behavior of certain persons in certain directions.

One dramatic example of this is the person who pays for newspaper advertisements to spread his message about peace, proposed legislation, government policy, or any other issue. A 45-year-old Tokyo man, for example, put his life savings into $63,800 worth of

183

advertising in five American and British newspapers in 1966. His 12,000-word message presented his views on ways of achieving peace, world affairs, fasting, and dealing with the fear of death. A writer in *Life* magazine declared that the Tokyo man "struck a splendid blow for the grandeur of the individual when he blew the 11 grand to have himself published." He had previously sent pamphlets to 5,000 important persons, but had received no response. Unfortunately, he paid dearly for his efforts to educate the public. Four years later, although he had once owned an apartment house and a prosperous mail-order business, he was "alone and broke, driving a truck in Yokohama." Also, "because of his idealistic extravagance, his wife divorced him, taking their sons with her" (*Time*, August 10, 1970).

Similarly, a man in London, Ontario, became convinced that a Canadian government White Paper on proposed tax reform was unfair and inaccurate. He spent $23,000 on advertisements in leading newspapers. His reason, according to the Toronto *Globe and Mail* (February 9, 1970), was his belief that "there are hundreds of thousands of Canadians who are not able to appreciate the frightening implications of the White Paper because it is so complicated." He was not backed by any organization or political party, but was willing to accept donations.

Other persons with strong views write letters to the editor or to their political representatives. Some write articles or brochures to express their views. Some seek interviews on television or radio.

Some people with definite views join a demonstration or protest. When demonstrators on both sides of an issue confront one another in the streets or on the campus, we have a clear example of a situation in which everyone wants to teach and no one wants to learn. Each side wants to spread its views through placards and a show of strength or numbers, but neither side has much interest in understanding the views of the other.

Certain political and religious groups have a strong urge to convert others to their views. Hoffer (1961) has suggested that the urge to proselytize is strongest in a movement when the believers feel some deep misgiving or deficiency, or when they see that their creed (communism, slavery, or whatever) is not really working out in practice. In other words, a confident and accurate belief that they already have an important truth is *not* their major motivation.

Alcoholics Anonymous provides another example of amateur teaching. The member who helps the alcoholic has already himself experienced the alcoholic's hopelessness and low self-esteem, and has found that the organization's principles, beliefs, and attitudes are effective.

Perhaps the most widespread amateur teaching can be found in child-raising. Many parents deliberately teach their children certain knowledge, skills, manners, habits, and even attitudes and emotional reactions. Some adults also set out to reform their marriage partner, often with negative results.

When neighbors have a noisy party, we wonder how to punish them or change their behavior. Selye (1956) has pointed out that revenge (the wish that another person not prosper) is "a savage distortion of the natural wish to teach others not to hurt us. . . . It is nothing but a grotesque malformation of our urge to teach [p. 286]."

References

Atkinson, R. C. Computerized instruction and the learning process. *American Psychologist*, 1968, **23**, 225-239.

Berzon, B., Reisel, J., & Davis, D. P. PEER: An audio tape program for self-directed small groups. *Journal of Humanistic Psychology*, 1969, **9**, 71-86.

Berzon, B., & Solomon, L. N. The self-directed therapeutic group: An exploratory study. *International Journal of Group Psychotherapy*, 1964, **14**, 366-369.

Bivens, L. W., Campbell, V. N., & Terry, D. F. *Self-direction in programed instruction: Effects on learning in low-ability students.* (American Institute for Research, AIR-D10-7/63-TR.) Washington: U.S. Office of Education; Department of Health, Education, and Welfare, 1964.

Bjerrum, C. A. Forecast of computer developments and applications 1968-2000. *Futures*, 1969, **1**(3), 331-338.

Blackburn, D. J. *Method orientations of adults for participation in educative activities.* (Doctoral dissertation, University of Wisconsin) Ann Arbor, Mich.: University Microfilms, 1967. No. 67-12,412.

Blackburn, D. J. *Guelph adult participation patterns: First report of the city of Guelph participation survey.* Guelph: Department of Extension Education, University of Guelph, 1968.

Bobbitt, J. F. *How to make a curriculum.* Boston: Houghton Mifflin, 1924.

Buhler, C., & Massarik, F. (Eds.) *The course of human life: A study of goals in the humanistic perspective.* New York: Springer, 1968.

Campbell, A., & Metzner, C. A. *Public use of the library and other sources of information.* Ann Arbor, Mich.: Institute for Social Research, University of Michigan, 1950.

Cardinal principles of secondary education: A report of the Commission on the Reorganization of Secondary Education. Bulletins of Bureau of Education, 1918, No. 35. Washington: Government Printing Office, 1918.

Channing, W. E. Self-culture: An address . . . delivered at Boston, Sept. 1838. In *The works of William E. Channing, D.D.* Boston: American Unitarian Association, 1890. Pp. 12-36.

Cohen, W. J. Education and learning. *The Annals of the American Academy of Political and Social Science*, Sept. 1967, **373**, 79-101.

de Sola Pool, I. Social trends. *Science and Technology*, April 1968, **76**, 87-101.

Dill, W. R., Crowston, W. B. S., & Elton, E. J. Strategies for self-education. *Harvard Business Review*, 1965, **43**(6), 119-130.

Dow, J. B. *Characteristics of noncredit university extension students.* (Doctoral dissertation, University of California in Los Angeles) Ann Arbor, Mich.: University Microfilms, 1965. No. 65-12,655.

Doxiadis, C. A. Learning how to learn. In *What I have learned: A collection of twenty autobiographical essays by great contemporaries from the Saturday Review.* New York: Simon & Schuster, 1968. Pp. 36-46.

Dumazedier, J. *Toward a society of leisure.* Translated by S. E. McClure. New York: Free Press, 1967.

Ely, D. P. New developments in educational technology for continuing education. In W. L. Ziegler (Ed.), *Essays on the future of continuing education worldwide.* Syracuse: Syracuse University, 1970. Pp. 72-81.

Ennis, P. H. *Adult book reading in the United States: A preliminary report.* Report No. 105. Chicago: National Opinion Research Center, University of Chicago, 1965. (Available from the ERIC Document Reproduction Service, order no. ED 010 754.)

Ewbank, H. L., Jr. Operation bootstrap: The American lyceum, 1826-1840. Paper presented at the National Seminar on Adult Education Research, Toronto, February 1969.

Fair, J. W. Out-of-school learning and beginning teachers. *Orbit,* 1970, **1**(3), 25-27.

Farber, J. The student as nigger. *This Magazine is About Schools,* 1968, **2**, 107-116.

Flaherty, M. J. The prediction of college level academic achievement in adult extension students. Unpublished doctoral dissertation, University of Toronto, 1968. (Microfilm copy is available from the National Library of Canada: Canadian theses on microfilm, no. 3554.)

French, W. *Behavioral goals of general education in high school.* New York: Russell Sage Foundation, 1957.

Fuller, R. B. *Education automation: Freeing the scholar to return to his studies; a discourse before the Southern Illinois University, Edwardsville Campus Planning Committee, April 22, 1961.* Carbondale: Southern Illinois University Press, 1962.

Gardner, J. W. *Self-renewal: The individual and the innovative society.* New York: Harper & Row, 1964.

Geer, B. Teaching. In D. L. Sills (Ed.), *International encyclopedia of the social sciences.* Vol. 15. New York: Macmillan and Free Press, 1968. Pp. 560-565.

Gibb, J. R. Is help helpful? *Association Forum* (YMCA), February 1964, 25-27.

Grattan, C. H. *In quest of knowledge: A historical perspective on adult education.* New York: Association Press, 1955.

Hackett, A. P. *Seventy years of best sellers 1895-1965,* New York: R. R. Bowker, 1967.

Hagstrom, W. O. *A study of deliberate instruction within family units.* Office of Education Comparative Research Project No. S-184, 1965. (Available from the ERIC Document Reproduction Service, order no. ED 003 070.)

Hall, C. A. Why Illinois women participate in home economics extension club programs. Unpublished doctoral dissertation, University of Chicago, 1965. (Available on microfilm from the Photoduplication Service of the University of Chicago Library.)

Hallenbeck, W. C. The role of adult education in society. In G. Jensen, A. A. Liveright, & W. Hallenbeck (Eds.), *Adult education: Outlines of an emerging field of university study.* Chicago: Adult Education Association of the U.S.A., 1964. Pp. 5-25.

186

Harvey, O. J., Hunt, D. E., & Schroder, H. M. *Conceptual systems and personality organization.* New York: Wiley, 1961.

Hilgard, E. R., & Bower, G. H. *Theories of learning.* (3rd ed.) New York: Appleton-Century-Crofts, 1966.

Hoeflin, R. The effect on child rearing practices of the various types of child care resources used by Ohio farm families. Unpublished doctoral dissertation, Ohio State University, 1950.

Hoffer, E. *The true believer: Thoughts on the nature of mass movements.* New York: Harper & Row, 1961.

Holt, J. *How children learn.* New York: Pitman Publishing Corp., 1967.

Houle, C. O. *The inquiring mind.* Madison: University of Wisconsin Press, 1961.

Houle, C. O. Adult education. In R. L. Ebel (Ed.), *Encyclopedia of educational research.* (4th ed.) New York: Macmillan, 1969. Pp. 51-55.

Illich, I. Education without school: How it can be done. *The New York Review,* January 7, 1971.

Jackson, P. W. *The teacher and the machine.* Pittsburgh: University of Pittsburgh Press, 1968.

Jacobs, D. W. The education of searchers in psychology. *Teaching of Psychology Newsletter* (Published by Division 2 of the American Psychological Association), November, 1969, 13-14.

Jahns, I. R. *The utilization of positional leaders by community members in a rural Wisconsin county.* (Doctoral dissertation, University of Wisconsin) Ann Arbor, Mich.: University Microfilms, 1967. No. 67-10,635.

Jahoda, M., & Thomas, L. F. *Search for optimal conditions of learning intellectually complex subject matter: Third progress report, September 1964 – September 1965.* London, England: Department of Psychology and Social Science, Brunel College, 1965.

Johnstone, J. W. C., & Rivera, R. J. *Volunteers for learning: A study of the educational pursuits of American adults.* Chicago: Aldine Publishing Company, 1965.

Jourard, S. *Disclosing man to himself: The task for humanistic psychology.* New York: Van Nostrand-Reinhold, 1968.

Kahn, A. J. *Neighborhood information centers: A study and some proposals.* New York: Columbia University School of Social Work, 1966.

Kearney, N. C. *Elementary school objectives: A report prepared for the Mid-century Committee on Outcomes in Elementary Education.* New York: Russell Sage Foundation, 1953.

Kempfer, H. *Adult education.* New York: McGraw-Hill, 1955.

Kidd, J. R. *How adults learn.* New York: Association Press, 1959.

Knoepfli, H. E. The origin of women's autonomous learning groups. Uupublished doctoral dissertation, University of Toronto (OISE), 1971. (Microfilm copy will be available from the National Library of Canada.)

Knowles, M. S. *The leader looks at self-development.* Looking into leadership monographs no. 4. Washington: Leadership Resources, Inc., 1961.

Knowles, M. S. Program planning for adults as learners. *Adult Leadership,* 1967, **15,** 267-279.

Knowles, M. S. Androgogy, not pedagogy! *Adult Leadership*, 1969, **16**, 350-352 and 386.

Knowles, M. S. *The modern practice of adult education: Andragogy versus pedagogy.* New York: Association Press, 1970.

Kolb, D. A., Winter, S. K., & Berlew, D. E. Self-directed change – Two studies. *Journal of Applied Behavioral Science*, 1968, **4**, 453-471.

Kuhlen, R. G. Motivational changes during the adult years. In R. G. Kuhlen (Ed.), *Psychological backgrounds of adult education: Papers presented at a Syracuse University conference, October, 1962, Sagamore, New York.* Chicago: Center for the Study of Liberal Education for Adults, 1963. Pp. 77-113.

Kulich, J. An historical overview of the adult self-learner. Paper presented at the Northwest Institute on Independent Study: The Adult as a Self-learner, University of British Columbia, Vancouver, February 1970.

Landsman, T. The beautiful person. *The Futurist*, April 1969, **3**, 41-42.

Leonard, G. B. *Education and ecstasy.* New York: Delacorte Press, 1968.

Litchfield, A. The nature and pattern of participation in adult education activities. Unpublished doctoral dissertation, University of Chicago, 1965. (Available on microfilm from the Photoduplication Service of the University of Chicago Library.)

Love, R. A. The use of motivation research to determine interest in adult college-level training. *Educational Record*, July 1953, **34**, 210-218.

Macdonald, M. Informal helping relationships among adults: A study of the reasons for choosing a helper and of the ways in which he helps. Unpublished doctoral dissertation, University of Toronto (OISE), 1968. (A summary of this study is available from the ERIC Document Reproduction Service, order no. ED 025 736.)

Machlup, F. *The production and distribution of knowledge in the United States.* Princeton: Princeton University Press, 1962.

Maslow, A. H. *Motivation and personality.* New York: Harper & Row, 1954.

Maslow, A. H. The farther reaches of human nature. *Journal of Transpersonal Psychology,* 1969, **1**, 1-9. (a)

Maslow, A. H. Toward a humanistic biology. *American Psychologist,* 1969, **24**, 724-735. (b)

Matson, F. W., & Montagu, A. (Eds.) *The human dialogue: Perspectives on communication.* New York: Free Press, 1967.

McClusky, H. Y. The relevance of psychology for adult education. In G. Jensen, A. A. Liveright, & W. Hallenbeck (Eds.), *Adult education: Outlines of an emerging field of university study.* Washington: Adult Education Association of the U.S.A., 1964. Pp. 155-175.

Miller, G. A., Galanter, E., & Pribram, K. H. *Plans and the structure of behavior.* New York: Holt, 1960.

Miller, H. L. *Teaching and learning in adult education.* New York: Macmillan, 1964.

Moses, S. *The learning force: An approach to the politics of education.* Syracuse: Educational Policy Research Center, Syracuse University Research Corporation, 1970.

Moustakas, C. The challenge of growth: Loneliness or encounter? In H. Otto (Ed.), *Human potentialities.* St. Louis: Warren H. Green, 1968. Pp. 199-211.

Mowrer, O. H. *The new group therapy.* Princeton: Van Nostrand, 1964 .

188

Murphy, G. *Human potentialities.* New York: Basic Books, 1958.

National Education Association of the United States, Educational Policies Commission. *The purposes of education in American democracy.* Washington: National Education Association, 1938.

Newman, S. E. Student vs. instructor design of study method. *Journal of Educational Psychology*, 1957, **48**, 328-333.

North, S. L., & Forgie, D. L. Multi-media program shows CUSO volunteers a new way to learn. *Canadian University & College*, 1970, **5**(4), 32-36 and 58.

Olson, W. C. *Child development.* (2nd ed.) Boston: Heath, 1959.

· Parker, E. B., & Paisley, W. J. *Patterns of adult information seeking.* Stanford: Institute for Communication Research, Stanford University, 1966.

Pearson, L. Humanistic psychology in teaching. *American Association for Humanistic Psychology Newsletter*, 1967, **3**, 2-3.

Peter, L. J., & Hull, R. *The Peter principle.* Toronto: Bantam Books, 1970.

Peterson, T. *Magazines in the twentieth century.* (2nd ed.) Urbana: University of Illinois Press, 1964.

Platt, J. R. *The step to man.* New York: Wiley, 1966.

Porcella, B. *A summary of research on the reading interests and habits of college graduates.* University of Illinois Graduate School of Library Science Occasional Papers, No. 74, December, 1964.

Rees, M. B., & Paisley, W. J. *Social and psychological predictors of information seeking and media use: A multivariate re-analysis.* Stanford: Institute for Communication Research, Stanford University, 1967.

Rieger, J. H., & Anderson, R. C. Information source and need hierarchies of an adult population in five Michigan counties. *Adult Education*, 1968, **18**, 155-175.

Roalman, Pete. How flipping through unusual books can help improve human relations. *National Observer*, December 2, 1963, p. 9.

Robinson, J. Exploring the range of adult interests. In R. L. Collison (Ed.), *Progress in library science 1965.* London: Butterworths, 1965.

Roe, A. *The making of a scientist.* New York: Dodd, Mead, 1953.

Rogers, C. R. *On becoming a person: A therapist's view of psychotherapy.* Boston: Houghton Mifflin, 1961.

Rogers, C. R. Graduate education in psychology: A passionate statement. In W. G. Bennis et al. (Eds.), *Interpersonal dynamics: Essays and readings on human interaction.* (2nd ed.) Homewood, Illinois: Dorsey, 1968. Pp. 687-703.

Rokeach, M. *The open and closed mind: Investigations into the nature of belief systems and personality systems.* New York: Basic Books, 1960.

Ryan, T. A. Testing instructional approaches for increased learning. *Phi Delta Kappan*, 1965, **46**, 534-536.

Schwitzgebel, R. A simple behavioral system for recording and implementing change in natural settings. Unpublished doctoral dissertation, Harvard University, 1964.

Selye, H. *The stress of life.* New York: McGraw-Hill, 1956.

Sharma, D. K. *Role of information sources and communication channels in adoption of improved practices by farmers in Madhya Pradesh State, India.* (Doctoral dissertation, Cornell University) Ann Arbor, Mich.: University Microfilms, 1967. No. 67-16,368.

189

Sheffield, S. D. The orientations of adult continuing learners. In D. Solomon (Ed.), *The continuing learner.* Chicago: Center for the Study of Liberal Education for Adults, 1964. Pp. 1-22.

Shorey, L. L. Teacher participation in continuing education activities. Unpublished doctoral dissertation, University of Toronto (OISE), 1969. (Microfilm copy available from the National Library of Canada.)

Smith, R. H. *The American reading public: What it reads, why it reads.* New York: Bowker, 1963.

Strong, L. How much is too much? The burden of executive reading. *The Management Review,* 1957, **46**, 60-70.

Terman, L. M., & Oden, M. H. *Genetic studies of genius.* Vol. 4. *The gifted child grows up: Twenty-five years' follow-up of a superior group.* Stanford: Stanford University Press, 1947.

Tough, A. M. The assistance obtained by adult self-teachers. *Adult Education,* 1966, **17**, 30-37.

Tough, A. M. *Learning without a teacher: A study of tasks and assistance during adult self-teaching projects.* Toronto: The Ontario Institute for Studies in Education, 1967.

Tough, A. M. *Why adults learn: A study of the major reasons for beginning and continuing a learning project.* Toronto: The Ontario Institute for Studies in Education, 1968. Also available on microfiche from the ERIC Document Reproduction Service, order no. ED 025 688.)

Tough, A. Some major reasons for learning. In *Self concept in adult participation: Conference report and bibliography.* Syracuse: ERIC Clearinghouse on Adult Education, 1969. Pp. 19-38.

Toynbee, A. Preface: Higher education in a time of accelerating change. In A. C. Eurich (Ed.), *Campus 1980: The shape of the future in American higher education.* New York: Delacorte, 1968. Pp. xix-xxiv.

Van Doren, C. *Benjamin Franklin.* New York: The Viking Press, 1938.

Verner, C. *A conceptual scheme for the identification and classification of processes for adult education.* Washington, D.C.: Adult Education Association of the U.S.A., 1962.

Wallen, N. E., & Travers, R. M. W. Analysis and investigation of teaching methods. In N. L. Gage (Ed.), *Handbook of research on teaching.* Chicago: Rand McNally, 1963. Pp. 448-505.

Warren, M. J. Trends in popular reading tastes, 1918-1958, as indicated by non-fiction best sellers. Unpublished master's thesis, University of North Carolina, 1960.

Werdell, P. R. Teaching and learning: Whose goals are important around here? In C. G. Dobbins and C. B. T. Lee (Eds.), *Whose goals for American higher education?* Washington: American Council on Education, 1968. Pp. 19-38.

Wesson, A. Discussion group schemes: The CAE scheme. Paper presented at the annual conference of the Australian Association for Adult Education, July 1966.

White, T. Editor's notes. *Adult Education,* 1965, **16**, 2.

Whyte, W. H. *Is anybody listening?* New York: Simon & Schuster, 1952.

Winter, S. K., Griffith, J. C., & Kolb, D. A. The capacity for self direction. *Journal of Consulting and Clinical Psychology,* 1968, **32**(1), 35-41.

190

Yadao, F., Jr. Learning orientations of adults for enrolling in the part-time B.A. program at the University of Guelph. Unpublished master's thesis, University of Guelph, 1968. (A summary of this study is available from the ERIC Document Reproduction Service, order no. ED 025 730.)